ACLU

The Devil's Advocate

The Seduction of Civil Liberties in America

F. LaGard Smith

Marcon
PUBLISHERS

ACLU—The Devil's Advocate
Copyright © 1996 by F. LaGard Smith
Published by Marcon Publishers
Requests for information should be addressed to:
Marcon Publishers, 770-101 Wooten Road, Colorado Springs, CO 80915.

Library of Congress Cataloging-in-Publication Data
Smith, Frank LaGard, 1944—
ACLU—The Devil's Advocate / F. LaGard Smith
     p. cm.
Includes Bibliographical references and Index
ISBN:1-886-547-03-3   (hardcover: alk. paper)
1. Current issues. 2. Church and state.
3. Religion and politics — United States.

This edition printed on acid-free paper and meets the American National Standards Institute Z39.48 standard.

Except where otherwise indicated, all Scripture quotations in this book are taken from the *Holy Bible: New International Version* ®. NIV ®. Copyright ©1973, 1978, 1984, by International Bible Society. Used by permission of Zondervan Publishing House.

Cover design, interior layout, and typesetting by Multnomah Graphics, Portland, Oregon.

Printed in the United States of America

95 96 97 98 99 00 01 02 — 10 9 8 7 6 5 4 3 2 1

Dedicated to

Dean Ron Phillips—

For his committed leadership of Pepperdine University School of Law for more than a quarter of a century,

For making it possible for me to do what I most love to do, teach and write,

And especially for his encouragement in the writing of this book.

With Appreciation

For their willingness to review and critique the manuscript, and in some cases contribute research assistance, I wish to thank David Davenport, Robert Destro, Eric Hedden, Liza Karsai, Joshua Kenyon, Bradley Kirk, Douglas Kmiec, Warren Kniskern, Phillip Johnson, Robert Mann, Suzanna Mitchell, Gregory Ogden, Ron Talmo, and Paul Wilkinson. Among these, I am particularly grateful to those who were gracious enough to make candid comments from the perspective of personal involvement in the ACLU. While often disagreeing significantly with views expressed in this book, each of them made insightful contributions to the ongoing dialogue.

Invaluable help in research and analysis came from my friend and colleague Richardson Lynn, whose ongoing encouragement ensured the completion of this project. He would want it known that he is not responsible for any noticeable ranting and raving.

To my wife, Ruth, goes my thanks for breaking up interminably long sentences, for insisting that I explain legalese to lay readers, and, most of all, for tolerating weeks of all–night writing sessions and missed social occasions.

No author is complete without an editor. My appreciation goes to Jamie Janosz, who juggled the commas, tweaked the grammar, and in other splendid ways brought order out of chaos.

More gratitude than I can ever express goes to Bill Roper, for his fraternal friendship, encouragement, and behind–the–scenes assistance.

My appreciation, finally, to Joe Finney, whose faith in this book and its message made it a reality.

Contents

Preface

It will be obvious as one begins to read through this book that I came to my task of evaluating the American Civil Liberties Union (ACLU) with a particular bias. As neither a member of the ACLU, nor a sympathizer with many of its policies, I can only plead guilty to having written from an outsider's point of view. Indeed, given my own differing perspective, I could not have done otherwise.

I regret not having had the insight of first–hand experience with the day–to–day inner–workings of the ACLU at some local level. To compensate, I have tried to import some of that insight through the personal experience of members of the ACLU who have graciously—and boldly—scrutinized the manuscript.

Yet, any loss which may have resulted from lack of closer association with the ACLU and a greater sense of identity with its policies may actually prove beneficial. Among the several purposes of this book, one goal was to challenge traditional civil libertarians within the ACLU to consider how radically the ACLU and its mission has changed, particularly with regard to political and social policies which one would think ought to be an affront to all true civil libertarians. Sometimes those closest to gradual change are in the least likely position to notice the change. An outsider, perhaps even an adversary, might well provide a fresh perspective.

What I have attempted to do through this book is to consider the policies and practices of the ACLU in a number of larger contexts, whether legal, political, moral, or even spiritual. For that reason, I have concentrated on the national organization and its policies rather than the actions of local affiliates. (References to ACLU policies are drawn specifically from the *Policy Guide for the American Civil Liberties Union*.) Anyone who is even slightly familiar with the ACLU knows that members of the ACLU disagree among themselves, sometimes vehemently, regarding what the ACLU's policies ought to be and even the meaning of civil libertarianism itself. However, the larger picture which emerges tells us something of where the ACLU as a whole is coming from. It is that composite picture which many of us on the outside find so troubling.

Given those purposes and inherent limitations, I have taken the liberty in the pages which follow to interact frequently with Samuel Walker's encyclopedic and sympathetic history of the ACLU, *In Defense of American Liberties* (Oxford University Press, 1990). As an insider with intimate knowledge of the American Civil Liberties Union, Walker has made a herculean effort to assess both the strengths and weaknesses of the ACLU over its 75-year history. I am greatly indebted to him for both his scholarship and candor, without which we could never hope to have so clear a window into America's leading civil liberties organization.

From the other side of the aisle, I am also greatly indebted to William A. Donohue for his two insightful treatises on the ACLU, *The Politics of the American Civil Liberties Union* (Transaction Publishers, 1990) and *Twilight of Liberty* (Transaction Publishers, 1994). Undoubtedly, there is no individual outside the ACLU who has a more thorough understanding of the ACLU and its policies than does Donohue. Although I have not often referenced his work specifically, my own thinking was prompted again and again by his careful research.

While the historical analysis provided by these two authors is invaluable, this book is an effort to engage the reader in a wider discourse. As a committed Christian, I am interested in the moral and spiritual implications of both traditional and radical civil libertarianism and in the impact each of those movements continues to have on our society. It is my central thesis that civil libertarianism can be a force for good or, indeed, a force for evil, and that the ACLU has been the source of both. Beyond that, the ACLU's articulation of various social and moral issues (like pornography and abortion) has made it an icon for political positions which are more widely shared among the liberal–Left.

Although political liberals and traditional civil libertarians are not always in agreement on every issue, the very points of intersection where they agree and where they don't are often telling. Overall (as one might expect), the generally shared beliefs of the liberal–Left represent a world view radically different from generally shared beliefs of the conservative–Right, and particularly the religious–Right. At the most fundamental level, those core differences—not just isolated issues—are what divide us and cause mutual suspicion. It is toward a better understanding of those conflicting perspectives that this book is intended.

At the most basic level, what most deeply divides us are not social or legal issues, but foundational spiritual beliefs which go to the very nature of who we are, where we came from, and whether or not we have an intrinsic purpose for being. That is why we simply have to speak more frankly about the role of religion and faith in society, and whether or not morality can or should be legislated—even examining what is at stake in the lessons we teach our school children about human origins.

In that larger context, there seems to be no end to the questions: Is free speech always, in every case, an absolute right, or should society be able to recognize moral limitations? Have we misunderstood the entire church–state controversy because we start off with different philosophical assumptions? Indeed, how does our view of origins or moral authority influence our hermeneutical approach to the Constitution? ("Original intent" versus "living document" is the sharpest possible dividing line.) Perhaps, most importantly, is there any common ground between the liberal–Left and the conservative/religious–Right; any hope for an end to the cultural war in which we are engaged?

In both the title and the text, I have purposely made explicit references to the devil in order to infuse a spiritual dimension into what is generally treated as nothing more than a secular dialogue. I believe that more is at stake than we normally assume. In most instances, one need not even believe in the devil to appreciate the broader spiritual context in which the issues are framed within these pages. However, whether or not we believe in the devil could be an excellent starting point for where we stand on any number of seemingly unrelated constitutional, legal, and moral concerns. If this book achieves nothing else, that point alone could be worth the exercise.

My hope is that, beyond providing a better sense about the mission and philosophy of the American Civil Liberties Union, this book will help each of us to reflect more closely upon our personal mission and beliefs. This is a book about freedom, responsibility, and, most importantly, about personal integrity.

Introduction

The title to this book suggests that the American Civil Liberties Union plays the role of devil's advocate in two very different senses—one good and one evil.

The American Civil Liberties Union describes itself as "the nation's foremost advocate of individual rights—litigating, legislating, and educating the public on a broad array of issues affecting individual freedom in the United States."[1] And that is true. Yet, the ACLU may also be described fairly as the legal arm of the liberal–Left, supporting any number of causes that seem to debase the noble ideals of civil libertarianism. Which of these pictures is more accurate?

As the nation's foremost defender of individual rights, the ACLU can proudly wear the title of being America's own devil's advocate. That title suggests more than simply a testing of one's ideas in perhaps an academic discussion wherein one person might say to another, "Let me play the devil's advocate for a moment...." Certainly, the ACLU does much more than that—something more akin to the origin of the term itself.

In Roman Catholic tradition, the "devil's advocate" plays an honorable and necessary role as general promoter of the faith. The office, first created under Leo X in the 16th century, was entrusted with safeguarding the rights of the faith and the observance of ecclesiastical laws in the canonization of saints. It was the duty of the *promotor fidei* to oppose the claims of the "saint's advocate," which explains the often misunderstood title of "devil's advocate."

In actual fact, the devil's advocate was an advocate for the Church, charged with the duty of vigorously investigating and critically challenging the evidence put forward on behalf of a person being considered for sainthood. The person's life and any miracles attributed to the individual were to be closely scrutinized. Anything unfavorable to the candidate was to be ferreted out and exposed.[2]

Far from being seen in any negative sense, the role of devil's advocate had a positive role in keeping the Roman Church from declaring someone a saint without possessing unquestionable proof. In modern terms, it would be the duty of the devil's advocate to make certain that there was proof of sainthood *beyond a reasonable doubt*.

Not only would the devil's advocate guarantee that the proceedings were conducted according to law (something in which the ACLU special-izes), but the mere potential of his objections compelled the patrons of the cause to do their homework carefully. That, too, could be said of the ACLU, whose very existence keeps police, prosecutors, and government legal advi-sors on their toes just to make sure they've got it right.

Devil's Advocate or Advocate for the Devil?

Despite that commendable legacy, it must be asked (if one may be per-mitted "to play the devil's advocate") whether, because of its increasingly radical liberal politics, the ACLU has betrayed its own *raison d'etre* and truly become an advocate for the devil.

Writing in 1984, Richard and Susan Vigilante stated the obvious, that the United States in our generation is "dizzyingly, gloriously free—the most radically free society in the history of the civilized world."[3] One can hardly question such a self-evident proposition, even while maintaining that free-dom is an ongoing battle.

Although there will continue to be civil liberties violations and the need for ongoing safeguards, there are really only two choices facing today's civil-libertarian watchdogs: "They can resign themselves to the noble but perhaps tedious job of conserving already secured basic rights, or they can become legal adventurers, discovering or creating ever more obscure and abstract constitutional liberties."[4]

What this suggests is that the ACLU has long since made its choice and daringly crossed the Rubicon. Already, it has exchanged its role as defender of the specific guarantees in the Bill of Rights for an activist expan-sion of civil liberties which reach beyond specifically articulated freedoms. Idle hands are indeed the devil's workshop.

To many, these newly-discovered "civil liberties" which have gained growing acceptance are as disturbing as the radical shift in the ACLU's mis-sion. Far from being easily recognizable and universally defensible, the "new liberties" do not always proceed from a moral foundation. Nor can the ACLU excuse itself by shifting responsibility to the courts and their interpretations. As the ACLU is proud to proclaim, many of the "new liberties" adopted by the courts were urged upon it by the ACLU through both amicus briefs and oral arguments.

Examples of the ACLU's adventurous forays into virgin libertarian territory are the ACLU's gratuitous defense of the sexual revolution, which, ten years on, now includes even gay rights; anti–family policies, pitting novel children's rights against traditional parental rights; and the defense of abortion rights.

The ACLU's almost fanatical stand on abortion and its pivotal role in bringing about *Roe v. Wade* are but inevitable steps along the way in the liberal–Left's inexorable march toward achieving unrestrained individualism. The march began with ACLU founder Roger Baldwin's personal commitment to political anarchy and will not end until, through the seductive notion of "privacy," it has won the final victory for personal autonomy.

Personal autonomy for what? Not to put too fine an edge on it—for *licentious behavior.* Enter, stage left, the devil. It should be shame enough that the ACLU actively and proudly facilitates the killing of 1.5 million unborn each year in the United States. But, if the ACLU had its way, there would also be no barriers to homosexual marriages, gay adoptions, prostitution, kiddy porn, or the unrestricted use of recreational drugs.

Is that sordid list of "civil liberties" what the framers of the Bill of Rights had in mind when they agonized over what ought to constitute our fundamental freedoms? Was it to secure the right merely to do as one pleases for which the founders of this great nation dedicated their lives?

Abandoning the High Moral Ground

The ACLU argues, of course, that unless there is complete freedom in the moral arena, all other freedoms—political, religious, or otherwise—will be equally at risk. Such a simplistic argument fails to account for the vast gulf between, on the one hand, societal interests in encouraging moral rectitude, and, on the other, the imposition of political tyranny.

If inculcating personal morality in individuals is not the government's business—and it is not—when was it ever in the government's interest to actively promote personal immorality? Therein lies the danger of any civil libertarianism that serves to promote moral decay. For some, political freedom is the convenient Trojan horse in a cultural war where traditional values are locked in a deadly struggle with libertine morality.

This is not to suggest that individual members of the ACLU are any less moral than a cross–section of the American people, religious or otherwise. There is no reason to believe that they are committed civil libertarians merely so that they can do drugs, watch pornographic films, frequent prostitutes, or personally have abortions. What it says is that, as an organization, the ACLU has adopted any number of policies which put it in league with clearly reprehensible moral behavior.

Perhaps more troubling is the fact that many in the ACLU would question whether, for example, prostitution, homosexual behavior, and kiddy porn are so "clearly reprehensible." That the immorality of these activities would have to be debated speaks volumes about why the culture wars are raging. It is not just a debate about the propriety of governmental action regarding certain activities. Competing moral value systems at the most fundamental level are in conflict.

That the American Civil Liberties Union has debased itself by supporting immoral causes gives new meaning to its role as the devil's advocate. We are no longer talking about an honorable duty wherein evidence is tested and hallowed rights are protected. Now we are well and truly within the devil's domain. Now we are talking about the realm of spiritual darkness and that which is by nature evil.

But here we are speaking the language of the Church, and the last thing the ACLU would want to be is an advocate for the Church. That, itself, tells the tale. Apart from the odd case where principled civil libertarianism has no option but to side with religious expression, the ACLU is the avowed enemy of the Church and virtually anything religious. Ignoring the obvious history and purpose behind the First Amendment's Establishment Clause, the ACLU has perpetuated a wall of separation between, not only church and state, but also between morality and state.

It's not just the controversy over school prayers or the teaching of creation versus evolution. It's not whether the local high school can put on *Jesus Christ, Superstar* as its spring play. Nor is it simply whether a cross can be erected on public property, or whether churches ought to be tax–exempt. The real issue is whether religion can be permitted to challenge liberal–Left values in the marketplace of ideas. How else does one explain the ACLU's appalling disdain of religious free speech?

If perhaps the ACLU might remotely agree with Tocqueville's assessment that religion provides Americans with a strong moral character without which democracy cannot function, it apparently sends shivers down its spine to think that Tocqueville might be right when he also concluded that "there are things which religion prevents them from imagining and forbids them to dare."[5] At that point, religion has overstepped its bounds and has interfered with the complete, uninhibited, unrestrained personal autonomy mandated by the First Commandment of Liberalism.

It is not simply the wall separating church and state that the ACLU feels compelled to maintain. (In a pluralistic society, there is no threat that either the federal government or any individual state would establish one particular denomination as its official church.) The wall that the ACLU is desperate to build higher and higher, brick by brick, is the wall fencing out any religious influence which might dare to inhibit personal moral autonomy. Because moral anarchy and liberal–Left politics are allies, religion—the common enemy—must be isolated from the public arena in every way possible.

Such being the case, it would be understandable if the ACLU were wholly dismissive of any suggestion that it literally acts as an advocate for the devil. Odds are, few of its members even take seriously the idea of a devil, unless perhaps he is personified for them in the red–suited, fork–in–hand religious–Right. But you can rest assured that if Satan really does exist, he rests easy knowing that the ACLU's guiding ideology represents an unreflective bias against religious morality, compromising the honorable mission which might otherwise continue to ennoble it.

I

The Many Faces of Civil Liberty

CHAPTER 1

When Terror Strikes
the Heart of Freedom

"MUST A GOVERNMENT OF NECESSITY BE TOO STRONG
FOR THE LIBERTIES OF ITS PEOPLE OR TOO WEAK
TO MAINTAIN ITS OWN EXISTENCE?"
ABRAHAM LINCOLN

Never are our civil liberties more at risk than when national security is threatened. From its own embarrassing experience in supporting the internment of Japanese-Americans during World War II, the ACLU knows that. It only takes a bomb, or a hijacking, or a surprise attack on Pearl Harbor, and we instinctively call on the government to go after the perceived "bad guys"—even, if necessary, at the expense of constitutional protections. It is here that, with rare exception, civil libertarians have split historically from their more liberal cousins. Liberals usually embrace policies of big government; civil libertarians harbor a deep-seated distrust of government.

This is where the issue becomes interesting. When the bad guys turn out to be on the radical right, the ACLU finds itself in bed with folks it would ordinarily abhor. (Whoever would have guessed that gun control advocates like the ACLU and the anti-gun control NRA would ever speak with one voice on a constitutional issue!) Some would consider it a badge of integrity to defend one's natural enemies. But if you look closely enough, you will see that the radical Right and the radical Left have more in common philosophically than either would like to confess. Therein lies a lesson for the ACLU: Civil libertarianism taken to an extreme can be as dangerous in its own way as gun toting radicalism. There is more than one way to threaten national security, including fostering misguided notions about civil liberties.

When Terror Strikes the Heart of Freedom

F or most of us, it was right up there with Kennedy's assassination and the Challenger disaster. At 9:02 a.m. on April 19, 1995, in the midst of choking smoke, nine floors of crumbling concrete, and unthinkable human carnage, America suddenly awoke to the reality that terrorism could happen in its own back yard. No longer was it confined to the predictable Middle East, or to the distant skies over Lockerbie, Scotland, or even to the much closer but always-potentially-explosive cultural melting-pot of New York City. With the bombing of the federal building in downtown Oklahoma City, the message was clear: Terrorism can happen anywhere, anytime—next week or today—in your town or mine.

As the smoke cleared from the air and the media rushed to record the heroic attempts at rescue, America's disbelieving eyes were riveted on the precious figure of tiny little Baylee Almon's lifeless body being gently carried out of the rubble in the burly arms of firefighter Chris Fields. With Baylee's death died America's innocence. With her death—and the scores of others who shared her fate on that unforgettable morning—there also surfaced a national anger that seldom has been so intense. "Terrorist" is one thing; "baby killer" is quite another.

In its righteous anger, America quickly pointed the finger of guilt at the most obvious perpetrators: "unknown persons of Middle Eastern descent." After all, was it not Islamic Fundamentalists who set off a bomb at the World Trade Center in New York just two years earlier? Had there not been an Islamic conference, full of fire-breathing rhetoric, right there in Oklahoma City?[1]

In Washington, President Clinton's response team was busy identifying possible targets of retaliation in the Middle East, assuming that it was just a matter of time before a foreign link would be uncovered. The President himself assured a shocked nation hungry for revenge that the "evil cowards" would be brought to a swift, certain, and severe justice. Secretary of State Warren Christopher announced he had sent Arabic interpreters to help investigators in Oklahoma.[2]

At Chicago's O'Hare International Airport, Jordanian-American Ibrahim Ahmad (who had just flown out of Oklahoma City) was questioned and released as he was about to board an Alitalia flight to Rome. By the time he was free to go, his flight had already departed—with his bags on board. (Inside the bags, the rumored "wiring capable of being used in bombs" turned out to be nothing more than connecting wires for a VCR.)

Ahmad was re-booked on a flight to London's Heathrow Airport where, upon arrival, he was arrested by British authorities, rudely strip-searched in violation of his religious beliefs, and denied food for hours before being sent back to Washington, D.C. After passing a lie detector test, Ahmad was released. Unfortunately, so too was his identity, for all the world to see. Back in Oklahoma City, his hometown for thirteen years, local residents dumped garbage on his lawn and spat at his wife.

By the time Ahmad returned home and magnanimously joined with other mourners at a memorial service for the victims of the bombing, the focus of attention was already moving rapidly away from "Middle Eastern men of dark complexion" to "right wing extremists." But in the interim, callers to local radio stations suggested that Middle Easterners should be put in internment camps, like the ones in which the United States incarcerated Japanese-Americans during World War II.

The talk next turned to Waco, the Branch Davidians, and the gun-toting Michigan Militia. Then, all of a sudden, came the fortuitous arrest of former U.S. Army infantryman Timothy McVeigh, whose only reaction to questioning, reportedly, was a terse name, rank, and serial number, as if he were a prisoner of war. Within hours of the bombing, America had to come to terms with the cold, hard fact that the horrendous loss of life was not the work of Middle Eastern terrorists, the Italian Red Brigade, the Sicilian mafia, or any other foreign terrorist organization. Timothy McVeigh was a red-blooded, clean-cut, all-American young man who had received a bronze star during the Gulf War. Here he was, the focal point for the worst act of terrorism in the nation's history.

Who among us would have believed that the homemade fertilizer bomb could possibly be marked "Made in the U.S.A."? Or, worse yet, that it would be painted with stars and stripes in patriotic red, white, and blue?

Who would have guessed that, as the result of one deadly bomb, America would become embroiled in a fierce national debate over the Second Amendment and civil liberties? Or that the pro-gun-control American Civil Liberties Union would join together with right-wing extremists and the gun lobby in rallying to the defense of constitutional freedoms? Or that Attorney General Janet Reno, a longtime foe of capital punishment, would say grimly, "The death penalty is available, and we will seek it"? In one brief explosive moment, the Oklahoma City bombing ripped through layer upon layer of sensitive political nerve tissue.

Rift Between Liberals and Civil Libertarians

It was one of those times when not all composite sketches of the liberal-Left looked alike. Sensing the nation's irate mood, a liberal President proposed legislation giving the FBI broader access to credit files, phone records, and hotel registers. Clinton wanted broader wiretap authority for federal agents searching suspected terrorists, and even called for the use of the military in investigating domestic security cases. When asked if these proposals might not encounter stiff opposition from certain quarters, Clinton asked, "Who are you talking about?" Upon hearing the response, "The ACLU," Clinton reportedly said nothing. He simply smiled.[3]

But the American Civil Liberties Union wasn't smiling. In an official statement, the ACLU said, "We are concerned about an overreaction that would threaten to sweep away the constitutional principles that have shaped our society and maintain the core of our liberty."[4] Apparently the ACLU didn't trust President Clinton when he said, "We still will have freedom of speech, we'll have freedom of association, we'll have freedom of movement, but we may have to have some discipline in doing it so we can go after people who want to destroy our very way of life."

"What we're afraid of," responded Phil Gutis of the ACLU, "is that history is once again repeating itself. During many times of fears and tragedy, we have seen the government harass and investigate and arrest innocent people solely because of their race, religion, origin, and political beliefs. It's the ACLU's fear that we are about to embark down that road again."[5]

The "history" to which Gutis referred includes Attorney General Mitchell Palmer's anti-Communist raids during World War I; the mob hysteria of the 1930s; the Joseph McCarthy inquisition in the '50s; the civil rights and Chicago Seven turmoil of the '60s; and the turbulent '70s, including Native American violence and Vietnam War protesters. Most of us have vivid memories of what happened in the '60s and '70s, if only by television replay.

Within hours of the federal building bombing, history was already repeating itself. Nobody knew that better than Ibrahim Ahmad. As his case demonstrates, it is indeed the toughest of all balancing acts to know what to do in times of national crisis—particularly when fear and hatred abound. If officials act too quickly, someone's civil liberties are likely to be violated; if officials act too circumspectly, the nation's security is put at risk.

In the wake of the World Trade Center bombing, which put the spotlight of scrutiny on Sheik Omar Abdel Rahman and other Islamic extremists, the Omnibus Antiterrorist Act was introduced by the Clinton administration to: (1) crack down on fund-raising activities in the United States that benefit organizations with terrorist connections; and (2) ease procedures for deporting aliens suspected of terrorism. (Little wonder that Britain was dumbfounded by Clinton's warm embrace of Sinn Fein President Gerry Adams and the lifting of restrictions on fundraising for the terrorist IRA!) The country was in no mood to tolerate terrorism on our shores—especially by a band of religious zealots wearing turbans.

Middle East bashing may be popular among political liberals and conservatives alike, but civil libertarians saw a deeper threat. James Zogby, president of the Arab-American Institute, complained that the anti-terrorism bill would "seriously erode civil liberties" and that "it would be terrible if the legislation passed in this [fear-charged] atmosphere."[6] For Zogby especially, the bill's provision against fundraising on behalf of nonviolent groups which also have paramilitary wings could seriously affect a number of Arab organizations. The ACLU quickly joined the chorus, warning that the Omnibus bill would violate the First Amendment's right of association.

However, few family members who lost loved ones in the Oklahoma City federal building were mourning some abstract lost right of association. What they continue to mourn even now is the loss of something far more tangible and personal—the right to life. I suspect they derive little comfort from ACLU President Nadine Strossen's concern that "repeatedly through history, we've seen how infringing civil liberties out of fear for public safety has done nothing to make us safer. Hysteria accomplishes nothing."[7]

While Strossen may be right about hysteria, she can hardly be taken seriously about the supposed non-connection between limitations on liberty and greater public safety. Merely consider increased passenger security on airlines since the installation of airport metal detectors (which the ACLU opposes).[8] If you are like me, you hate going through the metal detectors just as much as the next guy. (Worse yet, getting frisked.) But who among us is ready to board a plane without going through the drill?

As George Washington University professor Amitai Etzioni suggests, "It is disingenuous and ignorant to argue that if we introduce a few carefully crafted limitations on what individuals may do, we will slide down a slippery slope into a police state."[9] For the ACLU, it would be terribly complicated to argue otherwise. After all, the ACLU favors gun control, which is surely a greater infringement on more citizens than Clinton's new get-tough-on-terrorists proposals. If, as Nadine Strossen insists, public safety is never helped by infringements on individual liberties, how does one explain the ACLU's support of gun control?

The rift exposed by the Oklahoma City bombing is not just between political liberals and civil libertarians (who are otherwise usually in the same bed). It is also between diametrically opposed strands of civil libertarianism itself. Or, to be more precise, between one arm of civil libertarianism that remains pure and committed to the cause (cautioning against broader investigatory power for federal agencies), and another arm of civil libertarianism that has typically sided with political liberalism (endorsing gun control).

Safety In Exchange For Liberty—The Easy Trade-off

Janet Reno's about-face on capital punishment says about all that needs to be said regarding political expediency in the face of public outcry. In that very turn-about, Reno may have proved the ACLU to be right in its concern about hysteria and civil liberties. The *USA Today* headline was itself the story: "Americans would give up liberties for safety."[10] Behind the headline was the USA Today/CNN/Gallup poll which found that "72% of Americans think federal law enforcement agencies should aggressively probe and infiltrate suspected groups that aim to resist powers of the U.S. federal government."[11]

Probing Americans' feelings about the Second Amendment, the poll also found that "71% reject the constitutional argument that individuals have a right to buy and stockpile firearms," and that "78% say citizens should not be allowed to arm and organize themselves to resist government power."[12]   Perhaps it is legitimate to ask whether the Second Amendment expressly gives individuals the right to buy and stockpile firearms. But it is difficult to know what else the Amendment could possibly mean if it is not the right for state militias to bear arms. (Even the ACLU's policy on gun control tacitly acknowledges the constitutionality of local organized militia.)

How then can nearly 80% of all Americans stare the Second Amendment squarely in the face and yet deny its plain meaning? The answer, of course, is that the Oklahoma City bombing—which seriously wounded all of us in a collective sense—was associated with a bunch of government-hating Rambos in camouflage fatigues, running through the woods on weekends carrying machine guns and assault rifles and calling themselves "militia." If that is what the Second Amendment is all about, then most Americans want no part of the Second Amendment.

Had it not been for the bombing, the Second Amendment would have seemed a harmless anachronism. Hardly relevant today. Vestigial. But there *was* a bombing. And there *was* death and mayhem. America's outrage would not be assuaged until the authorities pushed the Second Amendment aside and did whatever else it would take to bring the killers to justice. If necessary, Americans might even be happy to ignore the plain meaning of the Fourth Amendment's search and seizure language as well....

Of course, we have seen this cycle before, beginning with a period of covert intelligence between World War II and 1975 when federal agents spied on fellow Americans in the name of domestic security. Never was it more insidious than when the FBI's Cointelpro program infiltrated political groups in an effort to control and discredit them. Then, in 1976, came Attorney General Edward Levi's guidelines limiting FBI domestic surveillance to situations where the government could show probable cause that a crime had been, or would be, committed. But by 1983, Attorney General William French Smith issued new guidelines whereby law enforcement officials could pursue covert intelligence whenever anyone "advocated criminal activity."

To understand the changes in official policy, one had to keep a finger on the pulse of America's fears. With each new cause for fear—whether it be the Black Panthers, anti-war protesters, or critics of the government's policy in Central America—came a new target for investigative scrutiny. As UCLA professor James Q. Wilson reminds us, "Political support for intelligence work swings like a pendulum."[13]

The ACLU's Ira Glasser takes that thought a step further. "People's position on civil liberties depends on who the target is," says Glasser. "Now the likely targets of illegitimate government activities are people whose political interests the Republicans care about."[14] Or, as Sen. Joseph Biden put it, "It all depends on whose ox is being gored."[15]

The same could be said, of course, for Sen. Biden's liberal colleagues who want to make sure they aren't seen to be protecting civil liberties at a time when most Americans are demanding a serious crackdown on terrorists. Just listen, for example, to Congresswoman Pat Schroeder, whose liberal credentials are impeccable. (After winning a seat in Congress in 1972 on an anti-war platform, Schroeder learned that the FBI had broken into her home and spied on her.) In the aftermath of the Oklahoma City bombing, Rep. Schroeder said of Clinton's anti-terrorist proposals, "I have no problem if things are defined. If you have a reason for a search and seizure, there is nothing wrong with it."[16]

Why in the world would Rep. Schroeder doff her normal liberal togs and put on a conservative suit for her constituency back home? What could possibly prompt President Clinton to sound more Reaganesque than Reagan himself? What allows political liberals to put civil liberties on the back burner and champion the cause of the FBI? In a word, *fear.* "Give us fewer rights, if necessary, but first and foremost give us safety," the people cry. And the politicians are not deaf.

Can Even Civil Libertarians Turn a Deaf Ear?

The American Civil Liberties Union would like to rise above the moment and take the high road of principle. Therefore, it does indeed protest. But it did not always do so. During World War II, the ACLU fell all over itself to burn the Red Flag it had so often carried and to wrap itself instead in the stars and stripes. To keep the FBI off of its back, the ACLU (through some of its key leaders) even named names of Communist sympathizers to the FBI.[17] In a time of fear, individuals, governments, and even civil liberties organizations often re-prioritize their highest values.

Nor was the ACLU's finest hour to be seen in the internment of Japanese-Americans. When fear, hatred, and prejudice led to the most flagrant violation of civil liberties in America's history, even the ACLU was compromised in its opposition. (While terribly tragic, the bombing of the federal building in Oklahoma City did not compare to the bombing of Pearl Harbor.) Although ACLU-founder Roger Baldwin and several others in the ACLU worked behind the scenes to help Japanese-Americans press their cause in the courts, the ACLU itself was split on how to react to the internment program.

After much debate, and by a vote of 52 to 26, the ACLU National Committee approved "Resolution 2," which expressed concern regarding several procedural matters relating to the internment process, but nevertheless formally accepted Roosevelt's Executive Order 9066 authorizing the internment.[18] (Even the Northern California ACLU—on the far left of all the affiliates—voted 119 to 65 to approve the internment.) In a moment of national crisis, civil liberties gave way to a threat against national security— even within the ranks of the ACLU.

But that is water under the bridge. Today the ACLU is urging caution regarding the relaxation of federal guidelines for investigating terrorism. As its own embarrassing history demonstrates, never are civil liberties more important than during times of national distress.

The High Cost of Free Speech

No sooner had President Clinton seized the moment with his quick sympathetic response to the Oklahoma bombing than he took the opportunity to lash out against talk radio and the conservative-Right. "We hear so many loud, angry voices in America today whose sole goal seems to be to try to keep some people as paranoid as possible and the rest of us all tore up and upset with each other," said an angry Bill Clinton. "They spread hate."[19]

Was Clinton cynically politicizing the tragedy, or was he telling it like it is? Not unexpectedly, his comments stirred up a firestorm of controversy. House Speaker Newt Gingrich and his Republican revolutionaries responded angrily, denying that their Contract With America to downsize the federal government had anything to do with the bombing of a federal building. And, indeed, any such implication would have been absurd.

At the center of the storm, conservative talk-show hosts voiced their outrage regarding the President's insinuation that they had provided motive and inspiration for right-wing extremists willing to kill and maim for what was, generally speaking, a common cause. They were particularly incensed when the President said, "They leave the impression, by their very words, that violence is acceptable." [20]

Though never specifically named, it appeared that Clinton's targets were talk-show hosts like "the Majority Maker" Rush Limbaugh, New York's racially-acrid Bob Grant, Oliver North (a newcomer to the talk-show arena), former Watergate burglar G. Gordon Liddy, and even Howard Stern— always anti-liberal and anti-establishment in his own schlock-jock, toilet-bowl style. Of these, Gordon Liddy came in for the harshest criticism, especially for his on-air advice that, if necessary for self-defense, one should use "head shots" when encountering federal agents wearing bullet-proof vests. "Kill the sons of bitches," Liddy urged.[21]

That bit of advice brought vociferous protest from the press, including an unusually biting editorial comment by congenial *Today Show* host Bryant Gumbel, who said radio stations and sponsors ought to cut off support for such inflammatory talk. Reasonable as his and others' similar comments may have been, one might have expected civil libertarians to argue that such a campaign would have a chilling effect on free speech.

Would the ACLU come to the defense of right-wing extremists as it had done for the Skokie Nazis? Judging from the ACLU's support of Howard Stern in his ongoing battle with the Federal Communications Commission over fines for obscenity and racism, the answer probably would be "yes." Likewise, had there been a serious attempt to impose legal restrictions on Gordon Liddy, it can be predicted that the ACLU would have lept to his defense. This, despite the enormous psychic cost it must be for civil libertarians—instinctively liberal—to come to the aid of political conservatives.

Or, quite to the contrary, is there really so great a distance between the extreme Left and the extreme Right? Of all the questions raised by the Oklahoma City bombing, that question may be the most intriguing and potentially insightful. To refine the question just slightly, is it possible that the ACLU itself has more in common with right-wing extremists than it would ever wish to admit?

Where the Two Extremes Meet

For starters, consider the irony of Clinton's linkage between voices of the conservative-Right and the bombing of the federal building in Oklahoma City. It was reminiscent of a report called *Revolutionary Radicalism*, published in 1920 by the New York legislature's Lusk Committee, which condemned the American Civil Liberties Union as "a supporter of all subversive movements....It attempts not only to protect crime but to encourage attacks upon our institutions in every form."[22] This report came amidst a series of terrorist bombings by Communist and labor union activists, whom the ACLU (philosophically wed on both counts) clamored to defend.

Then there was the sharp exchange in 1930 between Roger Baldwin and Hamilton Fish, who chaired the House Special Committee to

Investigate Communist Activities. When Baldwin argued that the First Amendment protected the *advocacy* of violence but not *acts* of violence, Fish asked Baldwin if it was permissible to openly advocate murder. Unhesitatingly, Baldwin answered "yes." What about assassination? Again, Baldwin said "yes," drawing Fish's attention to British law which allowed soap-boxers in Hyde Park to advocate the assassination of kings, but not the actual assassination of the current monarch.[23]

Did someone complain that G. Gordon Liddy was advocating "head shots" for federal agents? If perhaps the ACLU disagrees with Liddy's sentiments, presumably it would follow in Voltaire's shoes in defending to the death his right to use such inflammatory language. Should not the ACLU, then, also be put on Clinton's list of those who give aid and comfort to extremists bent on blowing up federal buildings?

Even when the line is crossed between advocacy of violence and an act of violence itself, neither the conservatives nor the liberals have a monopoly on terrorism. From the end of the 19th century until the 1930s, radical elements of the Left included bombings and political murders among its propaganda methods. During a labor dispute in 1910, the *Los Angeles Times* building in Los Angeles was bombed, resulting in twenty casualties. In 1920, a bomb in Wall street killed thirty people. Then there were the leftist "Weathermen" of the late '60s. On the opposite end of the spectrum, of course, is the Ku Klux Klan and other right-wing vigilante groups.[24]

The history books are clear: Whether on the Right or on the Left, political extremism begets violence. But to really understand what is going on, rewind the tape leading up to the violence only slightly and you will find an appetite for power. If you rewind the tape still further, you will discover an antagonism toward government, and, even further, a disdain for authority in general, if perhaps for very different reasons. (Perhaps a resentment of anything interfering with individual autocracy; or a rejection of any human authority that interposes itself between God and man.)

Nevertheless, if there is an ideological divide, there is much that also is shared. That is why, even in the absence of violence, the extreme Right and the extreme Left have more in common with each other than either has with political centrists. Left or Right, political extremists are, at base, anarchists. What they have in common is a problem with authority and a disaffection with government. Big government, especially.

Although he would later come to view government as an ally in the furtherance of civil liberties, Roger Baldwin initially despised the massive governmental bureaucracy of Roosevelt's New Deal. He warned that "the enormous increase of the power of the federal government under New Deal policies carries with it inevitable fears of inroads on the right of agitation." For Baldwin, civil liberties in the early years of the ACLU meant *freedom from government*. Even today, the ACLU's civil libertarian concerns continue to reflect a similar suspicion. In the wake of the Oklahoma City terror, for example, ACLU spokesman Phil Gutis warned that "Typically what the government tries to do is expand its power during times of national fear."[25]

In its antagonism to governmental interference, the ACLU finds itself in strange company. With the fall of Communism, midwest extremists, like the Michigan Militia who fanatically supported Uncle Sam in the fight against Communism, lost the one reason they had to support their government. The only remaining conspiracy they could find large enough to feed their voracious paranoia was the federal government itself.[26]

No, the ACLU doesn't share the strange paramilitary fantasy that believes Washington will bring in United Nations troops to establish a single world government; or that black helicopters have been buzzing Western states in advance of a U.N. invasion; or that the government has put electronic devices in cars to stall them when the invasion takes place. Nor does the ACLU believe that Russian troops are massing in salt mines beneath Detroit, or that barcodes are being implanted in babies so that the government can control everyone's behavior.

However, what the ACLU does share with the militant fringe of the extreme right is a pervasive, deep-seated distrust of government. Merely mention, for example, the FBI and CISPES (the Committee in Solidarity with the People of El Salvador) and the ACLU's blood pressure jumps by a factor of ten. Central America and the government's policies toward those who opposed U.S. involvement in the 1980's was to the ACLU and the liberal-Left what Waco was to paramilitary militias—*a cause celebre*. This shared distrust of the federal government largely explains why—despite vastly different ideologies—the extreme Right and the extreme Left have reacted almost in unison to warn against threatening governmental incursions into civil liberties.

The wonder of it all is that, on every side, the talk is of constitutional freedom. Those on the extreme Right speak of the Second Amendment as if it were the key to all freedoms. (If there is no right to bear arms, free speech is next on the government's hit list.) Radical civil libertarians prefer to concentrate on the First Amendment. (If free speech is not absolute, no other freedoms are safe.) Even Bill Clinton doesn't want to be left out, saying defensively, "I take a back seat to no one in my devotion to the Constitution." [27]

If one is to believe all the alarmist rhetoric, 169 people are killed in the bombing of a federal building in the midwest, and the greatest victim is the U.S. Constitution.

Britain's Margaret Thatcher (herself a target of IRA bombers while serving as Prime Minister) seems to have put it all in better perspective with her typical sharp-edged analysis. Speaking to faculty and students of Harding University in Arkansas shortly after the Oklahoma City blast, Thatcher was asked, "Is this country going to pay too high a price in liberty for its crackdown on right-wing extremists?" Said Thatcher curtly, "They're not right-wingers. They're brutes." [28]

If it weren't for the "brute element" of which Thatcher spoke, the ACLU might even be comfortable joining the ranks of the Michigan Militia. The camouflage fatigues and war paint probably wouldn't go down well, and packing around an AK-47 definitely wouldn't appeal to most civil libertarians, but their shared distaste of the government would make for interesting allies. One anarchist's camouflage fatigues and AK-47 is another's business suit and briefcase.

Terrorist brutes never have and never will understand the clear line between the political advocacy of ideas and cold-blooded acts of murder. Nobody needs terrorists. But right-wing voices and left-wing voices are the stuff of which democracies are made. In their own doctrinaire way, they each help to define more sharply the crucial issues of the day and thereby enable the moderate middle to maintain political balance.

What the ACLU seemingly fails to appreciate is that civil libertarianism, pushed to an extreme, gives a freer hand to those terrorist brutes who would violently destroy the very process of democratic dialogue. In its absolutist policies regarding free speech, assembly, and movement, the ACLU risks cutting off the nose of governmental intrusion to spite the face of governmental existence. When it is tempted to lean in that direction, the ACLU should take a good, hard look at the Michigan Militia. What it will see is a familiar face of anti-government sentiment not entirely unlike its own.

Anarchism can be philosophically proper or patently perverse, but it is still anarchism. Taken to its extreme—whether Right or Left—it leads not to freedom and liberty, but to public disorder and unthinkable tragedy.

In the bigger picture, public order must be maintained if we are to preserve civil liberties. Without order, liberty cannot survive. Perhaps one of the most important lessons little Baylee Almon's death can teach the ACLU, as well as the rest of us, is that civil liberties do not exist in a vacuum— whether social, moral, or even spiritual. Nor do they exist without limits.

It's Time to Ask Tough Questions

Now that the whole question of civil liberties has been dramatically re-ignited by the Oklahoma City bombing, it's time to ask some tough questions of the American Civil Liberties Union. Is the ACLU our greatest protector in times of national crisis, or has the ACLU's political extremism actually endangered social order by pressing civil liberties beyond their acceptable limits? Has it contributed to the breakdown in law and order by its relentless support of criminals' rights and its opposition to capital punishment? Does the ACLU bear any responsibility for undermining the nation's morals by its resistance to religious observance in the public arena? Has the ACLU endangered children like Baylee Almon by rushing to the defense of child pornographers? Indeed, does the ACLU have the blood of millions of unborn children on its hands for its militant support of legalized abortion?

The most frustrating thing for many of us is the feeling that the answer to the above questions is "yes." The ACLU is both America's greatest defender of civil liberties, and, at the same time, public enemy number one for defending causes that are ripping apart the very fabric of society. As the search and rescue teams discovered in the ruins of the federal building, sorting out the precious from the rubble is not always easy. But search and sort we must, for our time is short. Rarely has so much hung in the balance.

The Jekyll-and-Hyde ACLU

"THE TRUE DANGER IS WHEN LIBERTY IS NIBBLED AWAY FOR EXPEDIENTS...."

EDMUND BURKE

F ar too often, Americans take for granted both the plethora of civil liberties which we enjoy and the organizations which fight to preserve our liberties. What's so frustrating about the American Civil Liberties Union is that, no matter whatever else one might think of it, the ACLU defends the kind of liberties no one would ever want to give up. When travelling abroad to totalitarian countries, you are tempted to say of the ACLU (like the credit card commercial), "Don't leave home without it."

Back home, however, the ACLU often presents an entirely different face. Worse yet, two faces. For example, the ACLU proudly claims to be non-partisan and non-political, but without question it is the legal arm of the liberal-Left. Despite the ACLU's propaganda, any number of its civil libertarian policies confirm a leftward-leaning allegiance. Granted, a principled organization might at times find itself uncomfortably positioned on one side or another of a number of fences. But, ACLU policy is muddled in inconsistency. Oddly, such inconsistency is not terribly troubling for the ACLU.

Look behind the scenes and you will find a consistent ideology that justifies pragmatic waffling. For the ACLU, the underlying ideology is one of moral relativism, which naturally takes no notice of inconsistency or hypocrisy. In fact, it fairly demands it. The problem is that "relativized" civil liberties threaten to undermine our true constitutional rights—the very rights which make our country the envy of the world.

CHAPTER 2

The Jekyll-and-Hyde ACLU

I had just left "Checkpoint Charlie" and entered East Berlin. It was long before anyone could ever have imagined that one day the wall would fall and "Checkpoint Charlie" would be nothing more than a footnote in history. Crossing over into Communist territory, I was excited to see what it was like on the other side. But it was eerie. Here I was walking through no-man's land from West to East, where, only a few hundred yards away, East Berliners had been shot attempting to cross the wall in the other direction to freedom. My first impression of East Berlin was a sense of wide-open empty spaces, drab buildings, and abandoned streets. In fact, as I crossed the first wide boulevard with a couple of young Canadian tourists, there wasn't a car in sight.

We had hardly stepped up onto the sidewalk before, from out of nowhere, the three of us were accosted by a uniformed policeman. That was startling enough, but I could hardly believe my ears when I heard him say in broken English, "You're under arrest. Give me your passports." Naturally, it had crossed my mind even before I left my hotel that day that I would be going behind the Iron Curtain at a particularly sensitive point. Now, my worst fears had been confirmed.

In disbelief, we hurriedly asked why we were being detained and finally interpreted the officer's stern hand motions to mean that we had committed the highly serious offense of jaywalking. Apparently, we had missed the sign printed in German that directed us to cross the boulevard a few yards from where we actually crossed. This, despite the fact that neither cars nor other pedestrians could be seen for blocks! It was East Berlin's answer to America's patented speed traps.

Several anxious minutes went by before there was any hint that we might have our passports returned. Only at the mention of money did we finally get the point. It was a shakedown, plain and simple. Of course, none of us had any East German currency with which to bail ourselves out of trouble. Nevermind. The officer made it known that he would take virtually any currency we had, especially dollars. Ripped off and unnerved, we happily reclaimed our passports and proceeded quickly on our way. For three freedom-loving North Americans, it was just a small glimpse into a society where you could rest assured that the words "civil liberties" would not be found in the local phrase book.

Perhaps I shouldn't have been so surprised. Some years earlier, I had travelled extensively throughout the then-Soviet Union. Evelina, my Intourist guide and friend, had warned me that eyes and ears were constantly watching and listening in places frequented by foreigners, especially in the Intourist hotels. The frowning matrons sitting behind desks strategically placed at the end of the halls on each floor confirmed her warning about the all-seeing eyes. I took her word for it that the rooms were also bugged. In 1972, one got the distinct feeling that hotels in Moscow, Kiev, and Samarkand weren't exactly your basic Sheraton in the Western world. Nor that American-style "civil liberties" had any close translation in the Russian language.

Honor Where Honor is Due

Travelling to other countries and cultures makes one begin to appreciate the precious commodity of civil liberties which we too often take for granted. Try to imagine a country without a Bill of Rights, or an organization like the American Civil Liberties Union to rally to its defense, and you immediately think of any number of political regimes, none of which you would ever want to experience. The liberties we take for granted would not exist without vigilant guardians to protect us from the potential within every government to abuse its majoritarian, political, or military power. If America has the most secure rights and freedoms of any nation, it is in large measure because of watchdogs like the ACLU.

Is there an organization which has contributed more to the birth of our modern concepts of constitutional rights and liberties? One can hardly think of "civil rights" without the ACLU coming to mind—whether it be the fight for racial equality in the '60s, the dramatic changes in criminal procedure brought about in large measure through its influence on the Supreme Court, or the staunch protection of free speech—even for political dissidents. In the headlines and behind the scenes, the ACLU has been the leader among America's most influential forces in the defense of individual freedom.

It is easy to forget that when the American Civil Liberties Union was formed back in 1920, even basic civil liberties were virtually non-existent. Despite patriotic lip service paid to the Bill of Rights, persons accused of criminal offenses were regularly subjected to police abuse, and trials were conducted without legal counsel for indigents. Political speech was often exercised only at the risk of one's job, or worse. And the first rays of racial equality had yet to dawn on a widely segregated society.

It was into this civil liberties vacuum that the ACLU rushed headlong, winning for itself the praise of the underdog whom it defended and the scorn of those in power whom it usually irritated. Now, after 75 years, no civil liberties group can claim greater credit for the protection of our civil rights than the ACLU.

And yet, the story of the ACLU doesn't end where one might wish. Even its tangled history is an enigma, leading in its earliest years, ironically, to a wistful admiration for the very regime that gave birth to Soviet repression. It's an ever-changing chameleon, the ACLU: Sometimes principled; sometimes pragmatic. Sometimes political; sometimes not. Sometimes noble; sometimes mired in unworthy causes.

So just what are we to make of the American Civil Liberties Union? Is it the good guy, the bad guy, or simply the most schizophrenic character since Dr. Jekyll and Mr. Hyde?

Conflict and Controversy

A closer look at this unique organization, born of anti-capitalist union strife and never quite able to shed the taint of its early Communist connections, reveals that it is never far from controversy. Indeed, controversy is its life blood. Whether defending the Jehovah's Witnesses, or initiating the famous Scopes "Monkey Trial"; whether challenging the government in the Pentagon Papers case and Watergate, or opposing the nomination of Judge Robert Bork; you can always count on the ACLU to be right there in the middle of almost every rancorous public issue.

Well, perhaps not exactly in the *middle*. Despite its audacious claim—"Nor do we take political sides; we are neither liberal nor conservative"[1]—the agenda is patently political and clearly left of center. In the hands of the ACLU, "civil liberty" becomes what the ACLU wants it to be. And what the ACLU wants it to be is anything but conservative.

Can anyone seriously contend otherwise? Just look where the ACLU stands on some of the crucial political issues of our time. For the ACLU, a teenager's freedom to have an abortion is inviolable, yet she must not be permitted to pray aloud in her classroom at school. In the eyes of the ACLU, gay and lesbian couples should have the right to be married—perhaps in the local city park—but if those same couples were to erect a menorah or a nativity creche in the park, they'd best be prepared to defend their actions in court. Did someone really say, neither political nor liberal?

Beyond Simply Hype

It is not just the hype that is so troubling. It's the hypocrisy—at times breathtaking. Historically, there was the defensive about-face on Communism which prompted the infamous "1940 Resolution," barring from ACLU leadership positions any person supporting totalitarianism. Given the ACLU's adamant position against discrimination based upon a person's political beliefs, the Resolution itself should have been sufficiently embarrassing. But the hypocrisy reached new heights with the purge of Elizabeth Gurley Flynn who, despite being a founding member of the ACLU, was also a member of the Communist Party's National Committee. Flynn's heresy trial devolved into a procedural farce, in which political correctness made mockery of fundamental fairness.[2] Had it been a case in which the government was similarly involved, the ACLU would have been up in arms.

In his encyclopedic volume, *In Defense of American Liberties*, ACLU historian Samuel Walker says of this incident that when the anti-Communist fever swept through the ACLU, "it produced the one great deviation from principle in its history." That is a generous self-assessment, ignoring any number of other equally inconsistent positions taken by the ACLU.

There are, for example, instances in which—contrary to its absolutist position on free speech—the ACLU sued its detractors for libel. (When it comes to some forms of free speech—for example, pornography—the ACLU's absolutist position includes not only opposition to any prior restraint on speech but also to any after-the-fact legal consequences.)[4] To its credit, the ACLU has now adopted a policy against the use of libel actions when it is wrongly charged.[5]

When it comes to civil liberties principles that affect the ACLU itself, what's good for the goose—that is, everyone else—has not necessarily been good for the gander. Upon Roger Baldwin's retirement as Director of the ACLU in 1950, for example, the ACLU's staunch position against discrimination based on race or ethnicity suffered a momentary lapse. The search committee seeking to replace Baldwin decreed that "all things being equal...the ACLU director should not be one whose interest in civil liberties might be mistakenly ascribed to his being a member of an oppressed minority group."[6] Samuel Walker provides the frank translation—"In short, no Jews need apply."[7]

More currently, what are we to make of Walker's point that in 1977 the ACLU filed last-minute appeals "on behalf of and against the wishes of" Gary Gilmore (the first person to be executed in the United States in ten years)?[8] How could that be anything other than *against the wishes of Gary Gilmore and on behalf of the ACLU*, which so opposes the death penalty that it is willing to override the freedom of a condemned man not to contest his own execution?

It all gets very strange when one focuses on the ACLU's policy on euthanasia. The ACLU supports Kevorkian-like doctor-assisted suicide "as a legitimate extension of the right of control over one's own body."[9] The single exception, it appears, is if someone dares to exercise that right in the path of the ACLU's determined assault against capital punishment. It's a case of civil liberty for all but anyone who would stand in the way of civil liberty for all, as defined by the ACLU.

Consider also the ACLU's dithering in the Rodney King incident. When the four Los Angeles police officers were tried twice for the same act, hardly anyone seemed to take notice of the Fifth Amendment's protection against double jeopardy—least of all the ACLU, proud defender of the Bill of Rights. Back in 1990, the ACLU board had spoken out against multiple prosecutions and adopted a "no exceptions" policy in cases of double jeopardy. But after the Rodney King trial, the board decided to reconsider its policy in a tie vote broken by the executive director.[10]

When the board eventually re-affirmed its original absolutist position, the Southern California affiliate dissented from the national policy and supported the Justice Department in bringing the officers to trial a second time. *The Boston Globe's* Alex Beam remonstrated the ACLU about what should have been the obvious ACLU position all along, "that brutish, racist police officers," should one accept that characterization, "have civil rights too."[11]

Perhaps its most outrageous hypocrisy is the ACLU's refusal to come to the aid of the various "Baby Doe" infanticide cases. In 1982, when an Indiana child with Down's syndrome and an easily treatable blockage in his esophagus was denied treatment and slowly starved to death, the ACLU didn't want to know. Former ACLU member and anti-abortionist Nat Hentoff chided his colleagues in the ACLU for such a glaring violation of the ACLU's usual standards. Under any other circumstance where an individual was being denied the equal protection of law, the ACLU could hardly restrain itself. But, of course, infanticide cases tread disturbingly close to the ACLU's hallowed commitment to abortion rights.

As executive director Ira Glasser admitted to Richard and Susan Vigilante (authors of "Taking Liberties—The ACLU Strays From Its Mission"), "it was possible," as they reported his response, "that some ACLUers had not come out in favor of the Babies Doe because they didn't want to be on the same side as the right-to-lifers."[12] Harmless hypocrisy is one thing; deadly hypocrisy, quite another.

Fruits of a Liberal Bias

The common thread running throughout all these hypocrisies is the ACLU's partisan liberal-Left bias. If hypocrisy at its base involves crass inconsistency, there is a sense in which the ACLU could plead "Not Guilty." For there is indeed a consistency of sorts found precisely in the liberal-Left ideology which forms the umbrella over its more specific civil libertarian positions. In fact, the overarching relativist assumptions of liberal-Left ideology actually legitimize pragmatic and political inconsistency.

What was it that prompted the 1940 Resolution, the expulsion of Elizabeth Gurley Flynn, the angry libel suits, and the discrimination against Jews in the search for Baldwin's successor? Political pragmatism, pure and simple. Nevermind that it was precisely political pragmatism which created the monster of Watergate at which the ACLU recoiled in horror. In its own constellation of values, the ACLU's political pragmatism is not only easily rationalized, but philosophically mandated.

Liberalism is a kind of social Darwinism in which self-preservation at whatever cost is as natural as survival of the fittest, and in which temporary, convenient mutation may well be necessary for continuation of the species. Liberalism is born of moral relativism in which truth can be pushed either way like a swinging door. Relativism has nothing to fear from inconsistency.

In that light, no one should have been surprised at the 1940 Resolution, spawned by the anti-Communist fever which swept the ACLU after years of idealistic dalliance with Marxism and socialist revolution. It may have been a politically expedient confession of faith at the time, but it was never really a true conversion. Even today, the ACLU's philosophical liberalism continues to have far more in common with Marxist socialism than with right-wing anti-Communism.[13]

If liberal-Left pragmatism explains some of the seeming hypocrisy, much more is explained by the ACLU's ludicrously denied liberal politics. What else could account for the hypocrisy surrounding Gary Gilmore, Rodney King, and Baby Doe? When the choice had to be made between Gary Gilmore's civil rights and the ACLU's fight against capital punishment, politics won over civil liberties. When the ACLU had to decide whether to appease the racial lobby in the Rodney King case or to do the right thing and protest the officers' risk of double-jeopardy, politics again captured at least a partial victory over civil liberties. And, when the ACLU's abortion credentials seemed threatened in the Baby Doe cases, once again—tragically, cruelly, unthinkably—politics trumped both civil liberties and life itself.

The Berlin Wall of Ideology

There is, then, a high level of frustration when one attempts to evaluate the ACLU. Even if patently shocking inconsistencies are more easily understood in the larger context of philosophical assumptions, one cannot help but wonder how an organization dedicated to so noble a cause can fail to recognize the great moral quagmires in which it too often becomes bogged down.

My visit to the Berlin Wall, reminds me of another wall—the so-called "wall of separation between church and state." The ACLU is particularly fond of that wall—a wall which is symbolic of more than just the First Amendment's Establishment Clause, about which we will have much to say. On a far greater scale, it is symbolic of an ideological divide between two competing world views—views as different as east from west. So different are these two ideological perspectives that one almost needs a passport to gain access to the other side, as well as, perhaps, a tour guide and translator.

Beginning in the next chapter, we will attempt to scale the wall and discover the ACLU's unique identity and make-up. What is there about the ACLU that separates it so sharply from the conservative-Right and particularly the religious-Right? What kind of people are members of the ACLU, and what do they believe? What prompts them to be civil libertarians in the first place, and, more intriguingly, what tempts them toward leftist-leaning politics?

After decades of vicious cultural wars, surely it is time for an end to the impasse. If ever we are to break down the wall of suspicion that separates us, we've got to move beyond the deadly no-man's land of cynicism and ask the hard questions of hope.

Not Your Basic Blue-Collar Union

"AFTER NEARLY TWENTY-FIVE CENTURIES, ALMOST THE ONLY PEOPLE WHO SEEM TO BE CONVINCED OF THE ADVANTAGES OF BEING RULED BY PHILOSOPHER-KINGS ARE...A FEW PHILOSOPHERS."

J. ELY

Which best describes the ACLU: socially conscious and idealistic, or elitist with an air of superiority? The answer is both. The problem with idealism of all sorts is that it can be terribly out of touch with reality. In the case of the ACLU, it means being out of touch with the American public and its elected representatives. For the ACLU, elitism is pronounced anti-democratic. The people may have spoken, but the last word has not been uttered until the ACLU has had its say. Civil libertarian distrust of government has been replaced by complete trust in a small cadre of true believers who impose their collective superior wisdom upon lesser mortals. Some may call it an oligarchy of the liberal-Left.

The grand irony is that this small cadre of self-appointed mandarins—typically affluent, well-educated, and politically empowered—spend much of their time and energy railing against the very system that permits them so privileged a position. Historically, their rage against the system has led to wishful thoughts of replacing democracy with socialism. But since the fall of the wall, socialism has been embarrassingly out of vogue. Fortunately for nouveau civil libertarians, today's obsession with victim chic fills the gap. The ACLU even manages to provide the engine that's needed to make victimism work. When faux victims (especially group victims) require the invention of faux rights, the ACLU creates, invents, and provides.

Not Your Basic Blue-Collar Union

In her 1969 Oscar-winning performance in "The Prime of Miss Jean Brodie," Maggie Smith portrayed a politically avant garde, socially-conscious literature instructor at a posh English boarding school for young ladies. "Her girls" were always a cut above the students in the tutelage of others. Beyond the view of the strict headmistress, Miss Brodie assigned unconventional reading and promoted independent thinking on their part.

Brodie's brand of smug elitism was a combination of radical feminism, anarchism, and a particular soft spot for fascist regimes. She sought to instill an idealism and maturity that would have been uncharacteristic of ordinary students, and her small cadre of special disciples simply adored her for it.

Not unexpectedly, Miss Brodie's liberal ideas were eventually exposed, and she was dismissed by the stern headmistress. Worse yet, Miss Brodie's elitist thinking ended up causing a great deal of suffering in the lives of her students. One of her prize pupils, who had eagerly adopted Brodie's attraction to fascist causes, raced off with her fledgling idealism to participate in Spain's civil war and promptly got herself killed. Another (underaged) girl whom Miss Brodie had practically handed over on a plate to a lecherous male art teacher was all-too-easily seduced. Through it all, Miss Brodie maintained a complete air of superiority and equanimity, seemingly oblivious to the consequences of her liberal philosophy.

Whether or not intended, the film is an uncanny portrait of the great cultural battle being waged even today, pitting moral authority (represented by the prudish headmistress) against social rebellion and challenge to traditional mores (in the person of Miss Brodie). Whereas Jean Brodie comes across as the enlightened, progressive revolutionary, the church (predictably) is seen as not only the defender of the faith, but also the defender of a languid, corrupted status quo.

The sexual theme is thrown in, not just for good measure or box office success, but as it invariably is by the libertarian crowd—as the definitive example of what it means to be free from any overriding system of authority. (Miss Brodie even makes a passing reference to Marie Stopes, whose book about female sexuality, *Married Love*, drew both a Customs Service ban in 1929 and a staunch defense by the ACLU.)

The fact that the story of Miss Brodie is set in an educational institution is undoubtedly more than coincidental. For it is in the schools where the battle for the minds of the next generation seems always to be fought by those intent on bringing about radical social change. It is no surprise, of course, that the ACLU maintains a similar interest in promoting its liberal agenda through our educational system.

In both book and living technicolor, Jean Brodie rather strikingly personifies the American Civil Liberties Union: socially conscious, politically left of center, idealistic, elitist—yet seemingly indifferent to the victims whose broken lives lie strewn at the foot of its smugly maintained ivory tower.

From Brodie to Baldwin

The fictional Miss Brodie is in many respects brought to real life in the person of ACLU founder Roger Baldwin. ACLU historian Samuel Walker tells us that the Unitarian Church-raised and Harvard-educated Baldwin had family ties reaching back to the Mayflower, giving Baldwin "an elitist view of his role in society."[1] Speaking frankly, Walker says, "Baldwin had no contact with working-class or immigrant life and was always a bit of a snob."[2] So removed from blue collar labor was Baldwin that at one point he took off for three months to become a common worker in order to "study the psychology and conditions of labor at first hand."[3] Some might say three months was a rather optimistic goal for discovering the harsh realities of the working world!

For Boston-bred Roger Baldwin, an elitist upbringing translated into an elitist style of management. "He never felt he could trust anyone else to direct the civil liberties cause."[4] Baldwin's idea of ACLU governance was "autocracy tempered by advice."[5] Even in the daily affairs of the ACLU office, Baldwin was a clerical snob. No one who worked with him was in any doubt that mundane administrative tasks (like filing and correspondence) were beneath his dignity.[6] Despite being "a union man," Baldwin was "a terrible employer who treated his staff shabbily" and paid notoriously low wages.[7] (In fairness, Baldwin himself never took more than a token salary.)

More importantly, Baldwin's personal elitism seemed to set the tone for the fledgling civil liberties union. "Ever the elitist," says Walker, "he doubted whether there were very many genuine civil libertarians in the country. Better, he thought, to organize a small cadre of true believers."[8] Unlike special interest organizations representing specific groups like blacks and Jews, Baldwin and his board boasted that only the ACLU stood for a broader panoply of libertarian concerns. Precisely because they were a disinterested organization, they were, according to Baldwin, a unique and rare group of "public spirited citizens who are willing to fight for a principle."[9] In his eyes, the ACLU was, and probably always would be, a "small, self-appointed elite, committed to abstract principles."[10]

Baldwin's elitism was also reflected in his wider political perspective. Concerned initially about social reform, Baldwin's futile protest of the First World War caused him to sour on the inevitability of social progress and to abandon his majoritarian view of democracy.[11] He couldn't even handle the democratization of the ACLU itself in the mid-1960s. "Elitist to the end, Roger Baldwin warned that too much democracy could 'water down our principles.'"[12]

Who Are the ACLU Elite?

When Baldwin retired as the ACLU's executive director in 1950, he was succeeded by Patrick Murphy Malin who, says Samuel Walker, "shared many of Baldwin's elitist credentials: an Ivy League education, experience in international human rights work, a commitment to pacifism, and an independent income, thanks to his in-laws...."[13] In large measure, both Baldwin's and Malin's elitist credentials mirror the broader membership of the ACLU, even despite its diversity.

When Herbert McCloskey and Alida Brill set out to survey what Americans believe about civil liberties in their book, *Dimensions of Tolerance*,[14] they concluded that civil libertarians tend to be well-educated professionals; self-described liberals; strong advocates of business regulation and income distribution; and proponents of social change who believe in putting their faith in "theories, plans, and programs," and in "thinking people who have lots of ideas." By contrast, McCloskey and Brill report that civil libertarians are most likely indifferent to patriotism; generally uninterested in religion; and not terribly concerned about law-breaking by citizens.[15]

From the other side of the culture war, William Bennett describes today's cultural elites as "most often found among academics and intellectuals, in the literary world, in journals of political opinion, in Hollywood, in the artistic community, in mainline religious institutions, and in some quarters of the media."[16] The point is that we are not dealing here with a cross-section of the population, but with a small, highly-influential corner of society.

Power to the People? Not So Fast!

Because the "small cadre of true believers" which Baldwin and Malin gathered around themselves in the ACLU were, for the most part, also elitist, there was a distinctly anti-democratic slant to their politics. Never was that collective elitism more evident than when Chuck Morgan, the widely respected director of the ACLU's Southern Regional Office during the turbulent civil rights '60s, dared to say, "Give power to ordinary people, and they will do the right thing." Says Samuel Walker, "Few other ACLU leaders shared his populist vision. Rather, they were deeply skeptical of majority rule; curbing the majority, after all, was the purpose of the Bill of Rights."[17]

Interestingly, that same anti-majoritarian spirit nearly cost the ACLU its very existence. In a bitterly fought referendum in 1954 about whether the Communist party was itself anti-democratic and thus not entitled to civil liberties protections, the anti-Communists on the board were out-voted. Ironically, they invoked a clause in the ACLU's bylaws allowing the board to ignore referenda results when "it believes there are vitally important reasons" for doing so.[18]

If the ACLU subsequently became more internally democratized, nevertheless civil liberties have continued to be closely linked to America's elite, as the previously-mentioned surveys have indicated. More telling still is the ACLU's lack of populist diversity when it comes to implementing civil libertarian concerns into law.

As retired Judge Robert Bork notes, "The constitutional culture—those who are most intimately involved with constitutional adjudication and how it is perceived by the public at large: federal judges, law professors, members of the media, public interest groups—is not a cross-section of America politically, socially, or morally."[19] Bork invokes Robert Nisbet's phrase, "the clerisy of power," to suggest that the clerisy (intellectual class) is greatly distanced from the American public and its elected representatives.[20]

Libertarians or Reactionaries?

The question arises, "Why are America's elites so distanced and alienated from the rest of society?" The answer is surprising to say the least. We're obviously not talking about people who are among the homeless, the unemployed, or the uneducated underclass. In each category, it is just the opposite. Yet the word on the street is that America's elite are disenchanted with "the system," and even distrustful of it. As William Bennett puts it, "The liberal elite call into question what is commonly thought of as 'the American dream.'"[21]

We learn even more from a study by S. Robert Lichter and Stanley Rothman which measured the attitudes of the intellectual class and the liberal-Left. Included in their survey were the leading lights in 74 public interest organizations, including: the Center for Law and Social Policy, Common Cause, the Consumers Union, the Environmental Defense Fund, Public Citizen, a number of major public interest law firms, and—the most relevant organization to our purposes—the ACLU.

The survey revealed that "the liberalism of public interest leaders shades into profound dissatisfaction with the American social and economic order....Three out of four believe the very structure of our society causes alienation."[22] One of the most fascinating observations in the survey was the fact that 96 percent of those sampled had voted for George McGovern.[23]

That last statistic alone shows that not only are the liberal elite woefully out of step with their fellow citizens, but their perspective is characterized by a kind of bloc-vote solidarity. In that regard, America's cultural elite are not altogether unlike rebellious, independence-seeking teenagers who all end up wearing the same punk clothes, dyed hair, and nose rings. In fact, the "liberal establishment" (if that's not an oxymoron) has something else in common with the anti-establishment punkers. As Irving Howe would say of the liberal elite, theirs is "an unyielding rage against the official order."[24]

The problem with the disenchantment articulated by civil libertarians and other elites is that there is typically more outrage against what they regard as an oppressive system than clear-headedness about what ought to be the alternative. Thus, social critic Lionel Trilling describes them as the "adversary culture." They major in deconstruction, not reconstruction.

Of course, the only comprehensive alternative to majoritarian democracy to which the disenchanted elite can point is socialism. As captured by Charles J. Sykes in his compelling book, *A Nation of Victims*, their adversarial stance "was reflected in the intelligentsia's lingering romance with Marxism."[25] Certainly, this dovetails perfectly with the ACLU's historical flirtation with communism.

The problem facing America's elite, however, is that among this country's few remaining taboos is the use of the word *socialism*. John Dewey's *liberalism* perhaps; but not *socialism*. It is not surprising, then, that apart from specific issues of trendy political correctness, socialist-like liberalism has not been well articulated by the change-agents of the liberal-Left.

The reluctance to spell out more specifically what might be included in a full-fledged liberal agenda is explained by the fact that socialism, by whatever name, has proved again and again to be an abysmal failure. Still, the elite can never quite rid themselves of the fantasy that somehow, some way, some day it *might* work!

Washington Times correspondent Richard Grenier opines that "youngish American idealists like President Bill Clinton have never seen applied in their own country anything resembling conventional socialism, so they are consequently still entranced by the socialist vision."[26] As Grenier reminds us, the Clinton administration has more Rhodes scholars and graduates of Harvard and Yale than any administration in U.S. history. No wonder they are so well endowed with what Frederick Hayek called "intellectual hubris." No wonder, too, says Grenier, that "they are undeterred, and along with America's entire elite culture still embrace an enlarged notion of the state, naturally under their control."[27]

Different Costumes; Same Actors

Samuel Walker would likely take exception to Grenier's assessment that all liberals embrace the idea of big government. Walker goes to some length in his history of the ACLU to differentiate between mainstream, "do-gooder" liberals—who do want a welfare state—and ACLU libertarians, who want less government, not more. ("The Kennedys...had little concern for civil liberties," says Walker in aid of his distinction between traditional liberals and civil libertarians.[28]) Whereas mainstream liberals focus on programs, civil libertarians are concerned about form rather than substance, procedure rather than result. Whereas traditional liberals are bureaucrats, true civil libertarians are, at heart, anarchists.

If those distinctions were ever valid, today's overtly political ACLU has forfeited the mantle of true civil libertarianism and merged the two streams of liberalism into a single, cause-oriented agenda. The resulting marriage is a kind of love-hate syndrome. Civil liberties thrive best when government is small and non-intrusive yet still in control of how America thinks and acts. The result is neither democracy nor anarchy, but oligarchy—the rule of the few. And who else would that "few" be, but American's liberal-Left elite?

That is exactly the point at which any assumed distinctions between mainstream liberals and civil libertarians break down. All along, there were more similarities than differences. Take the liberal principle of egalitarianism, for example. For mainstream liberals egalitarianism means big government programs, if necessary, in order to enforce equality through social engineering. For civil libertarians, it meant the implementation of egalitarian principles through an elitist court system. But the difference is only a matter of tactics. The goal—socialist egalitarianism—is the same.

In either instance (as with every socialist or Communist regime that has ever existed), what results is a kind of egalitarianism in which some members of society—namely, the ruling elite—inevitably end up being *slightly more equal* than everybody else. They, not the people whom they claim to represent, are in control. All in all, it's a patently fraudulent egalitarianism for those who demand it on behalf of every segment of society with such strident moral certitude.

The most important common denominator between traditional liberals and civil libertarians is their shared elitism. When Grenier refers to the enlarged liberal State, "naturally under their control," he mixes *tactic* with *aim*. If not all liberals desire an enlarged State, virtually all liberals share the desire to have their hands firmly clenched on the wheel of the ship of state. Columnist Barbara Amiel pegs it perfectly: "Our neo-feudalism is run by mandarins who take the view that it is simply not safe to let any of us decide much for ourselves."[29]

When the mandarins take over, red lights, bells, and whistles ought to be going off for any true civil libertarians who may be left. Amiel sounds a clear warning when she observes that "This magnificent aberration called liberty has only been around for a couple of hundred years during which time a great deal has been accomplished. But almost the minute liberty took root, the very forces of liberalism that gave rise to it developed totalitarianism and statism. One might conclude, rather sadly, that hierarchical autocracy rather than individual liberty is natural to our species."[30]

Rise of the Therapeutic Elites

If there is anything that characterizes the liberal elite, it is a yearning to be unconventional. Bennett opines that "*Odi profanum vulgus* ('I hate the vulgar crowd') is a fitting slogan. If the middle class likes it—be it conventional morality, patriotism, Ronald Reagan, or even *Rocky*, light beer, cookouts, or Disney World—that alone is enough for many of the elites to disdain it, often with an aura of self-assured moral and intellectual superiority."[31]

The apparent irresistible impulse to be unconventional has always posed a great dilemma for elites: how to remain unconventional even when the unconventional becomes conventional. In his reprise of the 1960s, entitled *The Cultural Contradictions of Capitalism*, Daniel Bell addressed the dilemma of cultural insurgents who at one point were "no longer outcasts, or a bohemian enclave in the society."[32] When "outsider" anti-majoritarians finally dominate the cultural, artistic, and intellectual life of the nation, they themselves become the very establishment against which their protesting liberalism earlier railed.

Extrapolating that observation to the past two decades, it has meant that the civil liberties victories of the 1960s are now no longer able to satisfy the restless elitist soul. Hence, the anything-but-civil-libertarian causes fostered by the ACLU. Hence, too, the seeming insatiable need to constantly push the edge of the civil liberties envelope. If ordinary (i.e., constitutional) freedoms are now obtainable, liberalism must become ever more inventive. As Norman Podhoretz said of the Knowledge Elite in 1960, there was "a hunger for something new and something radical."[33]

Today, that "something new and something radical" is *therapeutic victimism*, a kind of new, improved, and—most important—repackaged socialism.

Charles Sykes explains the metamorphosis this way: "Like the other ideologies of the century, the therapeutic culture provided a sort of *faux* community to replace those genuine communities that had disappeared from the modern world. But while the utopian ideologies withered away, the therapeutic ideology survived and flourished."[34]

Translated into civil libertarian terms, it means that traditional (constitutional) rights have given way to faux rights in aid of groups and individuals never contemplated by the Constitution to be within the realm of its protection. It also means that there has been a tactical shift from utopian ideology (egalitarianism) to therapeutic ideology (victimism). Or to put it more graphically—from objectively understood "civil rights for blacks" to more subjective notions of "racism."

Motivated by Elitist Guilt

One quickly begins to understand that there is a natural bond between elitist liberals and the therapeutic ideology of victimism when one considers the movement for racial equality. The economic, educational, and philosophical backgrounds of those who comprise America's liberal elite hardly defines them as a group naturally outraged by injustices against blacks.

Taking nothing away from the ACLU-led civil rights activists (whose finest hour was to do what their conservative detractors should themselves have done), this much can be said: If they chose a noble cause, nevertheless—even unbeknownst to themselves—they may not always have had the purest of motivations.

It is not unfair to say that much of the motivation behind the civil rights movement was white liberal guilt. Not a *collective moral guilt* for the official and unofficial racial injustice imposed upon Afro-Americans from slavery onward, but rather an *individual elitist guilt* for having been raised with a silver spoon in the mouth when others considered themselves lucky just to have a *spoon*.

For many elites, the civil rights movement was as much about making *themselves* feel better, as it was about making racial minorities feel better. On one hand, there is what University of Chicago sociologist James Coleman calls the politics of "conspicuous benevolence" designed to "display, ostentatiously even, egalitarian intentions."[35] That seems almost a harsh judgement of motives, rather than motivations. On the other hand, there is Sykes' observation that the counterculture of the 1960s saw the movement for racial equality "as a powerful weapon with which to strike out against a smugly repressive, materialistic, soulless society."[36]

Look closely at that last sentence. Let the words "smugly," "materialistic," and "soulless" hold your attention. They capture in a nutshell the elite persona, and probably tell more than most elites would care to admit about what has shaped their outrage against "the system." A person does not normally bite the hand that feeds him—unless, perhaps, he is being grossly overfed. Surely, that explains both the otherwise inexplicable elitist resentment of the social order and the true origin of white liberal guilt. In short, for many elites the civil rights movement met a pressing personal need to fill a spiritual vacuum created by their very elitism.

Shifting from the battle over civil rights to the campus upheavals surrounding the Vietnam War, it is easy to see that—whatever the current cause—elites need victims almost as much as victims need the elite. In his 1967 article, "The Sources of Student Dissent," Kenneth Keniston pointed out that "one of the apparent paradoxes about protests against current draft policies is that the protesting students are selectively drawn from the subgroup *most* likely to receive student deferments for graduate work."[37]

So why were easily-deferred elitist students so worked up over the draft? Charles Sykes explains that "theirs was a sort of proxy outrage in which they appropriated the grievances of eminently draftable blacks to strike a moral pose of their own, one that became an essential part of their self-identity and was all the more gratifying since they could then imagine themselves sharing in the oppression and struggle of their brothers."[38]

That analysis is echoed by none other than former ACLU member Nat Hentoff, commenting on anti-war protesters who had interrupted mass at Saint Patrick's Cathedral in New York. "I would suggest that their act's essential effect was to make *them* feel relevant, to make them feel that some of their guilt as Americans had been atoned for by this witness. I am all for self-therapy, but if that's what it is, let us call it that."[39] If Hentoff was right about the shift from *Cause* to *Self*, surely that same shift could not have been better demonstrated than when ACT-UP protesters took a cue from their antiwar predecessors and disrupted mass at Saint Patrick's on behalf of gay rights.

Yet another illustration of liberalism's fascination with therapeutic politics is provided by Gerd Behrens in his *Time* essay regarding "Africa's Uphill Battle." On its face, the article has little to do with civil liberties, but it has everything to do with liberalism's "conspicuous benevolence." Referring to decades of misguided development aid, Behrens says it is "a policy that tends to be more concerned with the emotional comfort of the donor than the material welfare of the recipient."

Although that could be said virtually anytime someone gives a gift, the punch line here is crucial. "Frequently aid for Africa amounts to little more than an exercise in egotism," Behrens continues. "By giving alms, the West can exorcise its postcolonial guilt complex and play the pleasurable part of the benign savior. 'Charity,' notes Nigerian writer Chinua Achebe, 'is the opium of the privileged.'"[40]

One final illustration ties together both the self-serving idealism of the elite and one of the ground-gaining areas of concern for nouveau civil libertarians—namely, euthanasia. (Unfortunately, the ACLU's policy on euthanasia—Policy 271—is nigh unto incomprehensible. However, the language arguably would permit Kevorkian-like, doctor-assisted suicide, which is not simply the passive withdrawal of treatment, but, typically, the active injection of a lethal drug into the patient's body. The ACLU views euthanasia as the ultimate extension of the much-vaunted right to control one's body.)

The poignant illustration comes from Stephen Carter, who tells the story of an anonymous letter written by a physician claiming to have administered a lethal injection to a 20-year-old woman (identified only as "Debbie") who was dying of cancer. A furor of protest emerged in the *Journal of the American Medical Association*. The consensus was that, in failing to obtain unequivocal permission, the physician had overstepped his bounds. "Indeed," says Carter, "it was suggested by some critics that he had acted to alleviate not the patient's suffering, but his own."[41]

What could more clearly illustrate the danger of establishing a civil liberties agenda potentially based on nothing more than the deep-seated need of America's elite to ease what it *says* to be the suffering of a moribund society, but which, in reality, is a desire to ease its own angst?

At the very least, if America's elite would wait long enough to "obtain unequivocal permission" from the rest of America's citizens, perhaps they could proceed from an unsuspicious consensus. As it is, one is hard-pressed to know who stands to gain the most from therapeutic liberalism: Is it America's many well-recognized victims groups, or is it those who, for their own needs, would cavalierly capitalize on the plight of true victims in the name of civil liberties?

The Brave New Libertarians

This latest mutation of socialist ideology—therapeutic victimism—is the best of both worlds for the liberal elite. While *victims* give the new generation of civil libertarians a calling, *victimism*, quite wonderfully, provides an ideology more politically palatable to today's generation than the too-easily-discredited socialist platform of days gone by. Call it *therapeutic civil libertarianism*, if you will. In a culture where virtually everyone is some kind of a victim, therapy and victimism certainly have more curb appeal than any impersonal, economics-based ideology hinting of socialism. So, yes, indeed—a leopard *can* change his spots!

Perhaps. But, if so, he is still a leopard.

Likewise, whether clothed in the old rags of socialism or in the trendy *haute couture* of victim chic, the motivating force behind all civil libertarianism is still very much an elitist animal.

The Great Illusion of the Elitist Soul

Give the devil his due. He knows how to use people who have all the best intentions. Why *shouldn't* we press for equality and human rights all across the board? Egalitarianism stripped of its strained socialist manipulation is, at its core, a proper way to regard our fellow humans. And *how can we not* empathize with the underdog victims of this world? Caring for the poor, the rejected, and the downtrodden is what true social justice is all about.

Here, however, is where the problem lies. It is said that the devil "masquerades as an angel of light."[42] It should not be surprising, therefore, that he would rush to exploit what seems to be enlightened ideology and progressive thinking. Under close scrutiny, it is clear that liberal ideology also masquerades as an angel of light in a world darkened by unjust victimization of all sorts. The difficulty, of course, is knowing true light from the false.

Sorting out that difficult distinction is where the devil could also tell us much about the elitist soul. It is a soul that, because of its great social, educational, and economic advantages, has every potential for good. It is also a soul that is often tortured by its own lack of perfectibility and the guilt which comes from being overblessed. It is a soul easily seduced by a kind of pride and conceit that rails against ordered authority, and then arrogantly appropriates that self-same authority in an effort to create others in its own image.

The Achilles' heel of liberalism and civil libertarianism always and ever will be *elitist pride*. About that kind of destructive pride, the devil himself knows full well. Before his great fall into the abyss of evil, he had held the highest position attainable among the angelic elite.

CHAPTER 4

An Amicus Curious Assault on Democracy

*"IT IS USELESS FOR THE SHEEP TO PASS RESOLUTIONS
IN FAVOR OF VEGETARIANISM WHILE THE WOLF
REMAINS OF A DIFFERENT OPINION."*
DEAN WILLIAM R. INGE

Considering that the ACLU is an elitist, anti-democratic organization, perhaps we shouldn't be surprised at the methods which it employs in order to achieve its goals. A person could guess right away that the ACLU has more faith in the courts than in the legislatures of our land. After all, the ACLU is dominated by lawyers. But few seem to be aware of the punch that is packed in the quiet, behind-the-scenes *amicus curiae* briefs filed by the ACLU in one high profile case after another. It's as if the ACLU were doing the Court's homework.

For much of the ACLU's history, *amicus curiae* ("friend of the court") has had a fortuitous double meaning. Less by design than by common interests, the ACLU has enjoyed a fruitful cronyism with high court judges in an Old Boy, Old Liberal network that at times has bordered on conflict of interest.

But at least the ideological war in the high courts is tempered by legal constraints. Not so when you look at the day-to-day battles that go on in the trenches. Ask almost any school board or local government official, and they'll tell you about the threatening letters they get from the ACLU anytime they tread too close to a constitutional violation. Well, at least by the ACLU's own, vastly expansive definition. You can be sure that the practice of threatening costly law suits is one "chilling effect" that the ACLU will never fight. Apparently, the ACLU believes it is exempt from what it requires of everyone else.

An Amicus Curious Assault on Democracy

S o what do you do when you are an elitist, liberal organization on the fringe of a majoritarian society that, for the most part, thinks differently from you?   How do you promulgate your ideology and cutting-edge policies? How do you ensure that your programs are implemented in the face of far more conservative law-makers?

Go directly to court. Do not pass "Go." Do not collect $200.

But it was not always so. At the dawn of the ACLU, its founder Roger Baldwin was not in the least convinced that the judicial system could be relied upon to preserve and protect civil liberties. Even when the Supreme Court handed the infant civil liberties movement two important First Amendment victories in 1931, Baldwin's skepticism was not dispelled. (In *Stromberg v. California*, the ACLU had successfully defended the display of the red Soviet flag at a Communist summer camp for children; and in *Near v. Minnesota*, a law muzzling the press was struck down.)

Of course, it is difficult to know whether Baldwin's skeptical view of judicial process was born of experience or emanated naturally from his left-wing political ideology which trusted more in power than in law. As he read history, said Baldwin, "all progress has been made by the struggle of oppressed economic classes for a greater share of political and economic power. Power preserves rights. Pieces of paper do not."[1] Given that ideological premise, one is not surprised to hear Baldwin's conclusion: "Rarely do results come through court decisions."[2]

When he wrote those words in 1936, Roger Baldwin could never have imagined the phenomenal impact of groundbreaking court decisions like *Brown v. Board of Education* (school integration), *Miranda v. Arizona* (strict police guidelines), and Roe v. Wade (abortion rights), in which the ACLU would play an active part. But, encouraged by the Supreme Court's increasing receptivity to civil rights over the ensuing decade, Baldwin was eventually convinced. From that point onwards, there was no turning back. Under Baldwin's leadership, the ACLU established a litigation program, hired a permanent staff counsel, and appointed its first lawyers panel. By the mid-1940s, constitutional litigation had become a central feature of the ACLU.[3]

Speaking Briefly to the Court

It soon became obvious that the ACLU's commitment to constitutional litigation needed some kind of vehicle by which to present itself to the courts. After some casting about, the ACLU seized upon *amicus curiae* briefs as the most effective vehicle for carrying its agenda to the courts. These so-called "friend of the court" briefs permit various interest groups to contribute their own research and analysis to the arguments being made on behalf of either party to a dispute.

In case after case, the ACLU began lobbying the courts through the amicus process, and its successes have been legendary. In fact, says Samuel Walker, the ACLU has been involved in more than 80 percent of all landmark cases; and, in several key cases, the Supreme Court's opinion was drawn directly from the ACLU's brief. At any given moment, the ACLU is involved in perhaps 1000 suits, and—perhaps most telling—appears before the Supreme Court more often than any organization except the federal government. On the basis of that track record, the ACLU is proud to confirm what its critics have always contended, that "the ACLU has exerted 'an influence out of all proportion to its size.'"[4]

Dealing as they do with abstract issues of law, amicus briefs seem innocuous enough. (Who could object to whatever might produce a more thoroughly considered, well-informed opinion from the court?) But their popular use by special interest groups (more often claimed to be *public* interest groups) have a profound impact on how major social issues will be decided. And the problem is that it all takes place quietly behind the scenes in the shadow of national attention, with little opportunity for populist scrutiny.

By making what ought to be a *review* process the *starting point*, those who use the amicus approach are thereby able to avoid traditional public debate in the legislative halls by representatives of the people. In fact, more often than not, its whole purpose is to be an end run around what the people's representatives (or the people themselves by direct referenda) might determine the law to be. Indeed, that is why the courts are used instead of normal democratic processes: the courts are friendly; the legislatures are not.

Getting Cozy With the Court

When it comes to the ACLU, the term "friend of the court" takes on new meaning. At least until the Reagan era, the nation's appellate courts (which have the greatest impact on the state of the law) were mostly filled with America's elites who shared the same liberal vision as the ACLU. Judges on America's highest benches were often from a similar Ivy League, Eastern, affluent background, and tended over the years to interact more than just coincidentally with the ACLU and its leaders.

Consider, for example, the relationship between Roger Baldwin and Justice Louis D. Brandeis. When Baldwin graduated from Harvard in 1905, he had little idea what he wanted to do career-wise. Seeking advice, he turned to his father's own lawyer, then corporate attorney Louis Brandeis. Brandeis would go on to write a number of the Court's most expansive free-speech opinions, some in cases brought by the ACLU.[5]

In the early 1920s, prompted by his concern about the FBI's spying on Communists, Baldwin met personally with J. Edgar Hoover and Harlan Fiske Stone, Hoover's boss at the Justice Department. That meeting was made possible at least in part by the fact that Baldwin and Stone had met during the First World War, apparently through their shared interest in conscientious objectors. Baldwin had previously sent Stone a copy of *The Nationwide Spy System Centering in the Department of Justice*, an ACLU pamphlet. Stone was later appointed to the Supreme Court, and, as was typical of his civil libertarian bent, he was the lone dissenter in the *Gobitis* flag-salute case. (Stone's dissent held that the flag need not be saluted when it would be in violation of one's religious conscience.)[6]

Charles Evans Hughes—later Chief Justice Hughes—also had a peripheral Baldwin-ACLU connection. Speaking as president of the American Bar Association in the wake of the *Scopes* "monkey trial," Hughes warned against "growth of an intolerant spirit," particularly by those who would impose their religious beliefs on others. Ironically, it was Hughes whom Baldwin had hoped would try the ACLU-initiated *Scopes* trial rather than Clarence Darrow.[7] Only Scopes' own decision kept that from happening.

Justice Frank Murphy, while still U. S. Attorney General, was invited to be the keynote speaker at the 1939 ACLU Conference on "Civil Liberties in the Present Emergency." In his speech, Murphy pledged to respect civil liberties—a pledge he would keep while on the bench.[8]

Oliver Wendell Holmes, whose famous dissent in the *Abrams* case marked a significant shift in First Amendment thinking, had not taken so strict a line on free speech in the prior *Schenck* case. Samuel Walker suggests that "Holmes' change of heart between *Schenck* and *Abrams* may have been stimulated by a summer meeting with Harvard law professor Zechariah Chafee...."[9] Chafee himself was a noted free speech scholar who worked on a number of cases and free speech projects with the ACLU.

When the ACLU published a 1959 study entitled *Secret Detention by the Chicago Police*, Justices William O. Douglas and Tom Clark requested copies. Shortly afterwards, in a widely reported speech in St. Louis, Justice Douglas favorably cited the ACLU report and its recommendations.[10] Clark's opinion in the groundbreaking search and seizure case, *Mapp v. Ohio*, also appears to have been based upon *Secret Detention*.[11]

If some of the connections between the ACLU and the Supreme Court are more tenuous, other connections are direct and close. There is, for example, Justice Thurgood Marshall, who won 29 of 32 Supreme Court cases on behalf of the NAACP Legal Defense Fund before being appointed himself to the high Court. The ACLU had filed amicus briefs in most of those cases. As with all of the NAACP's top leaders, Marshall had also been on the ACLU board.[12]

One of the most interesting ties between the ACLU and the Supreme Court came in the person of Washington lawyer Abe Fortas. In 1947, Fortas helped coordinate the ACLU's lobbying campaign to counter the government's anti-Communist loyalty program. Then, in 1963, Fortas was appointed by the Supreme Court to represent Clarence Gideon, who had been denied the assistance of counsel in his burglary prosecution. The Court, apparently wishing to overturn its earlier *Betts* decision (which had denied court-appoint counsel for indigents), gave the case to Fortas, undoubtedly aware that his civil libertarian instincts would lead him to argue that the Court should do what it was already poised to do.[13]

That job accomplished, Fortas was then appointed to the Supreme Court. During his distinguished tenure, he wrote the majority opinion in

Tinker v. Des Moines, a landmark students' rights case filed by none other than his former colleagues at the ACLU.[14] At times, frankly, the intimate interbreeding between the ACLU and the Court seems to go beyond having merely a shared point of view and actually borders on conflict of interest.

On the other hand, such intimacy doesn't always play out as one might expect. In 1920, Felix Frankfurter, a labor injunctions expert, was an active member of the ACLU's National Committee. He was also involved in the ACLU's behind-the-scenes strategy in the famous *Scopes* case.[15]

Given that background, one might have expected that Frankfurter, once appointed to the Supreme Court, would be securely within the ACLU's pocket. To the contrary, Frankfurter became one of the Court's strongest advocates of judicial restraint. Samuel Walker reveals that "a distressed Baldwin approached [Frankfurter] on Martha's Vineyard and gingerly expressed the hope that he was 'still carrying on his traditions with us.'" Frankfurter's curt response was that, on the Court, he was no longer an advocate.[16]

The irony of Frankfurter's departure from the ACLU fold is that, during his confirmation hearings, he was attacked for his ACLU connections. Yet, even as counsel for the ACLU, Frankfurter had argued that *legislative* protections of civil liberties (as compared with *judicial* protections) were more democratic and more conducive to the maintenance of civil liberties.[17]

Of course, even considering the eventual estrangement between Baldwin and Frankfurter, the intimacy between the ACLU and the Supreme Court is evident even in respect to Frankfurter. Over the years, from private conversations on Martha's Vineyard, to close family connections (as seen in the Baldwin-Brandeis relationship), to collegial associations with fellow civil libertarians eventually appointed to the bench, the ties between the ACLU and the Supreme Court have been interwoven like an intricate web. Call it an "Old Boy network."

With the arrival of Ruth Bader Ginsburg on the Supreme Court, it may be more appropriate to talk about the "Old Liberal network." After her legal studies at Harvard and Columbia, Ginsburg went on to teach at Rutgers and then Columbia (becoming the first woman law professor ever appointed there). Her ACLU connection began in 1972 when she became director of the ACLU Women's Rights Project. She also served as general counsel for the ACLU from 1973 until 1980. On behalf of the ACLU, Ginsburg filed briefs in nine of the major sex discrimination cases decided during that period, made the oral arguments in six of those cases, and filed amicus briefs in fifteen other cases. *Reed v. Reed*, in particular, was a breakthrough for women seeking equal protection under the Fourteenth Amendment.[18]

Whether the connection is Old Boy or Old Liberal, the ACLU's ties with activist jurists on the high Court has served the ACLU's civil libertarian cause well. Considering the almost clannish links among the liberal set, one begins to appreciate how such intimate networking has led to mostly predictable results. Without question, when amicus briefs are submitted by those who are truly "friends of the court"—ideologically, culturally, and even personally in some instances—there simply has to be a warm receptivity not naturally available to others.

"The Amicus Brief"—Everybody's Doin' It

Sensing the inside track and special relationship which liberal special interest groups have established and curried over decades, conservatives and the religious-Right have begun to realize the importance of the amicus brief. Having gone to school on the ACLU and the other liberal interest groups, conservatives are now doing all they can to bring balance to the amicus process. Yet, in some ways, their monkey-see-monkey-do involvement merely serves to compound the problem. Now, with both sides lining up at the courthouse door, the task of resolving America's most crucial public issues is more likely than ever to result from something other than a purely democratic process.

If the ACLU is truly concerned about issues of constitutionality, it would do well to consider the patent unconstitutionality of judicial activism (both liberal and conservative) whereby the Court preempts Article I, Section 1, granting all legislative powers to Congress—not to the Court. Because of this now-common departure from constitutional mandate, the legislative and judicial branches of government have been reversed. Rather than the Court keeping Congress' legislative power in check, now it is Congress which must often keep the Court's legislative power in check.

Consider, for example, the Religious Freedom Restoration Act of 1993[19] which Congress passed in the wake of the Rehnquist Court's aberrational decision in *Employment Division v. Smith*.[20] In that case, the conservative Court had mysteriously eliminated the requirement for a showing of "compelling governmental interest" before a state could pass a law impinging upon one's free exercise of religion. Sensing disastrous results, Congress (with the support of the broadest religious freedoms coalition ever assembled, including the ACLU) hit the brakes and quickly restored the time-honored constitutional test.

Whether it is through a conservative Court or one more liberal (and more often it has been a liberal Court), a politicized use of the courts to push an organization's pet agenda puts the legislative and judicial shoes on the wrong feet. Far too often, use of an amicus brief has been the tactical shoe horn that has made such a wrongfooting possible.

Amicus Curious, An Evolving Species

Something has been happening to the amicus brief since its discovery by the activist liberal-Left. It has changed, almost chameleon-like, from a theoretically nonpartisan voice to a tool of partisan advocacy. It should no longer be called *amicus curiae* ("friend of the court"), but *advocatus curiae* ("advocate of the court").

Along with this mutation has come a noticeable change in the eyesight of the evolved species. It now sees all social issues in terms of constitutional law. When *advocatus curiae* was viewed under a microscope by Samuel Walker, it appeared that "The Bill of Rights became a set of secular principles for governing American society. As the Court assumed a larger role...the ACLU's ability to shape public policy increased along with it."[21]

The ACLU's Aryeh Neier articulated the strategy succinctly: "Identify a problem and frame it in civil liberties terms."[22] The strategy worked. It wasn't long before the courts had intervened in a broad range of social issues, "recasting them in civil liberties terms." Says Walker proudly, "In the long run the ACLU's role in helping the Court 'constitutionalize' so many public controversies represented perhaps its greatest impact on American life. The process of 'constitutionalization,' in turn, was one of the most important trends in American society."[23]

The process of "constitutionalizing" America meant, for example, that abortion was not merely a question of criminal law for each state to decide, but a "constitutional right" forbidding states from regulating abortion beyond the supposed constitutional guidelines. It also meant that sexual harassment in the workplace was no longer a moral and social issue to be worked out between employers and employees, but was an issue for the courts to decide, looking somewhere within the expansive language of an evolving Constitution. Hardly an issue of controversy could be viewed without being cast in constitutional terms.

It wasn't long, of course, before—just as the dog had wagged the tail—the tail began to wag the dog. Once "constitutionalization" of social issues became acceptable in the courts, the nation's number one constitutional organization (the ACLU) had no choice but to come to the defense of all those constitutionalized social issues. What resulted within the ACLU itself was the politically expansive Biennial Conference. At first, the conference was a forum for such new issues as capital punishment and the rights of the poor. It then devolved into a platform for the "constitutionalized" defense of more politically correct issues like abortion and gay rights.

But that was not the end of the cycle. There were two significant spinoffs from the ACLU's new political commitments. Strangely, the first was a move away from the amicus brief itself—or at least any exclusive attachment to it. As Executive Director Jack Pemberton explained, "We're no longer satisfied to win a few test cases which establish a matter of principle. We're finding that we have to...take a lot of cases at lower court levels—to make the principle work."[24]

This perspective led to much soul-searching within the ACLU, because it changed the very nature of the organization. But since the move from the ivory-tower amicus brief to the trenches of direct representation was already a *fait accompli*, no formal vote was ever taken. Official national policy soon merely recognized what was already happening in one local chapter after another.

The second spinoff from the "constitutionalization" of social issues meant yet another assault on the American democratic process. As the Great Protector of the innovative and expansive "civil liberties concerns" (like gay rights), it became incumbent upon the ACLU to challenge even the most democratic of political institutions—the referendum and initiative processes. Consider, for example, Colorado's anti-gay-rights initiative, Amendment 2. When the citizens of Colorado soundly rejected attempts by gay rights activists to gain special rights in their state, the liberal community went into high gear to overturn the will of the people.

What a long way the ACLU has come since Roger Baldwin first fought for the right of referendum, initiative, and recall. As secretary of the Civic League, he led a campaign to adopt these three Progressive Era reforms which had the purpose of placing government more directly into the hands of the people.[25] If those democratic reforms seemed inconsistent with Baldwin's elitist instincts, they were nevertheless consistent with his early anarchistic, populist leanings. Only later did both Baldwin and the ACLU realize that their own elitist ideology was generally out-of-step with the people they claimed to represent, and that genuine democratic processes were not to be trusted.

So when the citizens of Colorado voted to reject the assertive demands of homosexuals, the ACLU was not content to let democracy have its way. For the ACLU, after all, perverted sexual conduct had now become a respectable "constitutional issue" on par with racial justice.

Nor would support of efforts to overturn the amendment on appeal be enough to satisfy the now-thoroughly-politicized ACLU. One begins to understand just how far the ACLU has removed itself from its traditional defense of civil liberties when you learn that the ACLU vigorously supported, not just the legal appeal, but the highly publicized Colorado boycott which was organized in the wake of Amendment 2's passage.

What is going on here? The ACLU has now moved from the *courts* to the *marketplace*? (The answer, of course, is yes. And to facilitate this move, each local affiliate is organized into two separate corporations—one of which is a tax-exempt legal entity and the other a partisan lobby group.)

It all gets really weird when you listen to Ramona Ripston (Executive Director of the ACLU-Southern California chapter) explain why the ACLU was compelled to back the boycott. "We know that a boycott does economic damage to all residents of Colorado, not just those who supported the message of hate embodied in Amendment 2. But the fact remains that a majority of Colorado voters approved Amendment 2, 53% to 47%...We have no choice but to respond."[26]

Not only does Ripston dramatically underscore how undemocratic the ACLU's position is, but she also reveals the ACLU's complete elitist disdain for those who might suffer innocently for the "sins" of the majority. It would be difficult to imagine a case that better demonstrates how far civil libertarianism has travelled—from principled amicus briefs to the "constitutionalization" of social issues; from politicization of the ACLU itself to economic sanctions against guilty and innocent alike, particularly when things don't quite go the ACLU's way.

Is this still a civil liberties organization that any true civil libertarian can conscientiously have any part of?

A Case Study in Tactical Maneuvering

Sometimes it is easier (or just more interesting) to evaluate an organization in the grand scheme of things. But if one wants to get acquainted with the American Civil Liberties Union up close and personal, it is helpful to dig deeper. To discover how the ACLU operates on a day-in-and-day-out basis, a lesser-known lawsuit may be more helpful than high-profile cases. The case of *Akron v. Akron Center for Reproductive Health*[27] provides a good example of a mundane case, and yet there was something both ordinary and extraordinary about this suit.

It wasn't surprising that the ACLU sued to overturn an Akron, Ohio ordinance requiring parental notification prior to a minor having an abortion. Historically, the ACLU has challenged any number of laws relative to abortion. What made this suit different was not its beginning, but its conclusion.

The government's case in defense of the notification requirement was joined by a group of Ohio parents who contended that their rights as parents would be violated if the law were overturned as the ACLU desired. By joining in the government's case, the parents became "intervenors." That is, they were individuals concerned, not simply with sovereign acts of government, but with their own individual rights as parents.

As it turned out, the ruling in this particular case was in favor of the ACLU and against the government and the parents. In and of itself, such a result would have been unremarkable. Other courts have decided the same issue in exactly the same way. What was remarkable was the action taken by the ACLU at the conclusion of the case.

Under normal circumstances, it would be right and proper—even customary—for the ACLU to have sued the government for attorney's fees. It is assumed that the individual who sues the government is having to bear a great financial burden in doing so, and, further, that the government is in a position to afford such costs when it loses. Therefore, sticking it to the government was, by law, altogether permissible.

What was surprisingly different about this case was that the ACLU also stuck it to the parents who had intervened, to the tune of $100,000![28] The ACLU apparently did not appreciate that their own side in the case had hardly been a matter of individuals suing the government. The ACLU's very presence in the case meant that the issue had escalated from a simple civil suit among individual plaintiffs and defendants to a socially-significant civil action being fought between a special interest organization and a governmental body.

Nor, more importantly, did the ACLU appreciate—or seemingly care—that such punitive action against the parents had every potential for causing a chilling effect on future litigation by any individuals who might wish to challenge the ACLU's position on abortion or any other issue. Indeed, to the more cynical among us, that was precisely the reason for the ACLU's having taken such a harsh line. In any future cases, it would amount to a preemptive victory by prior intimidation. After all, what parents can afford to join in litigation against a massive special interest organization like the ACLU at the risk of having to pay sizable attorney's fees in the event that they lose the case?

When a Letter from the ACLU Brings Chills

There are more ways than one to have a chilling effect on free speech, free exercise of religion, and other constitutionally-guaranteed conduct. None has been more successful for the ACLU than its use of intimidating letters threatening costly litigation against those who do not comply with its agenda. In church-state matters especially, school boards, principals, and teachers have been targeted by the ACLU. They have been convinced by the ACLU's barrage of liberal "letter bombs" that conduct which is perfectly constitutional is not worth the risk.

Typical of such letters is one received by the superintendent of a school district in Spanaway, Washington, from the president of the local ACLU chapter. The superintendent was censured for permitting Bethel High School to put on *Jesus Christ, Superstar* as its spring play. According to the ACLU president, the school was "engaging in religious instruction." It was total nonsense, of course, but his parting shot was that "further violations of this kind may result in more direct and more drastic action by the ACLU."[29]

As a result of letters like this one, many school officials are running scared, even though they have no legal reason to be. What the ACLU has done is to build a barbed fence of its own making around the Constitution—although at considerable distance from it—and threatened anyone who would dare violate, not just the Constitution, but their own privately held beliefs about what ought, or ought not, to be permissible.

Anyone else engaging in such legal blackmail would be marked by lack of integrity. For a civil liberties organization to do so is unconscionable. How the ACLU would howl if a Christian legal organization made similar threats based upon nothing more than its private interpretation of a court decision!

True Friends of the Court

Whether it be a threatening letter to the local high school principal; or punitive attorney's fees for parents who would dare stand up to the ACLU's abortion Juggernaut; or an economic boycott against a state whose citizens vote their consciences in a democratic initiative; or the strained "constitutionalization" of social issues presented in partisan amicus briefs to cozy colleagues in the Old Liberal network—there is something unseemly about the manner in which the ACLU has allowed itself to operate. Such elitist tactics are patently highhanded, but all the worse for evidencing a fundamental lack of respect for the democratic process.

If the courts of America are gracious enough to receive amicus briefs on matters of great national importance, then let them hear millions of other "friends of the court." It is time for government to be handed back to the people—*all* of the people—not just the privileged few unfairly empowered by a liberal-Left cronyism. It is time, too, for judges to resist the heady notion that all social issues are questions of constitutional interpretation for people in robes alone to decide.

Given the dangerous trend towards anti-democratic civil liberties, surely it is also time for true civil libertarians to take back the ACLU from the radical social engineers whose political perversion of the Constitution and strong-arm bullying tactics desecrate the honorable name of civil liberties.

CHAPTER 5

Dancing to a New Hermeneutic

YOUR CONSTITUTION IS ALL SAIL AND NO ANCHOR."
LORD MACAULAY

L egal philosophy can be the stuff of dry law school lectures, or the hidden reason for the ACLU's frenzied opposition to the Supreme Court nomination of Judge Robert Bork. Why was Bork such a threat to the ACLU and its liberal allies? Because he personified a particular view of the Constitution that promised to undermine the liberal-Left political agenda of the ACLU. Not that his view of the Constitution was either novel or unique to himself. His view was the predominant view of virtually all legal scholars—as well as the ACLU—until relatively recent times. But times have changed, or so says the ACLU.

Today's battle is between those who view the Constitution as a document having a fixed meaning, and those who see it as a "living document," capable of being broadly reinterpreted. Restricted to the face value of the Constitution's original intent, many of the ACLU's current policies would have no constitutional basis whatsoever. Knowing that, the ACLU has become adept at undermining the Constitution's authority, while simultaneously paying lip service to it. Through a subtle process of textual revision, the ACLU alternatively adds to the text or takes it away. The ACLU specializes in inventing elastic concepts, like the notion of privacy, from which any number of novel civil liberties are then derived. In the end, the Constitution is what the ACLU says it is. With that, why bother to pass a Constitutional amendment?

Dancing to a New Hermeneutic

W hen on July 1, 1987, President Ronald Reagan strode to the podium in the press room of the White House and nominated Judge Robert H. Bork as the next Associate Justice of the U.S. Supreme Court, the American Civil Liberties Union went ballistic. So did the People for the American Way, the National Organization of Women (NOW), the Feminist Men's Alliance, Planned Parenthood, the National Women's Law Center, the AFL-CIO, the National Abortion Rights Action League, the National Association for the Advancement of Colored People (NAACP), and Senators Biden, Metzenbaum, and Kennedy.

Within forty-five minutes of Judge Bork's nomination, Senator Edward Kennedy appeared on national television, denouncing Bork in the shrillest terms ever leveled against a Supreme Court nominee:

> Robert Bork's America is a land in which women would be forced into back-alley abortions, blacks would sit at segregated lunch counters, rogue police could break down citizens' doors in midnight raids, schoolchildren could not be taught about evolution, writers and artists would be censored at the whim of government, and the doors of the Federal courts would be shut on the fingers of millions of citizens for whom the judiciary is often the only protector of the individual rights that are the heart of our democracy.[1]

How Senator Kennedy thought anyone could believe such a wild characterization of a respected United States Court of Appeals Judge in the rights-conscious 1980s is a mystery. Nevertheless, Kennedy's vicious tirade was but the opening volley in what would turn out to be a merciless massacre of Judge Bork's chances for confirmation, and—on a grander scale—an epic battle between liberals and conservatives in a far-flung culture war.

The intensity of the ACLU's own hysteria is most strikingly evidenced in a fundraising "telegram" sent by the director of the ACLU via "Western Union priority letter." Among its many expressions of outrage were some of the following statements, presented in full capitals: "DETAILED RESEARCH REVEALS BORK FAR MORE DANGEROUS THAN PREVIOUSLY BELIEVED...WE RISK NOTHING SHORT OF WRECKING THE ENTIRE BILL OF RIGHTS...HIS CONFIRMATION WOULD THREATEN OUR SYSTEM OF GOVERNMENT....TIME IS SHORT....URGE YOU TO RUSH EMERGENCY CONTRIBUTION AT ONCE."[2]

Yet it was the behind-the-scenes internal ACLU crisis prompted by Judge Bork's nomination that best demonstrated the extent to which the ACLU felt threatened by Bork. With but one exception throughout its history, the ACLU had steadfastly refused to support or oppose candidates for elected or appointed office. The single exception, the ACLU's opposition to the elevation of William Rehnquist to Chief Justice, afterwards proved to be an embarrassing deviation from what had been a fundamental organizational policy against political endorsement.[3]

Apparently for that reason, the ACLU was conspicuously absent when a national anti-Bork coalition—spearheaded by People for the American Way and others—was formed shortly after Judge Bork's nomination. But it was clear to most board members that Judge Bork represented an unprecedented threat to the ACLU's very mission, and something would have to be done about it. At the urging of board member Frank Askin, an emergency Executive Committee meeting to reconsider the ACLU's policy was hastily called for August 29 and 30. Most members arrived having already made up their minds that the ACLU should oppose Bork.[4]

Last-ditch efforts by a minority of board members who believed that the staff report distorted Bork's views and who feared what they saw as a slippery slope toward even more widespread partisan politics proved futile. The board voted 47 to 16 to permit ACLU opposition of any Supreme Court nominee "whose record demonstrates a judicial philosophy that would fundamentally jeopardize the Supreme Court's critical and unique role in protecting civil liberties."

On the following day, Sunday, the board voted 61 to 3 to oppose Bork's nomination.[5] By Sunday evening, staffers at the New York office had already begun phoning local affiliates. The ACLU's partisan, frenzied assault against a Supreme Court nominee had begun.

What was it about this man Robert H. Bork that incurred the wrath of the liberal-Left? What could possibly provoke the ACLU into reversing one of its most fundamental organizational policies, particularly in the face of recent embarrassment over the Rehnquist aberration? The answer depends upon whether one wishes to believe only the propaganda, or to pierce through the propaganda to understand the real threat.

Lies From the Left

The propaganda barrage itself focused on three main issues: racial justice, women's rights, and, of course, the pivotal issue of abortion. Anti-Bork forces specifically targeted the black community by intentionally spreading vicious rumors throughout black churches (particularly in the South) that Bork would "turn back the clock" on civil rights.[6] Employing scurrilous innuendo from two cases not even involving racial discrimination, it was said that Bork had ruled in favor of poll taxes and literacy tests in an attempt to limit voting rights for blacks. (What he did was to object to the two decisions involved for reasons wholly unconnected with either poll taxes or literacy.) Even ACLU historian Samuel Walker acknowledges that "there were some serious distortions. Bork was not a racist, as some critics suggested...."[7]

In another piece of pure fiction, the *Biden Report* appealed to the women's vote, claiming dramatically, "Judge Bork Has Indicated That The Constitution Does Not Protect Against Mandatory Sterilization."[8] Planned Parenthood joined in the deceit with ads accusing Bork of "sterilizing workers."[9]

Bork's unforgivable sin against women's rights was simply to rule, as part of a three-judge panel in the *American Cyanamid* case, on a company's dilemma about what to do when its manufacturing process endangered the fetuses of pregnant female employees. The panel ruled that the company had not violated the Occupational Safety and Health Act when it gave women employees the option of remaining in their jobs if they chose voluntary sterilization, rather than having to be either transferred or discharged for their own protection.

This decision should not have been even the least bit shocking in light of the Supreme Court's own holding in *Dothard v. Rawlinson* that women could be refused jobs as prison guards in male-only prisons because of their capacity to be raped.[10] Whether or not a person happens to agree with that ruling, it highlights the unwarranted paranoia over Robert Bork as somehow being uniquely unfit to serve as a Supreme Court Justice. The deliberate distortion of the narrow ruling in *American Cyanamid* conveniently served to provide a desperate excuse for the war cry—"the women of America are afraid of Judge Bork"—which in great measure helped to derail Judge Bork's confirmation.[11]

The propaganda was neither factual, nor honest. As characterized by Professor Robert W. Jensen, a Lutheran theologian, the campaign against Judge Bork was "notable not only for its volume but for its scurrility and mendacity."[12] Pulling no punches, Jensen observed that "the misrepresentation has been so pervasive and its detection requires so little investigation, that either the sponsors and authors of these ads are astonishingly incompetent conceptually or they have simply lied."[13]

In the end, of course, the liberal coalition's massive conspiratorial deception proved successful. On October 23, the Senate rejected Bork's nomination by a 58-42 vote.

The whole sad Bork affair reveals much about the morality of the liberal-Left, which permits truth to be so blithely sacrificed to ideology. If the devil is "the father of lies,"[14] he has many children. It should also be particularly shaming to civil libertarians that Judge Bork was put on national trial but never given a fair hearing. Had the conservative-Right smeared Senators Biden, Metzenbaum, and Kennedy in the same libelous manner, we would still be hearing a loud chorus of objection.

Behind the Propaganda

Ultimately, the battle over Bork had little to do with the headlines or hot-button issues, or even the liberal-Left's Watergate-like dirty tricks. We begin to get a feel for the real issue when we consider that much of the text of the newspaper and television ads was composed of deliberate falsehoods suggesting that Bork believed the stated goals themselves were not to be desired.[15] Bork did not object to the "ends" sought in a given situation, only to the "means" of achieving those "ends." Naturally, for those who wished to scuttle Bork's appointment, such subtle distinctions seemed but a pesky nuisance. Better to tar Judge Bork with the charge that he objected to the worthy goals themselves.

These important distinctions begin to point us in another direction, away from specific issues like racism, women's rights, and abortion toward Bork's underlying legal philosophy. The specific issues had been secondary all along. What rattled the liberal community was Bork's commitment to a view of constitutional interpretation that potentially would have had a devastating impact on the liberal-Left's entire political agenda.

Planned Parenthood alluded to the real issue (which it otherwise camouflaged) when it painted Bork as "an ultraconservative judicial extremist" who "uses obscure academic theory."[16] Of course, there was nothing the least bit obscure about Bork's philosophy. In truth, it was the very clarity of his philosophy that sent the liberal-Left into its frenzy. Bork's understanding of constitutional interpretation was the same as that held by Madison, Jefferson, and Story, and represented the classical view of constitutional interpretation until relatively recent times.

Ironically, it is the trendy academic theory of constitutional interpretation spawned by liberal activism which is obscure. Its results-oriented methodology depends almost entirely upon fanciful innovation of otherwise-clear constitutional text, a process which often takes one into the nether regions of creative abstraction. The more traditional approach, on the other hand, takes the Constitution at face value and employs both rational rules of logic and common sense in drawing its conclusions.

What was at stake in the Bork nomination was not just abortion rights, but the whole concept of privacy rights, having potentially negative effects on a wide array of liberal issues. On an even deeper level, what was at stake was not just privacy rights, but the choice in methods of constitutional interpretation that would either validate or condemn revisionist, extra-constitutional concepts such as "privacy."

Pure civil libertarianism could survive—even thrive—under traditional rules of interpretation; the political and social agenda of the liberal-Left could not. Hence the battle over Bork, who personified through his legal philosophy the one truly crucial issue in the larger cultural war.

Or should we say, the larger *spiritual* war? It should not be forgotten that the devil himself was the first textual revisionist. "Did God really say, 'You must not eat from any tree in the garden'?" he wryly asked an unsuspecting Eve. "You will not surely die," he reassured her with a creative rationalization worthy of the best legal minds who have ever ingeniously convoluted the obvious meaning of the Constitution.[17] For those who would be advocates for the devil, textual revision is a tool of the trade.

The Struggle Over Hermeneutics

However else the differences between Left and Right may have been articulated, the philosophical watershed is fundamentally a matter of hermeneutics. *Hermeneutics* is defined as the interpretive viewpoint from which you approach the text—any text, although it most often refers to the process of interpreting and applying sacred texts.

In this case, constitutional hermeneutics has to do with the words of the Founders: How are we to interpret what they meant when writing over two centuries ago? More difficult yet, how are we to apply the Constitution as we rapidly move into the 21st century?

It depends on what kind of lens we are using when we focus on the Constitution. Or, what tint of glasses, if you prefer. Depending upon one's choice of hermeneutics, two persons may read exactly the same words, and, in good faith, interpret their meaning altogether differently.

Naturally, there is a sense in which one's personal hermeneutic extends to one's entire world view. Without question, that philosophical panorama will have a profound effect on virtually everything else, including the particular hermeneutic being brought to a given text.

The correlation between one's world view and a particular textual hermeneutic is never closer than when one's world view affects underlying assumptions regarding the nature of the document itself. Is the United States Constitution, for example, imbued with a kind of divine inspiration akin to Holy Scripture; or is it, although extraordinary, merely a human document? Anyone claiming the former would naturally treat the Constitution with near reverence, while others would temper their assessment in light of human fallibility.

In truth, few, if any, would claim direct, divine inspiration on behalf of the Constitution. *Blessed by God*, it may well be; but hardly God-breathed, as is the case with inspired Scripture. And the difference is important, especially for many conservatives who also happen to be Bible-reading, Scripture-exalting believers. Because both documents are "constitutional" in their own way, it is easy to forget that the U.S. Constitution is not in fact on par with Holy Writ. Both may be authoritative—one in spiritual matters, the other in law—but only one, the Constitution, may be altered through an authorized amendment process.

That said, it is understandable that those who have one eye trained on Scripture would choose a constitutional hermeneutic not wholly unlike the one they would apply to their own faith text, the Bible. In all likelihood, their hermeneutic would view the Constitution as static, authoritative, and restrictive.

Those who are not believers are likely to choose a quite different constitutional hermeneutic, in part because their world view does not give them a comfort zone with any comprehensive authoritative document like the Bible. Whereas the Bible purports to present absolute truth revealed from on high, a person who does not accept the Bible in that light may well be more comfortable with a constitutional hermeneutic that allows for flexibility, relativism, and change.

If we move down a level at this point and leave behind the larger hermeneutic of one's world view, we continue to find considerable divergence, but in more familiar terms. Given the mutual tribute paid to the Constitution by both sides, the fundamental struggle between liberals and conservatives revolves around whether we are limited to the "original intent" of the Constitution or whether it is a "living document" which allows for expansive new rights. The distinction between those two approaches is critical, especially for the liberal-Left. Samuel Walker, for one, is quick to admit that the "original intent" approach "would invalidate most of the civil libertarian activism of the past several decades."[18]

"Original intent," the *old hermeneutic* if you will, calls for judicial restraint and affirms the belief that legal truth can be derived objectively from a careful reading of the Constitution. The *new hermeneutic*, by contrast, views the Constitution as merely a starting point historically, from which we launch out into unknown territory as demanded by the changing circumstances of our times. Put more sympathetically, in the eyes of the ACLU, it is a question of asking the Founders how they would resolve a particular issue if it were before them now as opposed to *then*.

This brings us to yet a third level of hermeneutical diversity—a more practical expression of the factors we have already noted. Wholly apart from one's philosophical presuppositions, it is the precise textual hermeneutic—one's methodology—that is crucial for the moment. Do we approach the text to see what it says and only then attempt to apply it to the specific case at hand; or do we draw our own conclusions about the case at hand and go to the text hoping to find justification for our conclusions?

The Cultural Argument

Naturally, you don't hear anyone talking out loud about adopting a revisionist view of the Constitution. That would spill the beans and forfeit any chance of credibility. Instead, the talk is about change. Change is a cultural icon. Presidents get elected on a platform of change—particularly when the past is couched in terms of soulless tradition. Particularly, too, when one castigates the moribund values of a dying generation. At base, the call for change is a cultural argument in which the Constitution must be interpreted in the light of new circumstances. What was good for *them* in the then and there is not good enough for *us* in the here and now.

No better illustration of the cultural, antihistorical argument could be found than that provided us by legal scholar Paul Brest in aid of his proposition that the death penalty is a violation of the Eighth Amendment's clause prohibiting cruel and unusual punishment. Writes Brest:

> The adopters of the clause apparently never doubted that the death penalty was constitutional. But was death the same event for inhabitants of the American colonies in the late 18th century as it is two centuries later? Death was not only a much more routine and public phenomenon then, but the fear of death was more effectively contained within a system of religious belief.
>
> Twentieth-century Americans have a more secular cast of mind and seem less willing to accept this dreadful, forbidden, solitary, and shameful event. The interpreter must therefore determine whether we view the death penalty with the same attitude—whether of disgust or ambivalence—that the adopters viewed their core examples of cruel and unusual punishment.[19]

How much clearer could it be than that, when viewed with a cultural hermeneutic, the original language of the Constitution counts for little? Indeed, one might ask, "Why even bother with paying lip service to constitutionalism?" Surely it would be better to simply transform the nation's highest tribunals into courts of equity. Each case could then be, quite straightforwardly, "equity is as equity does."

Of course, hardly anyone, whether liberal or conservative, would deny that the law must change with the times. We simply are not the same nation as when the Constitution was first drafted. The question remains, however, whether those changes ought to come about by democratic processes—namely, by local, state, and federal legislation through the people's elected representatives—or, rather, by judicial legislation from the nation's courts. Typically, so-called "judicial activism" is shorthand for the latter choice, although, surprisingly—given the usual philosophical align-ments—there have been conservative "activists" as well as liberal "activists" on the bench.

What *can* be said in complete fairness is that judicial activism is more natural to the liberal-Left than to the conservative-Right; and, furthermore, that most liberals would not be offended in the least by that assessment. Invariably, they are proud of their activism and take their activist role as seri-ously as the next person's religion. So activism, as such, can be a misleading clue in the search for what divides us.

Nor should one confuse judicial activism with the common law tradi-tion. That tradition, which predates the Constitution, emphasizes case precedent, not activism. When changes come through the common law process, they come primarily as the result of distinguishing a fact situation from prior cases, necessitating a different result. It is all the difference between evolution and revolution.

Judge Bork himself brings us back to the crucial hermeneutical issue and its relation to cultural influences around us:

> At some point, every theory not based on the original under-standing (and therefore involving the creation of new constitutional rights or the abandonment of specified rights), requires the judge to make a major moral decision. This is inherent in the nature of revisionism. The principles of the actual Constitution make the judge's major moral choices for him. When he goes beyond such principles, he is at once adrift on an uncertain sea of moral argument.[20]

In short, a hermeneutic of "original intent" will significantly prevent the kind of subjective analysis that would permit individual judges to read into the Constitution their own culturally-influenced ideas about what "ought to be." *Maybe* they could be right, and *maybe* we might agree with them. But what does it say for the rule of law when individual judges can overrule the express will of the people even in areas where the Constitution itself has not spoken?

Importing one's own cultural values without a license is the surest way to turn a "living document" into a dead one. A Constitution that is expan-sive enough to accommodate any values, no matter how trendy, loses its very essence as a Constitution. It survives only as a convenient wall against which to bounce ideas—hardly a lofty statement of commonly accepted fundamental principles on which a government is founded.

Being Objective About Subjectivity

The key component of the new hermeneutic is subjectivity. Explicit appeal to a subjective hermeneutic was perhaps most vividly seen among ACLU supporters during a policy struggle within the ACLU itself during the 1970s and 1980s. During that time, the ACLU's Biennial Conferences had become the principal forum for activists within the ACLU who wanted to move beyond the traditional First Amendment, due process, and equal rights issues. For those intent on further politicizing the ACLU, the Biennial resolution became the fast track to sweeping change in the realm of social and economic policy. Resolution after resolution was passed, mostly regarding groundbreaking economic rights but also including (get ready for this one) the "civil liberties dimensions" of nuclear war.

In the end, the resolutions were mostly rejected by the board and the electorate. Nevertheless, the debate between the activists and the moderates takes on increasing importance in light of today's resurgence of ACLU political activism. In response to moderates who contended that the ACLU could best serve the poor by sticking with the ACLU's original mission, "the activists," Samuel Walker tells us, "replied that the ACLU was bound by no fixed agenda. As many of them put it, the scope of civil liberties is what we say it ought to be, not what the Supreme Court says it is at this moment."[21]

Of course, the activists were right about the ACLU itself. Nothing says an organization can't change its mission in mid-stream. But what they were really saying was that the *Constitution* was not "fixed." The operative words in this exchange, "the scope of civil liberties is what we say it ought to be," exemplifies perfectly the subjectivity of the new hermeneutic which has now been comprehensively adopted by the ACLU.

The response of the activists to this charge of excessive subjectivism is revealing. "True," they say, "the Bill of Rights did not mention economic rights, but the word *privacy* did not appear either, and the ACLU was vigorously pursuing privacy rights."[22] (Certainly a damning admission if there ever were one.) The activists were not at all bothered by charges that they had introduced a hermeneutic which could lead wherever a person might want to go, even without any genuine constitutional support.

This contrasts, of course, with the constitutional authority to which the ACLU points when constitutional language suits its own agenda. The Constitution is binding when it agrees with the ACLU—but not otherwise. Where the Constitution is silent when the ACLU wishes it were not, the ACLU figures out a way to make it speak on the ACLU's behalf. Through its practice of selective usage, the ACLU demonstrates that it couldn't care less about the authority of the Constitution. Yet defensively, the ACLU wouldn't dare proceed without at least a pretense of constitutional backing. Constitutionalism thus becomes nothing more than self-serving rhetoric, and the process of interpretation little more than a hermeneutic of convenience.

The seeds for this new hermeneutic were sown as early as 1919 when Oliver Wendell Holmes argued in his *Abrams* dissent, that the Constitution was "an experiment, as all life is an experiment."[23] Samuel Walker is proud of the ACLU for playing "a leading role in that experiment since 1920, continually pressing for an expansion of individual rights."[24]

The problem with a civil rights organization that departs from "original intent" is that its own agenda is in a constant state of flux. Worse yet, it becomes an organizational dog chasing its own ideological tail: The Constitution is what civil libertarians want it to be; and what it thereby becomes, in turn, fixes the current agenda for civil libertarians.

Again, Walker provides the perfect illustration of the fluidity of constitutionalism that results from such a subjective hermeneutic. "Many ACLU members," he writes candidly, "will be surprised to learn that the organization did not always take an 'absolutist' position on censorship or the separation of church and state."[25] Why the shift? Because under the old hermeneutic, which the ACLU and virtually everyone else formerly acknowledged, the Constitution was taken at face value for what it obviously said or did not say. Using the hermeneutic of "original intent," there was simply no textual basis for anyone taking an "absolutist" position on either censorship or the separation of church and state. An objective approach leaves no room to find in the words of the Constitution what one merely *wishes* to find.

Sadly, the ACLU thinks of the Constitution in much the same way it regards the unborn child in the womb. If the mother *wants* it to be a baby, then it *is* a baby, and the law should do everything in its power to protect the baby from intentional harm. But if the mother *doesn't* want it to be a baby, then it is not a baby, and the law should do everything in its power to permit the mother to "terminate the pregnancy."

For the ACLU, the Constitution becomes whatever it subjectively *wants* it to be. The reality of what it actually says hardly seems to matter. One can simply read into the text whatever cultural, political, or personal values one wishes to find.

If perhaps the American dream was a grand experiment, the Constitution itself is much more than simply an experiment. It was, and is, law—the highest law of the land. It both delineates our freedom and limits the powers of government. If we choose a subjective, experimental expansion of our freedom, we open the door for others to choose an equally subjective expansion of the powers of government. In such a case, the grand experiment will have failed, and, with it, our civil liberties.

Inductive, Deductive, and In-de-ductive

Few interpreters of the Constitution are as open about their subjectivism as the ACLU's radical activists. Most liberals would never come right out and admit that "the scope of civil liberties is what we say it ought to be." What they will do, however, is subtly create an entirely new constitutional text from which they can more easily draw conclusions that are consistent with their political beliefs and goals.

Judge Bork talks about that disingenuous process in his book, *The Tempting of America*. (In fact, it is this very process which provides both the title of his book and the temptation of which he writes.) Referring to the 1937 case of *Palko v. Connecticut*, Bork points us to the seemingly innocent—even "splendid phrase"—for which that case is perhaps best known. In attempting to encompass the full scope of fundamental liberties worthy of protection, the *Palko* Justices said that our freedoms should include all those which are "implicit in the concept of ordered liberty."[26] Can there possibly be anything sinister about that formulation?

The answer, surprisingly enough, is "yes." Rather than identifying the specific bundle of liberties spelled out in detail in the Constitution itself, the *Palko* Justices created an elastic, user-friendly formulation which would permit unsuitable liberties to be invited into the Constitution's zone of protection. No, it's not that a judge might use such a hospitable formula to intentionally pervert the Constitution. It's just that what the *Palko* Court created in that brilliant formulation was a kind of *supratext* beyond the text of the Constitution itself.

It was, in effect, a completely different constitution—a concept, if perhaps not a document, which could be laid along side the original Constitution and interpreted freely without the tight restrictions of the more specific guarantees. In one fell swoop, it became the Grand Amendment, the Alternative Constitution. And for activist civil libertarians, the Constitution of choice in more than one respect.

Certainly, the *Palko* test was not the only formulation of its type. In *Moore v. East Cleveland* (1977) it was said by the Court that our protected liberties are those that are "deeply rooted in this Nation's history and tradition."[27] Commenting on that formulation, Judge Bork says wryly:

> The judge who states that tradition and morality are his guides, therefore, leaves himself free to pick through them for those particular freedoms that he prefers. History and tradition are very capacious suitcases, and a judge may find a good deal pleasing to himself packed into them, if only because he has packed the bags himself.[28]

Finally, there is Justice Blackmun's formulation in *Bowers v. Hardwick*, the Georgia sodomy case. If you thought "fundamental rights" just about said it all, listen carefully to Blackmun's masterpiece of creativity. The case, said Blackmun in dissent, was not about some fundamental right to engage in homosexual sodomy [which he recognizes, of course, that no one could find if limited to the specifically enumerated fundamental rights of the Constitution], but about "the most comprehensive of rights and the right most valued by civilized men,' namely, 'the right to be let alone.'"[29]

Think long and hard about that one. If the right to be let alone is *the most comprehensive of rights*, then the 5th Amendment itself is superseded. In fact, if consensual, non-public activity in this particular case reflects a more pervasive "comprehensive right to be let alone," by the same logic the government would never be entitled to impose justice in violation of the individual's right to be let alone. Consider, for example, crimes other than sodomy, such as burglary, robbery, and rape. Of itself, the right to be let alone makes no distinction between victimless crimes and those having identifiable victims.

Of course, the *Hardwick* case was not the first time that Justice Blackmun created a new supratext from which to glean novel civil liberties. Aided and abetted by the ACLU in *Roe v. Wade*, he fashioned from rarified constitutional air a general right of privacy, and then extrapolated therefrom a mother's right to kill her unborn child.

Perhaps the most insightful analysis of such supratext hermeneutics comes from Professor Gerard V. Bradley of the University of Illinois at Urbana-Champaign. Citing a single incident that precipitated World War I (the assassination of Austrian Archduke Francis Ferdinand), Professor Bradley begins a critique of the *Bowers v. Hardwick* case by noting that "Thus can small trickles unleash floods." The "small trickles," as he sees them, are the seemingly insignificant hermeneutical changes in the dissenting Justices' innovative extra-textualism.

Bradley points to catchwords like "privacy" and "autonomy," and even to an undifferentiated, all-encompassing "First Amendment" (wherein the specifically-listed liberties go conspicuously unmentioned). Referring to the seminal "privacy" case, *Griswold v. Connecticut*, he zooms in on what has become the most subtle hermeneutical ploy of the liberal-Left—what Bradley terms "in-de-deductive" reasoning:

> In 1965 *Griswold* set the standard for this kind of analysis, which I call the "in-de-ductive" method of constitutional law-making. "Induction" refers to a general analytical technique that first investigates all relevant phenomena and seeks in them a common principle. "Deduction" starts from an intu-ited or self-evident principle and proceeds to derive implication.
>
> *Griswold* did both. First, it surveyed the entire Constitution, particularly the Bill of Rights, and decided that "privacy" was a common element, following which a "general" right to privacy was dubbed an autonomous principle. From this principle certain desired conclusions—like use of contraceptives or abortion-on-demand—are confidently drawn.
>
> The special virtue of in-de-duction is that neither contra-ception nor abortion could persuasively be drawn from a single constitutional clause. Loosed from all moorings in the now-transcended text, the visionary jurist is free to pursue his extraneous commitments.[30]

Commenting further on Blackmun's extra-textualism in *Hardwick*, Professor Bradley calls the reader to "note the progression away from the text until it is completely out of sight."[31]

This departure from the text of the Constitution thus becomes the grand irony for the ACLU. In the midst of the civil liberties battle, they have gone over the wall to engage political enemies of their own choosing and are now defending distant ramparts which they themselves have built. Their support of a new, liberal-Left constitutional hermeneutic leads so far away from the Constitution that they can no longer legitimately claim to be its defender.

Parallels in Biblical Hermeneutics

One of the most intriguing aspects of the struggle over constitutional hermeneutics is its parallel in the field of biblical hermeneutics. Even the very issues that have divided our nation politically—women's rights, abortion, and homosexual rights—have brought schism to one church after another. As with constitutional hermeneutics, the battle is being fought over the authority of the biblical text. And the questions are much the same: How is the Bible to be read? Is its "original intent" still valid for the church about to cross the threshold of the 21st century?

Among liberal interpreters of Scripture, ways are being sought to make the Bible a "living document" able to keep pace with modern cultural changes. And with that, little is different from constitutional hermeneutics. The move is from an objective, truth-recognizing approach to a more subjective, intuitive, experiential approach. As is true of religious liberals' politically activist counterparts, relativism and pragmatism are the order of the day among activists in mainstream denominations.

One of the most interesting discussions of biblical hermeneutics is provided by the late Robert Williams, the first openly-homosexual priest to be ordained by the Episcopal Church. (He was later defrocked for saying that Mother Teresa's life would be significantly enhanced "if she got laid."[32]) In his theologically rambunctious book, *Just As I Am—A Practical Guide to Being Out, Proud, and Christian*, Williams linked together pro-gay and feminist theology, and demonstrated the hermeneutical tie which binds them. "Feminist Christian concerns and gay Christian concerns are, at root, the same," says Williams.[33]

For example, both feminists and gays employ what New Testament scholar Elisabeth Schussler Fiorenza calls a *hermeneutic of suspicion*. "The litmus test for invoking scripture as the Word of God," she says, "must be whether or not biblical texts and traditions seek to end relations of domination and exploitation."[34] Taking that approach, feminists and gays almost literally scissor out of Scripture any passage which they find offensive to their cause. Passages in the writings of the Apostle Paul about gender roles and the sin of homosexual behavior are excised as being particularly suspicious.

Robert Williams immediately spots the difficulty with any hermeneutic which focuses on original intent: "Sometimes the homophobic interpretation of a biblical text is a *correct* reflection of the writer's original intention—so simply reinterpreting the Bible is not enough. We must also *reevaluate* the Bible." What that "reevaluation" involves is made clear a few lines later: "There are parts of the Bible that should be trashed, period."[35] It's back to the scissors once again.

Using a not-altogether-dissimilar approach, the ACLU evidently finds some of the language of the Fifth Amendment sufficiently suspicious, and certainly counter to its political stance against capital punishment. It therefore blithely scissors out the explicit references to "capital crimes" and "jeopardy of life" as if such language never existed. All of which presents an interesting question: Is the ACLU really "America's Defender of the Bill of Rights?" Well, at least as to that part of the Bill of Rights with which it happens to agree.

Then there is the cultural argument used by feminists and gays. Says Williams, "The point is not really whether or not some passage in the Bible condemns homosexual acts; the point is that you cannot allow your moral and ethical decisions to be determined by the literature of a people whose culture and history are so far removed from your own. You must dare to be iconoclastic enough to say, 'So what if the Bible does say it? Who cares?'"[36]

It's back to the "then and there" versus the "here and now" argument. It's about keeping up with the times and accommodating cultural change. As noted, there is a fundamental difference between the Bible and the Constitution on that score. Whereas the Bible is divinely revealed and therefore cannot be changed by human amendment (if you buy the premise you buy the bit), the Constitution is continually subject to an amendment process. The Bill of Rights itself was born of that process.

So what could be wrong with using a cultural hermeneutic? Certainly, not that new liberties can't be added by the people through a well-delineated democratic process; only that it should never be done by the Court through its own highly subjective interpretation of cultural values. Where the amendment process permits change as a matter of representative legislation, cultural hermeneutics is a matter solely of judicial interpretation.

As seen in the previous chapter, amendment by judicial interpretation is preferred by the liberal-Left because it need never accede to the democratically expressed wishes of typically-more-conservative middle class voters. This elitist attitude, so well demonstrated in the ACLU, once again coordinates perfectly with the subjective biblical hermeneutics of feminists and gays.

Margaret A. Farley, for example, proposes as a test of canonicity: "It cannot be believed unless it rings true to our deepest capacity for truth and goodness."[37] Since what any number of biblical passages say about women and homosexuals does not "ring true" to them, those passages are obviously not to be considered as part of the sacred text.

For those civil libertarians who wish it to be so, the obvious corollary in law is: "It *can* be believed as belonging to the body of civil liberties guaranteed by the Constitution if it rings true to our deepest capacity for truth and goodness." And this brings us full-circle to the ACLU and its activist manifesto: "The scope of civil liberties is what we say it ought to be." With the advent of a subjective constitutional hermeneutic, each person becomes a law unto himself.

Professor Stephen Carter could have been addressing civil libertarians when he wrote of religious believers, "Few things are more trivializing to the idea of faith than for believers themselves to adopt an attitude holding that the will of God is not *discerned* by the faithful but *created* by them. To be sure, an important trend in contemporary hermeneutics argues that it is impossible for interpreters to do anything else, that all the reader will ever get out of a text is what the reader begins with."[38]

Substitute "civil libertarianism" for "faith," and "Bill of Rights" for "the will of God," and what you have is an apt description of the ACLU's own highly subjective hermeneutic. Whether biblical or constitutional, the trends in contemporary hermeneutics bear a striking resemblance to each other.

In that light, consider again Professor Bradley's critique of what he termed the "in-de-ductive" method of constitutional analysis whereby a transcended text is created wholly apart from the original document. He could just as easily have been speaking about what is going on in the world of biblical hermeneutics, and here the comparison could hardly be closer.

Perhaps the process is best seen in the recent brouhaha among Presbyterians over sexual ethics. It was spawned when the church's Special Committee on Human Sexuality recommended the adoption, among others, of the following resolution:

> That "all persons, whether heterosexual or homosexual, whether single or partnered, have a moral right to experience justice-love in their lives and to be sexual persons."[39]

The operative words here are *justice-love*. "Justice-love," like *Palko's* "concept of ordered liberty," is a lofty pronouncement that defies contradiction. After all, it is drawn from obvious biblical themes of justice and love. All you have to do is to pull out those two themes, add a hyphen to assure compounded respectability, and what you have is a ready-made formula for radical moral activism under the coveted pretense of scriptural approval. Like the extra-textual concept of "privacy," what you create is a now-transcended text by which you can approve virtually any activity, no matter how contrary it may be to biblical teaching or morality.

When you look at the precise terminology being used by pro-gay theologians and civil libertarian activists, the parallels get downright spooky.

Where liberal theologians talk about *justice-love* to erase homosexual behavior from the list of sins, David A.J. Richards of New York University Law School tells us in almost exactly the same language that "*the principle of love as a civil liberty*" makes it impermissible to prohibit "private forms of sexual deviance between consenting adults."[40]

It is instructive to note the title of Professor Richards' article: "Sexual Autonomy and the Constitutional Right to Privacy: A Case Study in Human Rights and the Unwritten Constitution." That, in a nutshell, is what the new hermeneutic of constitutional interpretation is all about: an *Unwritten Constitution*. No, not like England's nebulous, ever-illusive, yet plainly authoritative "unwritten Constitution" which, in reality, is the sum total of all its laws. Rather, it is an unwritten Constitution which lies deep within the breasts of activist civil libertarians, and is known only to them until such time as they choose to reveal it to the rest of us.

The Devil's Agenda

If a person is known by his fruits, a hermeneutic is known by its results. Any hermeneutic which can claim constitutional safeguards for obscenity, prostitution, recreational drugs, homosexual behavior, and abortion gives new meaning to a "hermeneutic of suspicion." It *ought to be* suspect.

As an indicator of how far we have come from the Constitution's original intent, simply consider that the Founders themselves would be aghast at the civil libertarian agenda of the ACLU and the liberal-Left. All we need do is to look at the laws which the Founders took for granted at the time they drafted the Constitution and the Bill of Rights. If they had considered such laws unconstitutional, it would not have been left to us two centuries later to discover the disparity and wipe the statute books clean of such unfitting laws.

Someone might suggest that the Founders also took for granted and perpetuated the institution of slavery, in which many of them personally participated. But, clearly, that is not a compelling argument for ignoring original intent in favor of unworthy moral causes. For, apart from purely moral considerations, there would be nothing wrong with slavery. Therefore, if morality is a factor to be reckoned with, the liberal-Left's patently immoral agenda would be quickly out of business. Liberalism's political agenda is no more morally based than the evil of slavery—ironically, an evil more closely associated with prostitution (sometimes involving so-called "white slavery") and homosexual behavior (often including sado-masochistic "bondage") than one might first think.

In the final analysis, it is no wonder that Judge Robert Bork represented such a great threat to the ACLU and the liberal-Left. Bork's philosophy of law shed interrogation-level light, not simply on the liberal-Left's devilish agenda, but on its destructive philosophical and methodological hermeneutic.

Instead of crucifying Bork, the ACLU should have awarded him a medal of honor. Without Bork on the Bench, it may not take long for the ACLU's heretical hermeneutic to so decimate constitutional authority that there is no maintainable Constitution left for the ACLU to defend. Unless one is prepared to do some serious textual revision, it takes only the briefest look at the ACLU's civil libertarian history to know that its current moral malaise was clearly not the ACLU's original intent.

II

Policies Your Mother Wouldn't Stand For

CHAPTER 6

In the Tortured Defense of Kiddy Porn

"IT IS BY THE GOODNESS OF GOD THAT IN OUR COUNTRY WE HAVE THOSE THREE UNSPEAKABLY PRECIOUS THINGS: FREEDOM OF SPEECH, FREEDOM OF CONSCIENCE, AND THE PRUDENCE NEVER TO PRACTICE EITHER OF THEM."

MARK TWAIN

The ACLU would have us believe that no speech is safe if pornography and obscenity are not protected. If the fringe cases are not protectable, so goes the argument, nothing in the center is safe. But there is another side to that story. By looking closely at how a policy is implemented in fringe cases, one can often spot flaws in the fundamental assumptions which underly the basic policy. Never is this more true than in the free speech area. When the ACLU feels compelled to defend all pornography, including kiddy porn, something is fundamentally wrong with its free speech policy. Outrageously wrong.

What's wrong is that the ACLU takes an absolutist approach to free speech. (Well, almost. Religious speech doesn't get as high a degree of protection as does kiddy porn.) The absolutist approach is made necessary, says the ACLU, because anything else would require us to make difficult distinctions. How, it asks, can we possibly define such a thing as pornography? But that is just a smokescreen. Juries decide cases every day using definitions which lack precision. And even if pornography could be defined with exact precision, the ACLU would still oppose any restrictions.

In the end, it is not a free speech debate, but rather a clash in cultural values. Aiding and abetting smut has nothing to do with political freedom. Any organization that can rationalize a tortured defense of kiddy porn merely demonstrates how far removed it is from middle America and the moral arena.

In the Tortured Defense of Kiddy Porn

Y
ou'd have to be blind, dishonest, morally desensitized, or perhaps a member of the ACLU to call it anything but kiddy porn. The video-tapes showed girls as young as ten. The camera zoomed in tight on various parts of their bodies—sometimes the face, but mostly the legs, chest, and crotch. Frequently, the camera focused on the girls' genital areas, breasts, and buttocks for prolonged periods of time. None of the young teens and pre-teens were nude, but they were provocatively posed in bathing suits.

The erotic pictures were taken at an amateur model shoot where aspiring teen photographers and models practiced their respective crafts.[1] Unbeknownst to the young girls, at least one cameraman was intent on capturing more than poses typical to the fashion industry. The Nather Company, based in Las Vegas, produced the tapes and advertised them in catalogues aimed at pedophiles, providing descriptions such as "bathing suits on girls as young as 15 that are so revealing it's almost like seeing them naked (some say even better)."[2] The intent was obvious: from start to finish, it was meant to be kiddy porn.

Among those who ordered the tapes was Stephen Knox, a 38-year-old graduate student at Pennsylvania State University. In 1990, Knox was found in possession of three of the tapes, titled "Ripe and Tender," "Young Flashers," and "Sweet Young Things."[3] He was convicted under the federal

Child Protection Act of 1984, which prohibits possessing or receiving depictions of sexual conduct, as well as lascivious exhibition of the genitals or pubic area of a minor. Knox was sentenced to five years in prison, and he appealed. Even Knox himself must have been surprised when his case ignited a political firestorm that went all the way to the Clinton White House.

Reinterpreting Porn Laws Right Out of Business

The controversy might have centered around the length of Knox's sentence; or the fact that in 1990 the government declined to prosecute the Nather Company itself for producing the videotapes. Instead, the controversy focused on the specific language of the child pornography statute—a signal to many that someone at the highest level of government was out to trash the child pornography law itself.

The Solicitor General, Drew S. Days III, filed a brief on behalf of the Clinton administration saying that the law was unclear as to whether the lascivious behavior needed to be on the part of the children themselves or only on the part of the producer or the viewer. But the government's concern didn't stop with examining a potential ambiguity in the law. The Justice Department affirmatively urged a novel interpretation, to wit, that a criminal exhibition exists only where "the minors who appear in the video tapes can be said to have been acting or posing lasciviously." Quite unbelievably, the government was attempting to shift the burden for being lascivious from morally-perverted pedophiles and child pornographers to the innocent children themselves!

That narrow interpretation—favorable to child porn producers and viewers—had been formulated in part, said critics, by former Arizona State University Law School Dean Paul Bender, who was serving as deputy solicitor general.[4] Mr. Bender had been chief counsel on the 1970 Presidential Commission on Pornography, which recommended the abolition of pornography laws.[5] "Is that what the innovative 'interpretation' was all about?" critics wondered aloud.

When the Supreme Court sent the case back to the Third Circuit for reconsideration in the light of the Justice Department's brief, the appeals court upheld Knox's conviction, holding that the child need not have been engaged in sexually explicit conduct with lascivious intent. But the court's ruling took time, and even as the case was making its way back to the Third Circuit, word of the Clinton administration's porn-friendly brief raced through the grapevine. Within 72 hours, there were so many irate callers to

Attorney General Janet Reno that the Justice Department's phone system was shut down for days. There was also a hurried resolution signed by 220 House members, and still another by the Senate (passing 100-0) which condemned the attempt to weaken the child pornography law.

In order to quell the storm, the Justice Department raced to Capitol Hill with curative legislation aimed at countering the charge that the Clinton administration was soft on child pornography. But almost no one was happy. Conservatives argued that the original legislation was already sufficient when reasonably interpreted, and furthermore, that any cloud cast on the original wording might threaten to undermine any prior convictions under the statute. At the Justice Department itself, both Mr. Days and Mr. Bender were so furious about their brief having been repudiated by the White House that they refused to sign the Justice Department's new brief.[6]

However, hardly anyone was more outspoken than the American Civil Liberties Union. Speaking disparagingly of the administration's quick climbdown, the ACLU's legislative counsel Robert Peck said, "This is a political pander rather than the result of any careful legal analysis."[7] But it wasn't merely political pandering that bothered Peck or the ACLU. It was the affront of any attempt to interfere with the possession or distribution of kiddy porn. The ACLU believes that such interference is a threat to free speech.

Brazenly (in light of the obvious intent of the videotapes), Peck claimed that the proposed legislation could allow prosecutions for possessing materials "that no one in their right mind would consider pornography—everything from medical texts to family pictures to ads for children's underwear and bathing suits."[8] Of course, Peck's own argument is the best argument yet *against* his paranoid conclusion. He is absolutely right: *no one in their right mind* would consider medical texts, family pictures, and ads for children's underwear to be pornography. So where's the threat to free speech? By contrast, *no one in their right mind* could look at the videotapes in question and conclude that they were anything but pornography.

Kiddy Porn—A Perverse and Twisted Policy

The ACLU's Policy 4, addressing Censorship of Obscenity, Pornography and Indecency, is a monument to convoluted logic and twisted values. Section (a) begins with the announcement that "The ACLU opposes any restraint on the right to create, publish or distribute materials to adults, or the right of adults to choose the materials they read or view, on the basis of obscenity, pornography or indecency."[9]

On its face, the ACLU's policy is absolute and unbending, with no exceptions. ("Freedom of speech and press and freedom to read can be safeguarded effectively only if the First Amendment is applied strictly—to prohibit any restriction on these basic rights."[10]) One can only ask, does this include the creation as well as the distribution of "snuff films" in which a woman is raped, tortured, and killed for the pleasure of the viewing audience? Incredibly, footnote 1 of Policy 4 asserts that "it is the intention of this policy to cover all meanings from merely sexually explicit material to constitutionally-defined obscenity to any group or individual's definition of pornography—*including violence* [emphasis added]."

So just how *absolute* is this "absolute" right of free speech? Hear again what the policy says: "*All* limitations of expression on the ground of obscenity, pornography or indecency are unconstitutional [emphasis added]." So, it certainly *looks like* "snuff films" get the ACLU's seal of approval. What's more, there seems to be little, if any, apology offered. "Much expression may offend the sensibilities of people and indeed have a harmful impact on some. But this is no reason to sacrifice the First Amendment. The First Amendment does not allow suppression of speech because of potential harm."[11] Really? Even when it comes to yelling "fire" in a crowded theater?

Of course, all of this absolutist verbiage is tough talk when it comes to pornography—all the tougher, perhaps, because the ACLU is surely aware of how outrageous its absolutist policy is. But "absolute" free speech can get pretty selective for the ACLU. For example, where is all the brash absolutist talk when it comes to commercial advertising? Under the same heading of free speech, ACLU Policy 16 permits "communications that are objectively false and fraudulently motivated" to be enjoined.[12]

Why this deviation from "absolute" free speech? Says the policy manual, "There are occasions when public interest in health and safety permit valid restrictions on commercial advertising."[13] *Health and safety?* Commercial speech is hardly yelling "fire" in a crowded theater! And yet somehow commercial speech can find its way into a free speech exception when pornography cannot. The same goes for perjury, or maybe libel and slander (at least where there is "reckless disregard for the truth"), or threats, extortion, or "fighting words." But not pornography. Pornography is always out of reach. "Public health and safety" is one thing; "public morals" is quite another. When it comes to pornography, the ACLU would assert that there must be no limitations whatever on free speech.

Absolutism—The New Kid On the Block

It might be difficult to believe in these days of free-wheeling free speech, but such a mindless defense of pornography was not always the case even with the ACLU. Samuel Walker reminds us that "Until the Boston [book banning] crisis, the ACLU had taken little interest in censorship of the arts. Following the dominant school of First Amendment theory...it had focused on political speech. Other forms of expression were not central to the process of self-government and so did not deserve the same protection."[14]

In 1925, there was still a sense of moral decorum that would have prevented any silly notion that pornography was somehow protected by the First Amendment. "Baldwin and his closest ACLU friends, Norman Thomas and John Haynes Holmes, were extremely puritanical," writes Walker. "Holmes thought local communities could restrict 'indecent' material and expressed shock at 'all those four-letter words' in *Lady Chatterly's Lover.*"[15]

In its pamphlet *Censorship in Boston*, the ACLU decried prior restraints on free speech, but approved of after-the-fact prosecutions against indecent books and plays. "The ACLU was not yet ready to defend 'indecency,' much less obscenity."[16] Even as late as the 1950s, the ACLU was still as innocent as was the rest of the nation. "Contrary to its own subsequent mythology, at this point the ACLU did not take an 'absolutist' position on freedom of expression. It still placed libel and obscenity outside the scope of First Amendment protection. Most ACLU leaders accepted Alexander Meikeljohn's distinction between political speech, which enjoyed full protection, and other forms of expression, which were entitled to less protection."[17]

It was not until 1962, in the wake of the groundbreaking *Roth v. United States* decision,[18] that the ACLU embraced its now-firmly-entrenched absolutist stand. In *Roth*, the Supreme Court upheld an obscenity conviction, invoking the rule that "Obscenity is not within the area of constitutionally protected speech or press." If that sounded like a defeat for the First Amendment, the ACLU reveled in the opinion's ocean of ambiguity. Justice Brennan had held the test of obscenity to be "whether to the average person applying contemporary community standards the dominant theme of the material taken as a whole appeals to prurient interest." But, asked the ACLU, who was this "average reasonable person"? Were these so-called "contemporary community standards" local or national standards? How dominant must "dominant" be? What in the world was a "prurient interest"?

In asking those questions, the ACLU had at last found its rationale for embracing absolutism: *If no workable definition was possible, then all prosecutions were invariably arbitrary.*

Interesting, isn't it, that the ACLU derides pro-life advocates for taking an absolutist position on abortion when the argument is essentially the same. (Because there is no point along the path of pregnancy beyond conception which universally can be defined as the beginning of life, then all dividing lines—such as trimesters—are invariably arbitrary and meaningless in support of abortion.) And, of course, there is a quantum leap between an abstract idea like pornography (where there is margin for error) and a living, flesh-and-blood microcosm of humanity in the womb (where one dare not get it wrong).

It speaks volumes about the ACLU that it makes passionate use of the absolutist argument to justify its defense of kiddy porn, but rejects with equal passion the same argument when it comes to unborn children.

Is a Definition Always Necessary?

In what other realm do we deny the obvious simply because we can't truly define it? What about *justice,* for example? Or *"pursuit of happiness"*? Or even *free speech*? If we have difficulty defining what is essentially undefinable, we don't thereby deny its reality. Ask a young man who has just bought a dozen roses for his sweetheart to define "love," and you're likely to get a blank stare. But who among us doesn't know what it means to be "in love?"

If that illustration seems a bit schmaltzy for legal minds, try a word closer to the ACLU's heart: *privacy.* What could possibly be a more elastic concept? Surely, no word in the English language has undergone a more dramatic metamorphosis of meaning at the hands of civil libertarians. Or has been filled with such substance. Or has been more useful to the cause. And yet, the ACLU itself would be hard-pressed to fully define it.

That is why Justice Potter Stewart's famous line in the 1964 *Jacobellis* decision makes so much sense. Stewart concurred with the majority opinion which overturned an obscenity conviction involving the Louis Malle film, *The Lovers.* Like the ACLU, he too was concerned with the difficulty of attempting to define what was essentially undefinable. But that did not stop him from acknowledging the obvious.

Said Stewart, "I have reached the conclusion, which I think is confirmed at least by negative implication in the Court's decisions since *Roth* and *Alberts*, that under the First and Fourteenth Amendments, criminal laws in this area are constitutionally limited to hard-core pornography. I shall not today attempt to further define the kinds of material I understand to be embraced within that shorthand description; and perhaps I could never succeed in intelligently doing so. But I know it when I see it, and the motion picture involved in this case is not that."[19]

"I know it when I see it," was not meant to be cute, or tongue-in-cheek, or merely a quotable quip. If he might not be able to give precise definition to hard-core pornography, nevertheless Justice Stewart affirmed the obvious: It doesn't take a mental giant to recognize hard-core porn, and only a fool would pretend otherwise.

If the lines between "hard-core porn," "soft-porn," and "non-pornographic" are not always easy to draw, it is not to say that no lines can ever be drawn. Nor that such phrases lack content or definitive meaning. It just means that defining them is a tougher task than, say, peeling a tomato. But when was that a reason to shut the courtroom door? Isn't that the very stuff of litigation?

In her book, *Sex, Sin, and Blasphemy—A Guide to America's Censorship Wars*, the ACLU's Marjorie Heins (appointed director of the Arts Censorship Project in 1991) states that Justice Stewart's conclusion is reason enough to abandon all obscenity laws. Of Stewart's famous line, Heins sneers, "This is all very amusing, but it's a hell of a way to run a legal system."[20] Really? Isn't this the *very* way that the legal system is run?

And what is so amusing—or novel, or extraordinary—about asking twelve jurors to decide tough legal issues based upon language which is necessarily broad enough to encompass a wide variety of factors? Consider, for example, the issue of negligence. Any legal scholar will tell you that the definition of negligence is nigh unto mysterious. Are we talking ordinary negligence, gross negligence, or perhaps willful and wanton conduct? In my Criminal Law course, it is every first year student's nightmare: Where is the line to be drawn?

The answer, of course, is that negligence is what twelve good citizens, tried and true, *decide* it is. We first ask them to consider how a hypothetical "average reasonable person" would act under same or similar circumstances; then instruct them that any deviation from that standard is considered negligence, to one degree or another (which they must also decide). And so it goes with any number of other thorny legal issues.

The jury system is also the answer to Marjorie Heins' sophomoric question, "Who's to decide?"—which is really nothing more than a variation on theme regarding the difficulty of defining pornography. Without question, one jury in one part of the country might decide one way, while another jury in another part of the country might decide another way. But if we can tolerate differences with regard to every other legal issue under the sun, surely we can tolerate differences pertaining to pornography as well.

What is there to be afraid of, unless it's that jurors in middle America might have the good sense to recognize porn for what it is? Today's civil libertarians have apparently become so desensitized to shame that they wouldn't recognize pornography if it was their own ten-year-old son or daughter in the middle of an adults-only movie screen. Let no one indulge in the delusion that some grand and noble crusade is taking place in the defense of free speech. The inability to define pornography is not an intellectual argument on the high road of civil libertarian principle, but a lamentable commentary on the inability or unwillingness to make even the most fundamental of moral distinctions.

Aid and Comfort to Kiddy Porn Producers

Suppose that we could somehow all agree on a definition of pornography. The truth is that the ACLU would still object to any restriction upon its distribution or possession—even if the only purpose was to keep such trash out of the hands of children. According to ACLU Policy 4, section (b), "Laws which punish the distribution or exposure of such material to minors violate the First Amendment, and inevitably restrict the right to publish and distribute such materials to adults."[21]

Has the ACLU never heard of laws which prohibit the sale of alcohol and tobacco to minors? Is there any historical evidence to suggest that prohibiting sales to minors has in any way inhibited the right of adults to purchase alcohol or tobacco? Is there any reason to believe that the results would be any different when it comes to the dissemination of speech?

Quite incredibly, the ACLU opposes even the kinds of safeguards that traditionally have been associated with sales to underaged minors. In Policy 4, section (d) 6), the ACLU gives virtually anyone convicted under obscenity laws a sure-fire defense: "Distributors, exhibitors and retailers should not be obliged to risk punishment by misjudging the age of a minor. Such persons should not be required to keep records of evidence submitted by minors; *and should be entitled to rely reasonably on a minor's statement of age* [emphasis added]."

Why not just invite the local grade school kids in for a porn party and take their word for it that they are over 21! (The law accepts no defense of claimed ignorance when it comes to selling alcohol or tobacco.) It's another issue for another time, but since the ACLU opposes even voluntary film ratings for juveniles, it could intend no other result in this instance.

But it gets worse than the issue of distributing pornography to children. What about the *production* of kiddy porn? That was the question asked of ACLU president Nadine Strossen in an appearance on "Larry King Live." When a caller asked Strossen whether film of a two-year-old being raped was protectable free speech, Strossen replied that "The ACLU believes that the way to address violence and coercion against women and children is directly, by prosecuting and suing those who actually commit the violence and the discrimination. Therefore, we pour major resources into our childrens' rights project and our women's rights project."[22]

What Strossen so masterfully glossed over was that, even if the rapist spent time in jail for rape, by ACLU policy (read it for yourself) the producer of the film should nevertheless be permitted to create the film, and distribute the film without any restriction whatsoever. (There is, of course, more than a slight problem here with criminal conspiracy and aiding and abetting.)

Listen again to the patent absurdity of it all. Under section (g) of Policy 4, the ACLU "opposes on First Amendment grounds laws that restrict the production and distribution of any printed and visual materials *even when some of the producers of those materials are punishable under criminal law* [emphasis added]." How can a producer of pornography be punishable under criminal law if he has a First Amendment right to produce it? The ACLU wants to have its cake and eat it too. It wants to be able to say that there should be no restrictions whatsoever on the creation of pornography, but still maintain the appearance of respectability by not approving of what *necessarily has to be done* in the production of such sleaze. *That*, says the ACLU, contradictorily, can (and ought to be?) criminalized.

At this point we get mixed signals from policy 4(g). On one hand, even violations of criminal law should not be a bar to the production of pornography. On the other hand, we read that "The ACLU views the use of children in the production of visual depictions of sexually explicit conduct as a violation of childrens' rights when such use is highly likely to cause: a) substantial physical harm; or b) substantial and continuing emotional or psychological harm."[23]

Would that it were only linguistic waffling we're concerned about here. But a closer look at that last paragraph reveals a gaping loophole in the production of kiddy porn. It appears that the ACLU objects to the use of children *only when* there is likelihood of substantial physical, emotional, or psychological harm. Would the ACLU's objection to the use of children apply to the Stephen Knox films in which the young girls were *unaware* that they were being filmed obscenely? And what about the case of Douglas Gates?

In 1991, Glendale, Arizona, resident Douglas Gates invited 10-year-old Tianna to use the swimming pool in his apartment complex. He told her she could change into her swimsuit in his bedroom. (You can guess the rest.) Gates then secretly switched on his video camera and filmed Tianna getting undressed, something—as it turned out—which he had done with a number of young girls from infancy to puberty.[24] By the ACLU's policy, there would have been no violation of the childrens' rights, because they were merely unsuspecting victims. Not raped, not physically harmed, not psychologically scarred for life.

Listen to the ACLU, and you'd think that passive child porn was as innocent as motherhood and apple pie. Take, for example, Marjorie Heins' commentary on the 1990 obscenity trial of Cincinnati museum director Dennis Barrie, in which Barrie was prosecuted for exhibiting photographs by the late Robert Mapplethorpe. It was not just the infamous self-portrait of Mapplethorpe, "bare ass in the foreground, face turned toward the camera with an expression that was at once both sad and mischievous, and bullwhip inserted firmly in his anus."[25] Nor the "extremely large, lovingly photographed penises, and sadomasochistic sexual practices like dressing up in leather or urinating into another person's mouth."[26]

In the midst of all of this pornographic filth, masquerading as artistically-compelling National Endowment for the Arts-sponsored (i.e., taxpayer funded) "political statements" guaranteed by the First Amendment, were two photographs of children. One, titled *Jessie McBride*, showed a little boy, perched on the back of a chair, nude. The other, in the admiring words of Marjorie Heins, "was pictured sitting on a bench in a natural childlike pose, legs apart, her dress carelessly askew so that part of her vulva is exposed. The child had no look of fear or discomfort; the pose was not pornographic but 'guileless and charming.'"

Isn't it all lovely? Who could possibly object? But why all the pretense about there being no fear or distress on the part of the child? Would it make any difference under ACLU policy if the child was, in fact, fearful and distressed? Only sentimentally, not constitutionally. And how—if there is no way to define pornography—can Marjorie Heins assure us with such equanimity that the pose here was "not pornographic?" Then again, would it have made any difference if it were pornographic? Not in the constitutionally-opaque eyes of the ACLU. To the ACLU, passive kiddy porn—when viewed in an art museum instead of Joe's Adult Books and Peep Shows—takes on a look that is altogether "guileless and charming."

It simply has to be asked, "Why the obvious loophole?" How difficult would it have been for the policy to read: "The ACLU objects to the use of children in the production of kiddy porn under any and all circumstances?" Would that wholehearted defense of childrens' rights be giving away something precious concerning the freedom of speech?

Instead of giving aid and comfort to kiddy-porn producers, the ACLU could go a long way toward redeeming itself by invoking an exclusionary rule under such circumstances. The ACLU loves exclusionary rules when it comes to police misconduct, so why not follow the same line with child pornographers? How about a rule that excludes from distribution and possession any pornographic visual depiction that involves the use of children in any way?

It's no use for Nadine Strossen and the ACLU to pretend that they care about childrens' rights when they maintain a hopelessly contradictory policy on criminal activity in the making of kiddy porn, and even provide an obvious loophole for others to take advantage of unsuspecting children in the creation of indecent, obscene, and pornographic materials. Let no one be fooled about the ACLU's commitment to children. Whether it be kiddy porn or abortion, the ACLU is no friend to children, born or unborn.

The Burning Question: Why?

The real question in all of this is why the ACLU would find itself in what seems to most people to be such an embarrassing position? Is all this tortured defense of kiddy porn really necessary in the defense of free speech? Are we really to believe that the people who are campaigning to restrict kiddy porn are also intent on shutting down legitimate free speech?

Let's bring it back to the basics. How is the marketplace of ideas even remotely threatened by the removal from the shelves of adult book stores those magazines and films which have no possible purpose other than to arouse the libidinous nature of pedophiles? Is the ACLU seriously suggesting that America's freedom is dependent on the existence of kiddy porn?

One clue to the ACLU's insistence on defending kiddy porn may be found in its own hierarchy of free speech values. Strangely, the ACLU gives less weight to religious free speech than it does to kiddy porn. With kiddy porn, the ACLU takes an absolutist approach: there can be no censorship whatsoever. With religious speech, the ACLU is quite willing to find exceptions to free speech, including government censorship of everything from school prayers, to the teaching of Creation in public schools, to the presence of Bibles and other religious literature in school libraries, to the display of religious symbols on public property.

Hence, the clue: For the ACLU, free speech has less to do with absolutism, than with one's own peculiar set of values. This is not a free speech debate, but a cultural conflict. Sadly, the ACLU is pushing the envelope of indecency for its own self-serving ends.

For the ACLU, the primary purpose of defending pornography, and especially kiddy porn, is to give all indecent free speech elbow-room. Thankfully, not many folks will demand the right to create, distribute, or possess kiddy porn. But by stretching the boundaries of free speech to accommodate the worst kind of expression imaginable, one can thereby assure that any indecency or obscenity short of that is likewise protectable.

At a time when free speech was assumed to be only political free speech, no such elbow-room was felt necessary. (Political free speech needed no elbow-room. It was, after all, the precise object of the First Amendment.) It was only when society was seduced by the sexual revolution that anyone even would have thought to demand a constitutional right to speak and act obscenely.

As Samuel Walker observes, "The ACLU's growth [from 1955 to 1965] was symptomatic of the changing public attitudes. A new sense of freedom was in the air: An increasingly educated public expected the freedom to read without restrictions imposed by religious moralists. The sexual revolution challenged censorship in the arts and restrictions on birth control, eventually leading to a new concept of privacy."[27]

But there was also a dynamic synergism between the sexual revolution and changing notions of free speech. According to Walker, the ACLU was as much responsible for the sexual revolution as it was for reacting to it with a demand for greater free speech. "The issue of pornography illuminated the disagreement between the ACLU and its critics," writes Walker. "In large part because of the ACLU's long crusade against censorship, virtually all the old restraints collapsed in the late 1960s. Books, magazines, and movies depicting explicit sex—including 'hard-core' pornography—circulated as never before. Adult theater marquees openly advertised 'Live, Nude, Girls.'"[28]

It is worth noting here that Samuel Walker obviously had a particular category of pornography in mind when he specifically included "hard-core" porn within other forms of explicit sex. Likewise, Marjorie Heins goes all the way back to the word "pornography's" Greek origins to make a careful distinction between "pornography" (writing or pictures intended to arouse sexual desire) and "obscenity" (sexually explicit art and entertainment having no legal sanction). So why all the pretense about the impossibility of definition?

Whether it was the sexual revolution which prompted the ACLU's defense of pornography, or whether the ACLU's defense of pornography encouraged the sexual revolution, it is now clear that each washes the other's hands. It is also crystal clear that pornography has nothing to do with the preservation of democratic ideals, and everything to do with the empowerment of baser instincts. No democracy is dependent on the availability of kiddy porn!

In support of that proposition, political scientist Walter Berns formulated in the 1970s a defense of censorship which rested unabashedly on the importance of shame to a viable democracy. Shame, said Berns, implies a healthy self-restraint, which itself is necessary to any ordered society. (To make his point, Berns even cited ACLU charter member Morris Ernst, who had said that he "would hate to live in a world with utter freedom.") Far from any democracy being dependent on the availability of pornography, it was Bern's argument that democracy is dependent upon the public recognition of shame and, in turn, the very *absence* of pornography.[29]

It is obvious that the ACLU does not share much concern about shame. Nor could it be expected to. To the ACLU, morality (which provides the basis for shame) is but a tired and overworn platitude perpetuated by the religious-Right. Perhaps. But morality and liberty have an uncanny family resemblance. As long as the ACLU fails to grasp the crucial connection between political liberty and moral responsibility, it will continue to find itself defending the indefensible.

Undermining the Cause

The shame of it all is that the ACLU's true mission as a defender of constitutional liberties is unduly compromised by an unnecessary commitment to absolute free speech in the realm of obscenity and pornography. Has not every lawyer been taught, "Never use an obviously weak argument?" If a lawyer makes two strong arguments, and then throws in a third—clearly weak—argument just for good measure, you can bet that the jury will seize upon the obvious weak argument as an excuse to ignore the two strong arguments.

In defending the indefensible—kiddy porn—the ACLU weakens, rather than strengthens, its defense of free speech. Why should Americans be willing to honor *political free speech* when they are being told that *kiddy porn* stands on the same footing? If they have every right to reject kiddy porn (and they do), then, by that same token, they would have a right to reject every other form of free speech (which they *don't*).

Pornography is not only unnecessary to the defense of free speech, but it is inimical to it. Pornography does to good government what it does to good morals: It undermines it. It seduces entire nations with the notion that there are no limits. And what could be more out of step with the current mood of America than a philosophy which says that there are no limits? Ours is the generation of limitless government coming to grips with the horror of its legacy. How else can we explain the grass-roots movement for budget limits, term limits, and limits on how far the government can intrude into our affairs?

If that sounds like the best argument yet for protecting pornography, somebody's missed the point. Pornography, unlike political speech, has nothing whatever to do with the political process. There is neither an idea, belief, opinion, nor cause, that cannot be adequately expressed in the absence of pornography. (Whatever else one may think of it, when the court found the anti-war slogan, "F___ the draft" to be constitutionally protected free speech,[30] it was precisely that: *speech.*)

This is exactly where the Court lost its way in the flag-burning case. In *Texas v. Johnson,* the Court ruled that the First Amendment's guarantee of free speech protected a man who publicly burned the American flag to express his hatred for the United States.[31] Writing for the majority, Justice Brennan said that "the Government may not prohibit the expression of an idea simply because society finds the idea itself offensive or disagreeable."

Of course, it was not the *idea* that ran afoul of the law, but rather the *mode of expressing the idea.* Would the Court, using Brennan's logic, approve of indecent exposure at a shopping mall in middle America as graphic symbolism for some particular point of view? If not, why is pornography on the magazine shelf of a grocery store any more protectable under the First Amendment than acted-out pornography in a shopping mall? In most pornography, generally, and in kiddy porn, specifically, there is not even the slightest pretence of putting forward a point of view for public discourse.

What more proof does one need of the symbolic free speech fallacy than the recent spate of abortion doctor killings as an expression of anti-abortion protest? Is the ACLU prepared to defend homicidal acts by political activists as a form of symbolic free speech? Hardly. Nor should it. When backed into such a corner, even the ACLU surely must recognize that there are limits to how one should express his or her beliefs, political or otherwise. If that is the case with political expression, it must be all the more true of pornographic expression—especially if one equates the two as the ACLU does.

Such an unholy marriage between political speech and pornography desecrates the First Amendment. The ACLU's absolutist policy has not only undeservedly elevated pornography to the high altar of political free speech, it has thereby unwittingly dumped political free speech into the unspeakable gutter of kiddy porn. When the ACLU is unable, or unwilling, to distinguish between political speech and pornography, it makes the two practically indistinguishable. And when that happens, government is not just prudently limited, but dangerously reduced.

Which brings us to one characteristic virtually always attendant to pornography: a reductionist view of that which deserves more respect. Considering such dangerous reductionism, the American Civil Liberties Union is the greatest of all purveyors of pornography. It should be reprehensible enough that its free speech policy reduces the First Amendment to a protective cloak for sadomasochism, verbal excrement, and moral filth. But how can the ACLU ever be forgiven for its ungodly defense of kiddy porn, which reduces America's children to nothing more than objects of lust for the perverted pleasure of predatory pedophiles?

Did the ACLU say that its policies were never meant to hurt kids, but only to defend free speech? Of one thing you can be sure: If the ACLU's extremist views on free speech were ever to be fully accepted by the Court, then the constitutionalization of kiddy porn would mean that the state would have to stand idly by while real, live, vulnerable children—perhaps your own—were victimized with impunity. Sadly, with the ACLU's encouragement, such harm is already happening, and more is bound to happen.

Never have our civil liberties been so debased. And never has the devil been more successful in the corruption of innocence. But then, it figures. Wasn't it the devil himself who first took unwarranted liberties with free speech?

CHAPTER 7

Taking Sexual Liberties

"SEXUAL INTERCOURSE BEGAN IN NINETEEN SIXTY-THREE
(WHICH WAS RATHER LATE FOR ME)—
BETWEEN THE END OF THE CHATTERLY BAN
AND THE BEATLES' FIRST LP."
PHILIP LARKIN

I s there some necessary, indispensable tie between sex and civil liberties? Given the ACLU's keen interest in defending sex education, prostitution, and homosexual activity, apparently there must be some connection. Of course, one could point to common civil libertarian threads like *privacy* and *choice*, but looking first to those innovative concepts confuses the priorities. Sex was always first; civil liberties, second.

Place the many sex-related ACLU policies under surveillance, and you'll soon discover that the goal is permissive sex. Whether it be heterosexual or homosexual; romantic or commercial; private or public—what is at stake is total sexual freedom. Even the ACLU's policies in support of AIDS victims and abortion are necessary backstops to uninhibited sexual freedom. For, first and foremost, it's about consequence-free sex. Abortion, in particular, is an insurance policy. Just in case....

Consequences aside, liberated sex has become the ultimate symbol of unfettered freedom. Behind the scenes, the ACLU talks about—not just sex—but personal autonomy, private franchise, and defining one's own concept of liberty. Such liberation is contagious. If something as hedged about with natural barriers as sex can be liberated from restraint, then there is nothing that can't be given legal license. Not even, sadly, the killing of an unborn baby conceived in the heat of forbidden passion. That morality is a seamless web is a lesson the ACLU has yet to learn.

Taking Sexual Liberties

I t was not your basic sex education program. Unlike most programs in recent years, it did not begin with the assumption that teens and pre-teens inevitably would engage in sex. Over the past several decades, that approach has led to explicit "how-to" sessions, abortion counseling, and the Great Condom Giveaway—not to mention higher and higher rates of teen pregnancy and venereal disease.

Sensing the futility of traditional sex education programs, the Hemet School District in Southern California decided to make two radical changes. First, to put the primary responsibility on parents to educate their own children about sex. Second, to encourage abstinence.

It was a carefully-designed program, promoting self-control and fostering a sense of personal responsibility. And it was practical. It taught a sound reasoning process, including skills on how to say *no* to sex, and how to avoid intimidating another young person sexually by the use of verbal or physical harassment.[1]

Moreover, it was socially conscious. The study guide emphasized "that jokes, slurs, and derogatory statements made on the basis of sex, sexual orientation, disability, race, color, creed, religion or culture are demeaning and destroy the dignity of the affected individual."

Sound sensible? Reasonable? Progressive? Perhaps, but not to the American Civil Liberties Union. Along with Planned Parenthood, the ACLU sued the Hemet School District and each of the five board members to halt the innovative program. *Why,* you ask? Because to the liberal-Left establishment abstinence sounds suspiciously like morality, which itself sounds suspiciously like religion. And everybody knows you can't impose religious values on students in public schools.

Of course, the battle is not just in Hemet, California. The new wave of abstinence programs all over the country has engendered the wrath of the ACLU and Planned Parenthood wherever condoms have been removed from the cucumbers and put back in their boxes on the shelf. One of the most popular abstinence-based programs, "Sex Respect," has drawn particular fire, despite the fact that it has been eagerly adopted in more than 2,000 schools and enjoys widespread support from parents.[2] What other reaction could be expected from Planned Parenthood and the ACLU? "Sex Respect" spurns even the mention of contraceptives, Planned Parenthood's stock in trade.

Incredibly enough, the ACLU takes great umbrage when students are led in chanting, "Do the right thing! Wait for the ring!" or "Don't be a louse! Wait for your spouse!" (Not particularly catchy, but surely harmless enough.) And, at this point, it becomes obvious that church-state concerns have little to do with the rancor and hubbub after all.

It is not just a matter of religion, established or otherwise, that disturbs the liberal-Left, but more importantly a matter of inhibited sexual expression. Harmless little chants—when they suggest there are boundaries to acceptable sexual expression—are no longer considered harmless. By idealizing sexual purity, we might be condemning sexual freedom, and that simply won't do. In a sexually permissive culture, surely the teaching of abstinence can't be constitutional!

In fact, the ACLU sees it as downright subversive. Berkeley law professor Phillip E. Johnson suggests that, "If a school district were to announce a policy of preparing children for stable traditional marriages, and for two-parent child-raising, and also for discouraging high schoolers from developing the kind of casual attitude towards sex described by William Kilpatrick, the whole idea would be characterized...as a plot by the religious right and met with a mighty chorus of 'the grand sez who.'"[3] When it comes to sex and family values, the ACLU is hardly just a neutral civil liberties organization.

ACLU Backs Sex for Sale

Another battle has been brewing a bit further north in California—this time on the streets of San Francisco. After years of sexual tolerance which finally got out of hand, local citizens and businesses in the Tenderloin District demanded that the police do something about the open prostitution which had become a blight on the community. But the police were hamstrung by having to go undercover each time they attempted to bring sexual solicitation charges against the "working girls" and male prostitutes. The undercover game became an almost comical charade in which plain clothes officers tried to bait prostitutes into soliciting them, without going so far as to legally entrap their prey and have the case thrown out of court.

In light of the legal difficulties attached to enforcement of the solicitation laws, San Francisco police began using a state law which criminalized any conduct that was indecent, injurious to health, "offensive to the senses," or an obstruction of a street, and at the same time interfered with the "comfortable enjoyment of life or property by an entire community or neighborhood."

Anyone familiar with the history of vagrancy or nuisance abatement laws knows the almost inherent problem associated with such laws—that they are often "void for vagueness." So it was not surprising that the American Civil Liberties Union filed an amicus brief in this case, arguing excessive vagueness. But one would be short-sighted to think that a thorny constitutional concern about vaguely-worded ordinances was all that was at stake for the ACLU. Even if vagueness were not remotely at issue, the ACLU would still have a problem with any attempt to criminalize or regulate sex for sale.

The ACLU's Policy 211 is straightforward: "The ACLU supports the decriminalization of prostitution and opposes state regulation of prostitution." It does so on a number of bases, including concerns regarding discrimination against women, the use of entrapment, lack of due process in the enforcement of loitering or vagrancy laws, and the right of individual privacy. That last reason—the right of privacy—tells the real tale. Everything else is merely window-dressing.

Minutes from the board meeting of March 5-6, 1977, reveal the heart of the matter: "The ACLU reaffirms its policy favoring removal of criminal penalties for prostitution, and in support of *total sexual freedom among consenting adults in private* [emphasis added]."[4] Of course, the last two qualifying words—*in private*—aren't really that pivotal, because the ACLU believes that even public solicitation of prostitution is "entitled to the protection of the First Amendment."[5] It's not just the bedroom that the ACLU wishes to make off-limits to public censure, but also the local street corner, presumably even if that corner is regularly used by school children crossing the street.

Don't be fooled, either, when the ACLU cites the problem of gender discrimination. When former New York Mayor Edward Koch instituted a public broadcast, known as the "John Hour", to reveal the names of men who had been convicted of patronizing prostitutes, guess who cried foul? The New York Civil Liberties Union, of course.

Vagueness isn't the real concern. Nor police entrapment. Nor gender discrimination. Just as with sex education programs, it's *total sexual freedom* that is at stake in the eyes of the ACLU. Here again, we find many in the ACLU asking: Why is this so bad? No, not "Why should the government be in the sex regulation business?"—a legitimate question for civil libertarians to ask—but "Why is *total sexual freedom* bad?" Here again, we are reminded that what most divides us are our basic moral assumptions, not the tough legal questions which seldom get to the heart of the matter.

Straight or Gay, We Want Our Way

Perhaps no more bitterly fought battle has been waged in defense of total sexual freedom than the battle over homosexual activity in the military. From the tabloids to the Oval Office, "gays in the military" has been a hot topic. Of course, the American Civil Liberties Union is in the front ranks of those fighting for gay rights.

A flyer from the Southern California chapter, for example, boasts that:

> As the nation's oldest, multi-issue civil rights organization, the American Civil Liberties Union is a well known and respected voice for all minority groups denied equal treatment before the law, including lesbians and gay men. In the 1960s, long before most Americans had even heard of gay rights, the ACLU was challenging the federal government's exclusion of gay men and lesbians from civil service jobs and fighting to end post office censorship, police entrapment and bathhouse raids.[6]

The ACLU, and the ACLU Foundation, lists the following issues as matter of concern:

- discrimination against lesbians and gay men in housing and employment
- anti-gay ordinances in communities across California
- police brutality against gay and lesbian demonstrators
- restrictions on the custody rights of lesbian and gay parents
- homophobic police department employment policies
- exclusion from the military and the Boy Scouts[7]

Of great interest is the admission that the ACLU—proudly "non-political"—uses ACLU memberships as "the primary funding source for our legislative lobbying, public education and community outreach programs."[8] Additionally, the ACLU Foundation's Lesbian and Gay Rights Litigation Project has helped to achieve significant legal victories on behalf of homosexuals in the military. Included among its successes is the case of *Pruitt v. Cheney* which laid the foundation for the courts' favorable rulings in the much-celebrated case of Naval sonar instructor Volker Keith Meinhold who had been discharged from the armed forces because of his homosexuality.

What's most interesting about the ACLU's claim to be the first to jump on the gay-rights bandwagon in the 1960s is the ACLU's history relative to homosexuals. As late as 1957, the ACLU had determined that it was "not within the province of the Union to evaluate the social validity of laws" criminalizing homosexual activity.[9]

In fact, the ACLU went so far as to say that homosexual activity was a valid risk factor when security clearances were being sought.[10] To no one's surprise, the ACLU has reversed itself on this issue, saying now that "one form of security inquiry that should never be permissible pries into sexual activities and orientation, notably homosexuality."[11]

In 1964, hardly anyone at the ACLU's policy formulating Biennial Conference seemed to notice that, when Harriet Pilpel introduced gay rights as an issue about which the ACLU should be concerned, there was no historic civil libertarian basis for such a policy. At most, there was only a trendy solidarity with a group of persons defined solely by their aberrant sexual practices. But, when the tide of social opinion about homosexual activity began to turn among America's elite, then magically, mystically, *ipso facto*, deviant sexual behavior took on the respectability of a civil liberties issue.

If politics sometimes makes strange bedfellows, in this case strange bedfellows made politics the order of the day at the ACLU. The Constitution be damned; full speed ahead! Within two years of the Biennial

Conference, the ACLU formally recognized gay rights as a civil liberties concern, and hasn't looked back since. For the ACLU, *total sexual freedom* must be maintained at all cost—in the classroom, on the street corner, and with the partner of your choice, whether in or out of the closet.

Sex in the Cuckoo's Nest

To that list can also be added: *whether in or out of the mental institution.* According to ACLU Policy 246, "In matters of sexual expression, the mentally retarded should have the same rights as all other persons. In cases of severe retardation and legal incompetence, special care should be taken to maximize sexual freedoms."[12]

Funny how that works out when involuntary sterilization becomes an institutional option. Although there is great posturing about the need for a "full panoply of adversarial legal safeguards" before involuntary sterilization can take place, is anyone surprised to learn that *total sexual freedom* is still the goal? "We recognize," says the policy statement, "that, in certain cases of severe retardation and legal incompetence, sterilization may act to increase rather than reduce freedom."[13] Whatever stands in the way, whether morality, the Constitution, or even the need for involuntary sterilization, everything is justified in the pursuit of uninhibited, uncensured sexual expression.

Sex Has Deep Roots in the ACLU

One wonders what ACLU founder Roger Baldwin would have thought of all this energy being spent on behalf of sexual license in the name of civil libertarianism. Oddly enough, he might have approved. On one hand, Baldwin, who descended from Puritan roots, has been described as downright prudish. On the other hand, Baldwin was not exactly your orthodox Puritan. Puritans were not known to be nudists, as was Baldwin. Says Samuel Walker, "Nudism was a regular part of weekends at his New Jersey farm and vacations on Martha's Vineyard."[14]

When Walker reports that Baldwin was "squeamish about sex," that seems best translated as *private* about sex, as would have befitted the tenor of the times. Given those times, we may never know Baldwin's ideas about sexual expression behind closed doors. Twice married, he was also the subject of a rumored affair with Elizabeth Gurley Flynn (who was ousted from the board following the "1940 Resolution").[15]

To say the least, Baldwin's nudism suggests a freedom from restraint not altogether inconsistent with the ACLU's current mania regarding sexual

freedom. Moreover, any initial hesitancy on the part of the ACLU to challenge the censorship of material with sexual themes, as Walker suggests,[16]
must have dissipated rather quickly. As early as 1912, Baldwin had given
his first defense of free speech. It was on behalf of Planned Parenthood
founder Margaret Sanger, who was about to have her lecture on birth control shut down by the police.[17]

To whatever extent Baldwin might have been personally embarrassed
by public discussion of sex, as of 1927 there were others within the ACLU
who had no qualms of any kind about pushing the agenda of sexual freedom. Walker reports, for example, that Arthur Garfield Hays and Morris L.
Ernst led the attack against sexual censorship on behalf of the ACLU.
"Thoroughly secularized Jews, they shared none of the puritanism of the
ACLU Protestants. They were not embarrassed by sex and believed that
personal freedom extended into the realm of private sexual relations."[18]

Without question, the views of these two "thoroughly secularized"
ACLU members regarding uncensured sexual expression point to deep
roots for the ACLU's current commitment to total sexual freedom. For the
ACLU, sexual license was not just some newly-discovered truth emanating
from the sexual revolution of the sixties. If anything, it was the ACLU's
activism in defense of sex-related issues which laid an early foundation for
the sexual revolution itself.

What a telling commentary on the tie between a secularized world
view and libertine sex! Considering what appears to be an overwhelming
percentage of ACLU members today who would feel comfortable being
tagged as "thoroughly secularized," it is little wonder that total sexual freedom takes a high priority in the ACLU's liberal platform. Little wonder, too,
that the very sight of the words *morality* or *religion* in the same sentence with
sex makes the ACLU positively apoplectic!

Make no mistake. When it comes to sexual freedom, church-state
separation is not just an abstract Constitutional issue for the ACLU. The
ACLU recognizes all too well that sexual freedom is a matter of no little dispute between God and the devil. And on the issue of sexual expression, the
devil is "thoroughly secularized."

Safeguarding Libertine Sex

One could be excused for thinking that the ACLU's policies regarding
sex education programs, legalized prostitution, and gay rights are only coincidentally related, with no greater linkage than the common thread of sexual

activity. But you begin to see a much larger picture when you consider other significant ACLU concerns—namely, AIDS and abortion—which directly relate to the sexual theme. An unusual mix takes place when these various ACLU concerns are seen in a single light.

For example, who would ever guess that homosexual activity and abortion would have anything in common? It virtually goes without saying that few, if any, homosexuals will ever be personally affected one way or another by abortion laws. But just take a close look at those who turn out for the pro-choice rallies. Thousands of the demonstrators are lesbians and homosexual men!

Of course, there is obvious solidarity in the matter of choice. "The right to choose" is not only important to a pregnant woman who doesn't want to keep her baby, but also to anyone who guards the freedom of sexual alternatives.

And, of course, gay rights have been promoted under the same "privacy" umbrella as abortion rights in *Roe v. Wade*—although, so far, with less success. Yet even the "privacy" issue begs the question of which came first: faux rights desperately in search of a common constitutional patron; or a novel constitutional concept gradually mutating from a legitimate progenitor (marital privacy) into illegitimate species of libertarian concerns (abortion and gay rights)?

Still, those ties between seemingly unrelated issues of civil liberties miss the point. The true common denominator is neither "choice" nor "privacy," but the ACLU's commitment to total sexual freedom. Gay rights does it for homosexuals; abortion does it for heterosexuals. If the latter seems less obvious than the former, think in terms of *consequences*.

Abortion is the ultimate backstop for libertine sex. All along, of course, the ACLU (in conjunction with Planned Parenthood) has staunchly defended the right of access to contraceptives, not only for married couples, but also for the unmarried. But what's a woman to do when the condom breaks or the pill fails? It is at that crucial point that abortion becomes sexual freedom's most trustworthy ally.

The reality is that sexual freedom cannot be total until one can be guaranteed that there will be absolutely no consequences attached to the exercise of one's sexual freedom. Were it not for the ACLU's commitment to total sexual freedom, the ACLU would probably have only a passing interest in abortion as a civil libertarian issue. As it is, abortion is the flagship of a whole flotilla of sexual freedoms.

There is a similar—and certainly more obvious—pairing between the ACLU's concern with AIDS and its aggressive gay rights policies. Just as with abortion, AIDS would likely pass unnoticed as a specific civil libertarian concern were it not for its close association with homosexual activity. Again, it is a matter of having to deal with the consequences of sexual freedom. Rather than face head on the leading cause of AIDS (or even be honest enough to acknowledge the causal connection), the ACLU continues to demand on behalf of homosexuals a plethora of civil rights which only serve to further condone and encourage the very sexual activity which results in such dire consequences. Considering the shocking, unacceptable human loss involved, the ACLU's misguided policies on AIDS and gay rights make tragic mockery of *total sexual freedom.*

Sex, the Ultimate Personal Freedom

If someone were to ask you which of your many rights is most to be valued, you might immediately nominate the rights to speech, religion, and association. After all, these are positioned at the very beginning of the Bill of Rights. However, more and more people today would suggest that the right of privacy heads the list. In a nation besotted with rights-consciousness, we are downright heady with the wine of personal autonomy, for which "privacy" is but a nickname.

The ACLU (still staunch in the defense of speech and association, if less convinced about the value of free exercise of religion) both reflects and actively precipitates the cultural shift from traditional libertarian values (like speech, religion, and association) to more contemporary concerns about personal autonomy (like total sexual freedom).

What is more intriguing than the shift itself is the often proffered rationalization for the shift: Unless we have total *sexual* freedom, we risk losing our *traditional* freedoms such as speech and association. (Religion, naturally, is omitted from the equation, since religion is viewed as an obstacle to sexual freedom.) Nevermind that sexual freedom was nowhere guaranteed in the Constitution, as were speech and association. According to the ACLU, we simply can't afford to lose that "freedom." Lose one "freedom," so goes the logic, and we will lose them all. Amazingly, in just a few short years, sexual freedom has gone from being no freedom at all to becoming the icon of all freedoms.

Jefferson would never have imagined it. Madison would have been positively dumbfounded! But the essential connection between sexual freedom and all other freedoms has become an unassailable fundamental of the New Fundamentalism.

Sex as a Symbol of Liberation

Why has sex been elevated to such primacy? You begin to catch a vision of its importance from Russell Hittinger's cogent analysis of *Planned Parenthood of S.E. Pennsylvania v. Casey*, the abortion rights case which rather unexpectedly upheld the validity of *Roe v. Wade*.[19] Hittinger first cites the (Reagan-Bush appointed) plurality's novel definition of subjectivized, privatized, and personally customized liberty:

> At the heart of liberty is the right to define one's own concept of existence, of meaning, of the universe, and of the mystery of human life. Beliefs about these matters could not define the attributes of personhood were they formed under compulsion of the State.

He then proceeds to tell us exactly why sex, particularly in its ultimate manifestation—abortion—is so crucial to the liberal-Left. "The abortion right seems to recognize a private franchise over matters of life and death."[20]

Sexual freedom is crucial because it is symbolic of the individual triumphing over the State, community expectations, social norms, moral strictures, and indeed, if necessary, even over one's own offspring. Sex reaches to the heart and soul of private franchise, personal autonomy, and self will. Because nothing defines one's own self quite as intimately, intensely, or as powerfully as sex, freedom of sexual expression has become the epitome of the Unfettered Self.

The parting of the ways comes when the liberal-Left suggests that being sexually free is always and in every case a good idea. One need not be on the conservative-Right to view with caution the siren call of sex—sex with its infinite capacity to seduce us; sex with its temptation to forbidden passion; sex with its often false allure, promising relationship in a space occupied only by lust. In ways we sometimes least expect, sex can bring a freedom from commitments, values, and character that eventually betrays and enslaves us. It is not unbounded emancipation that sex needs, but, rather, carefully delineated boundaries of healthy expression. Seen in this light, traditional sexual taboos are an ally to be welcomed, not an enemy to be overcome.

This is not to say that traditional sexual taboos should necessarily be regulated by the government. What it does say is that the government should not be in the business of promoting sexual activity which is contrary to traditional taboos. For example, there need not be criminal punishment for homosexual activity. On the other hand, the state should not endorse homo-sexual marriage by treating it in the same way as heterosexual marriage.

Certainly, it is liberating to be released from anything (like sex, for example) which demands from us a great amount of self-control. Since hardly anything is more hedged about by restraints than sexual expression, the lifting of those restraints should indeed be liberating! If sex no longer has boundaries, limits, or obligations, then one can truly be free from restraint. And, by extension, free from *all restraints*, sexual or otherwise.

If the State issues a license for sexual liberties, that license is good in *any* sexual jurisdiction—whether for normative or perverted sex; whether for loving or commercial sex; whether even for consequence-free sex with its often fatal results.

Note the progressive nature of sexual license. It begins harmlessly enough (one may think) with heterosexual promiscuity; then downgrades to deviant homosexual activity; and finally takes a quantum leap to the killing of millions of unborn children, the Final Solution for sexual freedom. Ultimately, the consequences reach to the unborn child who will never survive the womb to experience the joy of sex.

Actually, if one thinks carefully about abortion, there really is no quantum leap at all. As the ACLU understands better than the rest of us, there is indeed a rather direct tie between sexual restraint and other forms of moral restraint. Or, to put it the other way around, a rather direct tie between total sexual freedom and total moral freedom in other seemingly unrelated realms as well.

No, this is not to say that fornicators, once having tasted of unbounded sexual freedom, would thereby demand the right to kill. What it does mean is that a Declaration of Sexual Independence, once signed, holds a certain truth to be self-evident. A rather different truth, to be sure— that other matters of personal morality are on an equal plane and deserve the same *laissez faire* treatment. Hence, for example, the ACLU's related policies on the legalization of drugs and gambling. Hence, too, the ACLU's abortion flagship, which treats the death of the unborn with as much indifference as its casual attitude towards unbridled sexual expression.

In a civilized society, few people would dare apply for a license to kill. By contrast, many would apply for an unrestricted sexual license. Sadly, the wholesale granting of unrestricted sexual license has led to the wholesale granting of a license to kill. Pull down barriers to the sexual beast within us, and we will soon discover the other beasts within ourselves which we never knew existed.

The Ties Between Sexual and Civil Liberties

Traditional civil liberties, such as speech, religion, and association, do not depend in the least on sexual liberty as some now propose. However, the ACLU is right to believe that there is a vital network (call it a moral internet) between the various individual liberties. What the ACLU apparently does not understand is that, when one liberty is exercised without restraint, the same spirit of excess can run virus-like throughout the entire system and cause it to shut down.

Such was the case, for example, when total sexual freedom worked its way insidiously into free speech. At that point, the logic of total sexual freedom dictated that there could be no such thing as pornography or obscenity, and in fact that there could be no prior restraint of any speech whatsoever. Once the ACLU philosophically committed itself to moral anarchy in the realm of sexual expression, one didn't need a crystal ball in order to predict that it would also take an absolutist position on free speech—with no holds barred. As with total sexual freedom, free speech could have no restraints whatever. Such thinking inexorably leads to a legal license for even greater sexual freedoms...even kiddy porn.

Total sexual freedom doesn't operate in a vacuum. Unlike any other human activity, there is something about sex that speaks to a wider audience than its own indulgence. It should be warning enough that sexual expression for any one individual has the potential for absolutely ruinous consequences when not handled with cautious rectitude. By its very nature, sexual freedom threatens to unravel the wider moral and civil order. Liberty, when seen through the eyes of sexual license, is soon debased into a libertine licentiousness unworthy of genuine libertarian concerns.

If the ACLU is still serious about following its historical civil libertarian instincts, it has no choice but to renounce its policy of protecting and promoting libidinous sexual instincts. As the devil himself knows, you can't sleep around forever without risking the loss of respectability.

CHAPTER 8

Nolo Contendre to the War on Crime

"AN EXCESS OF LAW INESCAPABLY WEAKENS THE RULE OF LAW."

LAURENCE H. TRIBE

Thanks in large measure to the ACLU, criminal justice has become a game. The police know it; the criminals know it; the courts know it. Yet through it all (just read its literature), the ACLU remains defiantly proud of its role in bringing about the criminal procedure revolution. If by the new rules the police shaped up and became more professional, so did the criminals. By now, they all know their rights and what they can get away with if the cops mess up. In prisons and penitentiaries, thousands of "jailhouse lawyers" are clogging the courts, demanding everything from the umpteenth appellate review of their case to the latest action movies and soap-on-a-rope. Thanks largely to the ACLU, America's criminals get more attention than their raped, robbed, and murdered victims.

It is well known that the ACLU hates capital punishment. Extraordinary efforts are made to keep serial killers from the chair. But is America aware that the ACLU basically opposes all punishment? No wonder the ACLU is so intent on giving persons accused of crimes as many bites at the procedural apple as possible. The irony is that, because of all the protections being provided for the accused, the justice system itself is now in critical meltdown. Worse yet, a younger generation has been taught that they can act irresponsibly and get away with it. And so, the rest of us lock ourselves in at night, terrified at the thought that the ACLU is proudly keeping vigil for our security.

Nolo Contendre to the War on Crime

In the "trial of the century," it had been billed as the "cross-examination of the century." For four dramatic days, a captivated nation almost forgot it was O.J. Simpson on trial. All eyes and ears were on Detective Mark Fuhrman as he came under a withering cross-examination by the scowling, ranting F. Lee Bailey. It didn't exactly live up to its pre-trial hype (and how could it have?). Nevertheless, it was gripping stuff.

Need anyone be reminded that it was Fuhrman who found the bloody glove at O.J.'s Rockingham residence? Or *planted it there*, depending upon whom you believed? The stakes could hardly have been higher. The glove in question was a perfect match with the *other* bloody glove—the one found at the scene where O.J.'s ex-wife Nicole and her friend Ronald Goldman had been brutally murdered.

So F. Lee Bailey had little choice but to slash into Fuhrman's testimony with as much ferocity as the killer himself had displayed in his frenzied attack. Wasn't Fuhrman angry about having been taken off the case? Didn't he go around to the north side of the fence by himself at a time when other officers couldn't see what he was doing? Hadn't he said at the preliminary hearing that he had seen *gloves*, not *a glove*?

Then the indignant Bailey went for the jugular. (Everyone, including Fuhrman, knew what was coming.) You're a racist, aren't you, Mr.

Fuhrman? You don't like interracial marriages, do you? How many times in the past ten years have you used the word "nigger?"

"No," "Not true," "Never," came Fuhrman's responses, carefully considered and cool as a cucumber. For all his fury, Bailey had hardly made a dent. Lead prosecutor Marcia Clark breathed a sigh of relief at how smoothly it had all gone. Not a hitch. Not a slip.

Little did she know then that Fuhrman's apparently-flawless testimony had set in motion a time bomb that would blow up in her face when the infamous Fuhrman tapes later came to light. As it became painfully clear to the prosecution, Fuhrman had indeed used the "N" word over the past ten years. And the "F" word, relentlessly. And words of brutality, deceit, and venomous hatred aimed at everyone from blacks, to Hispanics, to women. Here, at last, was explosive impeachment evidence, the prosecution's worst nightmare.

Why Fuhrman Didn't Lie About the Glove

So the "Dream Team" had managed a dramatic coup. It had caught the prosecution's star witness in a lie and made the most of it. Still, the defense had done little to prove its planted-glove theory. The evidence to the contrary was just too compelling. For starters, Fuhrman was the fifteenth officer to arrive at the murder scene, and not one of the officers who preceded him had seen more than the one glove. (You can't take a glove that was never there in the first place.)

And how in the world would Fuhrman have been able to carry the glove to O.J.'s house without other officers noticing it? (The ol' plastic baggie inside the sock trick was surely a bit of a stretch.)

Why would any officer risk his badge by trying to set up a suspect whose whereabouts—and possible airtight alibi—were unknown to him at the time? (It would be embarrassing, to say the least, if, after announcing the discovery of the glove, those four mythical young men in the vicinity of Nicole's condo actually confessed to having done the killing!)

Finally, don't forget that "Kato" Kaelin heard the three loud thumps behind his bedroom wall long before Fuhrman arrived at O.J.'s house. (Are we to believe that "Kato" and Fuhrman were somehow in cahoots?)

Face it, folks. Whatever else you might think of Detective Mark Fuhrman, there's not a chance in the world that he lied about finding the glove. *But he probably did lie about the search warrant.* As did detectives Phillips, Lange, and Vannatter. Even Judge Ito used the phrase "reckless disregard of the truth" in connection with their testimony about searching O.J.'s Rockingham compound.

Who did they think they were kidding? Is there anyone who doesn't believe that, as soon as they knew it was O.J.'s ex-wife, the four L.A.P.D. detectives were acting on a hunch that O.J. was the killer? (It obviously wasn't your basic drive-by stabbing; so—unthinkable as it may have been— who else but O.J. would have had a motive to kill Nicole so viciously?)

You can safely bet the ranch that the reason the four detectives went in force to O.J.'s residence is that—contrary to their collective sworn testimony—they did indeed suspect that O.J. was Nicole's killer. But, in their rush to confirm their hunch, the detectives didn't swing by night court for a search warrant as they made their way to Rockingham.

So Bailey was definitely onto something when he took his attack in the direction of the search warrant—or the *lack* thereof. And one did begin to wonder. Was the white Bronco really parked at such an angle that it would have drawn attention to itself? Could Fuhrman's much-talked-about little flashlight really have detected that small drop of blood on the Bronco's door handle? Was it really necessary to jump over the fence when their only reason for being there, supposedly, was to make a death notification?

And is there a chance in the world that Fuhrman wouldn't remember whether or not he pulled his gun as he walked down that back sidewalk in the dark? (He remembered every other detail, right down to the cobwebs.) Or that he really believed some injured person might be at the rear corner of the property? (Is that why he waited so long to go in search of this "injured person?")

Those questions should have had little appeal to the jurors at trial, whose job it was to determine O.J.'s guilt or innocence. But those questions stood to have great appeal on appeal, had Simpson been found guilty. If Fuhrman and his fellow detectives had lied about why they went to O.J.'s house, and had lied about why they went over the fence without first obtaining a search warrant, then their search was illegal. And, if the search was illegal, any evidence which they seized while on O.J.'s property— including the all-important bloody glove—should have been thrown out of court before the jury could consider it. Or at least so says the "exclusionary rule," the controversial court-made sanction designed to curb illegal police practices, particularly in the area of searches and seizures.

Searching for the Truth

The Fourth Amendment says that, "The right of the people to be secure in their persons, houses, papers, and effects, against unreasonable searches and seizures, shall not be violated...."[1] The burden, therefore, was on the four detectives to prove that their search of O.J.'s residence was reasonable under the circumstances. And, had reasonableness been the only standard, they just might have pulled it off. Mark Fuhrman's awareness of at least one prior instance of domestic violence between O.J. and Nicole could have supplied reason enough to make further inquiry. Given a horrific murder, *serious* inquiry.

But the Fourth Amendment additionally requires that "no Warrants shall issue, but upon probable cause, supported by Oath or affirmation, and particularly describing the place to be searched, and the persons or things to be seized."[2] As interpreted by the courts, it is permissible to make *unwarranted* searches and seizures when there are exigent circumstances that would not allow time for the police to obtain a warrant. (As where the evidence sought will most likely be destroyed, or where there is risk of immediate harm to the police or to others.) But even where exigent circumstances exist, there must still be a showing of probable cause, the same as if a warrant were being sought from a magistrate.

And, aye, there's the rub. Technically speaking, Fuhrman and crew had neither exigent circumstances nor probable cause to enter the premises. The latter explains why they didn't stop and get a search warrant before first going to the Rockingham residence. (Even an educated hunch doesn't amount to probable cause.) The former explains why they uniformly testified that they were concerned about someone possibly being injured at O.J.'s compound. (Nice try, but even their patient ringing of the buzzer at the front gate tends to indicate anything but an emergency situation.)

Yet the mystery remains: If Judge Ito himself wasn't fooled about the claim of exigent circumstances, and even alluded to dishonesty in the Affidavit which supported a search warrant obtained later in the day, then why did he uphold the seizure of the crucial evidence? The short answer is that he is privy to how the justice game is played: the police act reasonably, if perhaps without actual probable cause; officers then lie, if necessary, to transform hunch into probable cause, or non-exigency into exigency; and judges tacitly approve of the deception, in order to insure that unquestionably reliable evidence doesn't get tossed into a black hole of unconstitutionality.

Most courts acknowledge that wide latitude simply has to be given to the police in order to safeguard important evidence. The comfortable retrospect of the courtroom months following the investigation of a crime is hardly what police are facing on the street in the heat of the moment. If the roles were reversed, and F. Lee Bailey had been a detective on the O.J. case, there is probable cause to believe that he would have made most of the same decisions (and the same mistakes) as did Fuhrman and his fellow detectives.

So when Fuhrman testified that he wasn't looking for anything in particular when he took a stroll over to the Bronco, and later wandered down the back path alone, he was just playing the justice game the way virtually all other police officers play it. He knew he couldn't admit what was really going on in his mind, because he was only acting on a hunch, and that wasn't good enough for a legal search. Where he went wrong was in having a *good* hunch (the kind taxpayers *pay him to have* when he investigates brutal murders) which led to a damning piece of evidence against O.J., but without first having a warrant securely in hand.

The Good News-Bad News Exclusionary Rule

There is a grand irony at work in all of this. Police deception is winked at even by the courts to get around what otherwise would be potentially disastrous results were the exclusionary rule strictly applied in every case where court-mandated procedure was not followed. But the exclusionary rule itself was thought necessary by the courts to curb rampant deception regarding patently unreliable evidence in an era of widespread police abuse. It seems that the pendulum has now swung from one extreme (unsafe evidence) to another (the preeminence of procedure over even safe evidence), with each extreme being maintained by less than honest testimony on the part of the police.

If there is any distinction which legitimately might be made, the current practice of deception typically takes place in aid of *zealous* police work, whereas the former practice of deception too often took place in aid of *overzealous* police work. Yet, as a former prosecutor, I can assure you that civil libertarians are right to point out that there is a thin blue line between what is zealous and what is overzealous. There is a need for some kind of safeguard to insure that the line doesn't get crossed.

What makes the exclusionary rule so controversial is not its aim and intent, but its potentially harsh results. Protecting against unsafe, manufactured evidence is one thing. But when in a given case the rule does in fact lead to the exclusion of otherwise reliable, trustworthy evidence, it elevates form over substance, procedure over truth. As witnessed in the O.J. Simpson trial, the spotlight is all too easily shifted from the accused to the police. Any mistake the police might make is treated by defense counsel as if it were a greater evil than a heinous act of double-murder.

The distinction between legal process and actual truth has never presented much of a problem to the legal profession as a whole, much less to committed civil libertarians. For example, Ramona Ripston, executive director of the southern California ACLU, would not think it the least bit strange to say (as she did) "I don't think [Fuhrman] planted that glove," but then approve of the exclusion of the glove in the event its seizure were found to be illegal.[3] Nor would she be alone in taking such a seemingly bizarre position.

The legal profession has been almost unanimous in its view that the primacy of "the system" must be maintained even, if necessary, at the expense of freedom for someone who is undeniably guilty. "Better that ninety-nine guilty persons go free than one innocent person be wrongfully convicted," and so forth, goes the idea. Unfortunately, that noble ideal begins to have devalued currency when the abstract *theory* of ninety-nine percent of the guilty going free starts to become a *reality.*

Therein lies a problem of perception. Most Americans, understandably fed up with the crime problem, tend to focus their anger on the legal system in general and civil libertarians in particular. Right or wrong, they lay the blame for the evils of the criminal justice system on the exclusionary rule; and place the blame for the exclusionary rule on the ACLU.

The truth is that the exclusionary rule probably has less of an actual impact on individual cases than most people think. That's because, except in instances of truly outrageous police misconduct, the courts allow officers, like the Simpson case, to play the justice game just the slightest bit loosely and get away with it. Even so, hardly anything could be more symbolic of the evils of the criminal justice system and the wider crime problem with which it is associated than a rule which potentially can put a guilty person back on the streets to once again rape, rob, and perhaps even kill.

In the Simpson case, millions of people were outraged by a verdict which appeared to be contrary to the facts and rendered in order to "send a message" to the police. Ironically, the exclusionary rule itself is as much a "nullification" of the facts as is "jury nullification." Its exclusive purpose is to "send a message" to the police saying that they messed up. If you didn't like the verdict in the Simpson case, there is much to think about when it comes to the exclusionary rule. That rule stands as a striking symbol of facts suppressed, truth ignored.

Nor can the ACLU escape its association with that symbolism. If it didn't think up the exclusionary rule (and it didn't), the ACLU is nevertheless linked to all that the rule stands for and shares in whatever stigma may be attached to it.

Criminal Procedure, the ACLU's Baby

For better or for worse, the ACLU claims responsibility for having supplied the central arguments behind the criminal procedure revolution which took place primarily during the Warren Court era. Cases like *Rochin* (1951)[4], *Mapp* (1961)[5], *Gideon* (1963)[6], *Escobedo* (1964)[7], and *Miranda* (1966)[8], all wore the ACLU insignia.

Of all these cases, perhaps the most legally significant was the *Mapp* decision. The exclusionary rule had already been in force in federal cases since *Weeks v. U.S.* in 1914,[9] and by 1961 half of the states were also imposing the rule wherever there was evidence of police misconduct. However, when *Mapp* mandated the rule in *all* states, it set in motion a wide-ranging national standard for police conduct from which there was no retreat. Since then, searches and seizures, wiretaps, interrogations, excessive bail, and the entire array of police practices have undergone close judicial scrutiny.

Far more controversial than *Mapp* was the more-famous *Miranda* decision, from which the so-called "Miranda warnings" came. Those warnings: "You have a right to remain silent;" "Whatever you say can, and will, be used against you;" "You have a right to an attorney;" and "If you cannot afford an attorney, one will be appointed for you;" are so well known that criminals themselves have been known to recite them with contempt to the police.

Miranda v. Arizona was the result of a novel conceptual marriage between the Sixth Amendment's right to counsel and the Fifth Amendment's right against self-incrimination. The ACLU's Anthony Amsterdam was the matchmaker who proposed the marriage to the Supreme Court in the ACLU's amicus brief. To properly celebrate so important a union of constitutional concepts, Chief Justice Earl Warren personally presided over the marriage. In a strongly-worded opinion, the Chief Justice took as his text for the occasion the many police manuals cited in the ACLU's brief, as well as the ACLU's own publication, *Secret Detention*.[10]

The ACLU had taken its case for police reform to the highest Court in the land and won. Yet, it was not only in the appellate courts that the ACLU was making its presence known. It was the ACLU that also first came up with the idea of civilian review boards, and that published reports on police abuse together with brochures about what to do if you are arrested. The ACLU even opened up store-front offices to provide counsel for victims of police abuse.[11] For good or for ill, the ACLU played a singularly significant role in the criminal procedure revolution.

ACLU—Accessory to Crime?

No one could be prouder of that assessment than the ACLU itself. Speaking for the ACLU, Samuel Walker boasts, "As was the case with the church-state decisions, the Court's rulings on the police penetrated deep into the fabric of American society, altering public expectations and reshaping the behavior of public officials."[12]

If the ACLU can take deserved credit for the revolution in police professionalism from the 1960s onward, it must also share in its responsibility for public attitudes that have been fostered as a result of that revolution. Just exactly what public expectations were altered? In what way was public behavior, not only of officials, but also of ordinary citizens, reshaped?

Given a concurrent significant rise in crime since the beginning of the criminal procedure revolution, one simply has to ask whether there might be some causal connection between the two. Certainly there are *many* factors contributing to the crime problem (including the drug culture, a shifting economy, and the breakdown of the nuclear family). Perhaps Justice Louis Brandeis was right. In a way, we've not considered seriously enough his statement that the law is a "great teacher." Could it be that the criminal procedure revolution in general, and the exclusionary rule in particular, ended up teaching some lessons that were not at all intended?

Is it possible that we have educated an entire generation to believe that no one has an obligation to own up to what they have done against society? Or that everyone is entitled to hide behind a lawyer, no matter how heinous an act they've committed? Have we taught the public that the police are the real enemy, not thugs and hoodlums? That criminals are the real victims, not those who suffer at their hands? Or—worst of all—that you can commit a crime and still have a good chance of getting away with it if the police mess up?

Charges that the ACLU is anti-law and order don't stem merely from the ACLU's support for the exclusionary rule. Consider the ACLU's opposition to curfews for minors (which has been highly successful in curbing crime in a number of cities, including, Dallas, Atlanta, Roanoke, Austin, San Jose, and San Diego). And its opposition to roadblocks, such as the one in

Oakland, California (set up to stop cruising, public drunkenness and rude behavior on roads leading to Lake Merritt); and in Chicago (where drive-by shootings and drug trafficking were dramatically reduced by stopping cars near a public housing project); and in Inkster, Michigan (where the local sheriff shut down an open-air drug market by checking drivers for their operator's license and proof of car ownership).

To this list can also be added the ACLU's opposition to sobriety checkpoints, examination of school lockers, drug testing, and security screening gates at airports, schools, and courthouses. Are these the kind of policies which are naturally mandated by the ACLU's principled commitment to civil liberties, or is it possible that such anti-communitarian policies actually reflect the ACLU's anarchistic roots? Is it possible, too, that ACLU policies regarding criminal procedure have been formulated under the influence of the ACLU's pervasive policy on personal privacy—and perhaps, especially, the use of drugs?

As one might expect, the ACLU is incredibly sensitive about charges that it is soft on crime and is a lobby for criminals. In fact, so defensive is the ACLU that executive director Ira Glasser appears to have engaged in some Fuhrman-like "reckless disregard of the truth" regarding ACLU policy. In a letter to the editor of the *Wall Street Journal* (responding to an article by Professor Amitai Etzioni), Glasser said, "The ACLU has never opposed community crime watches, community antidrug patrols or airport metal detectors."[13]

Giving Glasser the benefit of the doubt, perhaps the ACLU has never instituted a lawsuit to prevent the use of airport metal detectors. (Is that what he was saying?) But, even if that were the case, it is difficult to take Glasser seriously when ACLU Policy 270 says explicitly, "The ACLU opposes the present and previous systems of airport searches because they violate the requirements of the Fourth Amendment."[14]

When questioned about Policy 270, former associate director Alan Reitman explained that the ACLU's opposition "is this dragnet nature of checking people who have not been charged when there's no indication that they are about to commit a crime. That weakens the Fourth Amendment protection."[15] To say the least, it is curious that Policy 270 was adopted in 1973, and, despite repeated challenges from the ACLU's critics, remains unaltered and unclarified to this day. One can only conclude that the ACLU is resolute in taking an absolutist position on the Fourth Amendment while taking great pains to downplay the irresponsible implications and extreme results of its opposition to airport metal detectors.

Victims? What Victims?

What is most disturbing about such deceptive propaganda is that the ACLU's hyper-sensitivity about its own policies stands in stark contrast to its callous lack of sensitivity for the victims of crime. That, surely, is the ACLU's greatest crime of all. (At a minimum, it raises a serious question as to where the ACLU's sympathies lie when it comes to the issue of crime.) ACLU observer William Donohue (author of the two most authoritative ACLU critiques: *The Politics of the Civil Liberties Union and Twilight of Liberty*) reminds us, for example, that the ACLU has eight policies addressing the rights of prisoners (reasonable enough) but not one policy on the victims of crime (mere oversight?).[16]

With such an imbalance of official concern vis-a-vis criminals, on one hand, and their victims, on the other, the ACLU owes the American people a better explanation than it has ever offered. For a nation of people who hide in fear behind locked doors, the ACLU must answer former Chief Justice Warren Burger's question: "Is a society redeemed if it provides massive safeguards for accused persons" but fails to afford "elementary protection for its decent law-abiding citizens?"[17]

In point of fact, the ACLU did answer the Chief Justice's question, and his recommendations to the American Bar Association, that there be "swift arrest, prompt trial, certain penalty and—at some point—finality of judgment."[18] Within an hour of Burger's speech, Bruce J. Ennis, then national legal director of the ACLU, went before the press and strongly denounced Burger's criticism of multiple appeals and tightened bail standards.[19] True to form, there was still not a word about the "elementary protection for decent law-abiding citizens," only myopic attention to the ACLU's continuing bias in favor of "massive safeguards for the accused."

Presumably, the ACLU's explanation for this bias is that it primarily opposes government action. Because the government does not directly create victims, there is nothing for the ACLU to oppose on behalf of victims. What that explanation ignores is an anti-law enforcement climate that the ACLU has helped to foster, which, arguably, has resulted in an increase in both crime and its victims. Certainly, hard proof of that proposition is lacking, giving the ACLU every reason to deny it. But at some point, those who take pride in having engineered the criminals' rights revolution must also take responsibility for any of its negative results.

A Capital Aversion to Punishment

Never is the ACLU's concern for criminals more out of proportion to its concern for their victims than in the issue of capital punishment, which the ACLU virulently opposes. In its Policy 239, "The ACLU opposes the death penalty because it denies equal protection of the laws, is cruel and unusual punishment, and removes guarantees of due process of law. The death penalty is so inconsistent with the underlying values of our democratic system—the pursuit of life, liberty, and happiness—that the imposition of the death penalty for any crime is a denial of civil liberties."[20]

The ACLU still doesn't get it: The ultimate denial of civil liberties is *the whole point* of capital punishment. One who has intentionally taken the life of another without justification or excuse has thereby forfeited any right he or she might have to civil liberties. Can't the ACLU see that it is the *murderer* who has deprived the *victim* of "the pursuit of life, liberty, and happiness?" That is the very reason capital punishment is a just penalty in such cases.

It is not simply a matter of deterrence (which as a practical matter one could legitimately question) or of societal revenge (a not altogether worthy motive). Rather, life is so important—indeed sacred—that only the taking of life can begin to atone for its deliberate destruction.

In as close as the ACLU gets to a moral argument, the ACLU's capital punishment policy complains that "the existence of the death penalty for crimes results in discrimination against the poor, the uneducated, and members of minority communities."[21] And that may well be true, although one must be careful to ascertain whether, in fact, there might not be a proportionally higher percentage of murders committed from such groups. (That there is more than a measure of truth in the claim of unequal justice is graphically seen in the prosecution's decision not to seek the death penalty against O.J. Simpson. Rather than his color or economic status, his fame was such that no jury was likely to convict if they knew "The Juice" might be executed.)

To whatever extent there is discrimination in the administration of the death penalty, the ACLU is right to protest, and so should we all. If conservatives want to maintain the moral high ground on capital punishment, they must redouble their efforts to insure that there is not even the hint of discrimination. It is clear, however, that the ACLU would be opposed to capital punishment even if it were administered with scrupulous fairness.

The ACLU's second objection is that "contemporary ideas of the significance of human life make imposition of the death penalty cruel and unusual punishment, which is prohibited by the Constitution."[22] Until Gary Gilmore's execution in 1977, capital punishment had been "unusual" for the better part of a decade only because the ACLU itself had made it unusual by successfully persuading the courts to impose a de facto "moratorium" on legal executions. But for the ACLU's dogged interference, capital punishment would have occurred with "usual" regularity whenever guilt was determined in capital cases.

As for the death penalty being "cruel," the ACLU is obviously past being persuaded. For starters, the ACLU seems to be wholly unmoved by the cruelty imposed on the victims of brutal homicides. Could the ACLU stomach making "extraordinary efforts" to block executions if vicious slayings were witnessed first hand in the same way that official executions are witnessed?

If, as the ACLU suggests, it is the possibility of unsafe convictions we're to be worried about, how could even life imprisonment (or any lesser sentence, for that matter) ethically be imposed? It is simply not good enough to argue that "we can always reverse a wrong decision to incarcerate, but we can't turn back the clock on an execution." The risk of making such an irreversible mistake is the reason why the verdict itself must be *beyond a reasonable doubt,* and why, in capital cases, even those tight verdicts undergo strict judicial review before a person is executed.

Would the ACLU be willing to apply the same "How can we be sure?" argument to whether the unborn fetus is protectable "human life?" If we can *never be totally sure* that it *isn't* human life, how can we permit abortions to be a legal choice? Like capital punishment, the decision to abort is also irreversible. Unlike capital punishment, innocence of the aborted fetus is always, in every case, absolutely assured.

Those concerns aside, the ACLU does not seem to take on board the explicit language of the Constitution, which tells us right up front that the Founders would never have considered capital punishment to be cruel. Just look at the wording of the Fifth Amendment, for example: "No person shall be held to answer for a *capital*, or otherwise infamous crime, unless on a presentment or indictment of a Grand Jury...nor shall any person be subject for the same offense to be twice put in jeopardy of *life*...nor be deprived of *life*, liberty, or property, without due process of law..."

Consider also the Fourteenth Amendment, which speaks directly to the due process and equal protection concerns pressed by the ACLU. When the Amendment says "Nor shall any State deprive any person of life...without due process of law," it is crystal clear that a State may deprive a person of life as long as there has been due process.

Naturally, the ACLU knows that it is spitting into the wind when it offers due process and equal protection arguments. The original intent of the Founders to the contrary is just too clear. So, the ACLU's fall-back argument is to cite "contemporary ideas of the significance of human life." Capital punishment wasn't cruel in the eyes of the Founders, but it is cruel in *our* eyes, goes the argument. If so, of course, the problem is no longer one of constitutionality, as claimed, but a matter for the people to decide through their legislators.

What is so repugnant about the "contemporary value of human life" argument is its commentary on abortion. In a loud and clear voice, this argument tells us that the ACLU values the lives of convicted murderers more than the lives of the innocent unborn. In the ACLU's bizarre hierarchy of values, it is not cruel for a mother to kill her own offspring through a process of saline expulsion, which burns the fetus and prepares it for dismemberment as it is forced out of the womb, but it is cruel beyond measure for the State to use lethal injection (which the ACLU would approve for doctor-assisted suicide) to take the life of one who has been convicted of a brutal murder.

In its anti-death penalty policy, the ACLU reveals itself to be out of touch with both the Constitution and "the significance of human life." Considering the culture of death which the ACLU promotes through its policies on abortion and euthanasia, it is striking that the only life the ACLU seems to value is the life of one who has engaged in senseless murder.

Punishment: A Philosophical Watershed

When one speaks of capital punishment, of course, there are many who would oppose the death penalty, yet would have no qualms about imprisonment. For the ACLU, by contrast, its policy against *capital* punishment is merely an extension of its more general policy against *punishment*, period. The gospel according to the ACLU teaches that it is wrong to punish persons who themselves are victims of society's ills and who are therefore not personally responsible for what they do. For the ACLU, *that* is the true heart of the matter.

Hence, the ACLU's preference for probation rather than incarceration: "Probation maximizes the liberty of the individual,"[23] says the ACLU's policy on sentencing. (Of course, truly maximizing the liberty of the individual would also preclude probation.) And don't be fooled by the ACLU's talk about imprisonment being "safer" than capital punishment. The ACLU opposes life imprisonment without parole as much as it opposes the death penalty. Again, it is *punishment* that the ACLU fundamentally opposes, not just *capital* punishment.

Wholesale opposition to criminal penalties of any type is theoretical anarchism of the worst kind—where even violent offenders are not worthy of punishment. Indeed, says the ACLU, because they are all "victims" in their own way, proven criminals cannot legitimately be said to be "offenders." Roger Baldwin once said he would never serve on a jury, because he would never take part in convicting anyone. Asked how society could function without punishment, Baldwin replied, "That's your problem."[24]

This brings us to yet another fork in the road between the spiritual and the secular. The secular path does everything in its power to prevent punishment of the sin which it denies even exists. The spiritual path doesn't wish for punishment, but recognizes that sin does exist and, therefore, demands vindication.

At the fork in the road, the issue of sin and punishment becomes central to human existence. On one hand we hear God speaking to Adam and Eve about what would happen to them if they ate the forbidden fruit: "When you eat of it, you will surely die."[25] Yet, from the other side of the Garden, we hear the devil denying the possibility of punishment: "You will not surely die," he urged confidently.[26]

The devil's opposition to punishment is not the slightest bit principled. He doesn't care one whit for either the offender or the process by which punishment might be imposed. It is the devil's anarchistic philosophy that is at stake. If he acknowledges the legitimacy of punishment, he is thereby forced to acknowledge the very concept of sin itself, and—worse yet—the sovereignty of a God who calls us to personal accountability.

Crime and punishment are difficult enough for the ACLU to accept. Sin and punishment hardly compute. But, like the devil himself, the ACLU must surely know deep down that the link between crime and sin is close indeed. So close, in fact, that criminal punishment hints of a kind of punishment far more significant than the prison cell or even the electric chair. Some would even dare to call such punishment *eternal*.

So, says the devil, let's hear no talk of punishment, capital or otherwise. Once let loose, it's the kind of thing that could get completely out of hand.

Gun Control, A Political Anomaly

In its opposition to capital punishment, the ACLU breaks ranks with a growing number of political liberals (many of whom, like California Senator Diane Feinstein, have to be concerned about winning the next election in an era of pro-death-penalty sentiment). However, the ACLU is in lockstep agreement with most political liberals on the issue of gun control. Although ACLU Policy 47 takes unusual pains to stress that the ACLU has no civil liberties basis for "affirmative support" of gun control legislation, nevertheless it finds gun control to be "justified."[27]

Were it not for the ACLU's nervousness about encouraging the police to search homes, cars, and persons for restricted weapons, there would undoubtedly be even more wide-open support for gun control. Yet, given gun control's substantial restriction of the individual's interest in freedom of choice, the ACLU's sympathy for gun legislation is altogether surprising.

Even more surprising is the dual justification offered for the ACLU's position. First, there is an uncharacteristic appeal to the *original intent* of the Second Amendment. ("The individual's right to bear arms applies only to the preservation or efficiency of a well-regulated militia."[28]) Unlike capital punishment, there is no attempt here to make a "living document" argument that would allow for "contemporary values" to override original intent.

Second, there is a most amazing and disingenuous disclaimer that "it is not the ACLU's role to commit the ACLU to involve ourselves in social issues by finding a constitutional basis where there is none."[29] Has the ACLU forgotten what Aryeh Neier said about identifying a problem and then couching it in terms of constitutional civil liberties? It is the ACLU's precise *modus operandi*!

In every way conceivable, then, the ACLU's gun control policy is strikingly anomalous—except, of course, for neatly fitting the agenda of the liberal-Left. But therein lies the even greater curiosity: Why is gun control a *liberal* cause? Or, put differently, why is opposition to gun control a *conservative* cause? Wouldn't philosophical consistency dictate just the opposite pairings?

At least with regard to hand-guns (as opposed to rifles), guns and crime statistics go very much hand in hand. (Among murders by teens, for example, a full 60 percent are committed with a handgun.[30]) One would think, therefore, that "law and order" conservatives would favor anything that would get guns out of the hands of gangs and other hoodlums, and that civil libertarians would oppose such governmental intrusions into one's zone of personal freedom.

Given the current crime problem, conservatives presumably believe that access to guns is necessary in order to defend oneself against the bad guys who are already out there carrying guns. But that argument is merely pragmatic, suggesting only a lack of faith in the government's ability to successfully take guns away from the bad guys. From a strictly philosophical perspective, opposition to gun control seems to run counter to normal conservative instincts.

Could it be, then, that "law and order" is not the crucial issue after all? From the standpoint of traditional liberals, there is a philosophical comfort zone with big government telling folks what they will or will not do—all in aid of a good cause. And, looking back to the opposite extreme, perhaps that explains something which is consistent with normal conservative instincts: an aversion to big government. The conservatives' opposition to gun control apparently has nothing to do with the crime problem and everything to do with telling Big Brother to take a hike.

Surely, that was the sense in which "the right to bear arms" was contemplated by the Founders. Madison, for example, wrote in *The Federalist* that "the advantage of being armed, which the Americans possess over the people of almost every other nation," provides them with an almost "insurmountable" barrier to tyranny. Militia or no militia, originally the point of bearing arms was a matter of insuring that a democratic government didn't turn despotic.

Of course, even that rationale has been twisted grotesquely in the recent Oklahoma City bombing, in which radical right-wing para-military types resorted to blowing up innocent children in an unconscionable paranoia about the federal government. Such cowardly bombing of soft targets is hardly what the Founders would have contemplated within the idea of local militias guarding against anti-democratic tyranny. Besides, more than two hundred years onward we are hardly facing the kind of tyranny that the country was ridding itself of during the American Revolution.

Given today's crime problem, it's not a matter of protecting against some big despot sitting in the seat of government, but of protecting against thousands of little despots threatening to gun us down in the streets and in our homes. In such a climate of fear, handguns used by hooligans hardly fit the original intent.

But where does that leave the ACLU? Oddly enough, it leaves the ACLU cutting against its civil libertarian instincts (born of anarchism and a distrust of government not unlike that of radical conservatives) and favoring, instead, its liberal political leanings (which embraces Big Brother statism whenever convenient to the cause).

The carefully nuanced wording of ACLU's Policy 47 confirms that analysis perfectly. The ACLU acknowledges that it has no purely civil libertarian basis for supporting gun control. If anything, it hints that it has a civil libertarian basis for being very concerned about gun control. But after all the sputtering, it comes down on the side of justifying restrictive gun legislation—a liberal *political* position, pure and simple.

And—surprise of surprises—it turns out to be a "law and order" position after all—but one that is not natural to civil libertarians, and for which they get no credit. (Why should they? For them, supporting gun control is apparently only a matter of maintaining credentials as political liberals.)

What a telling anomaly the gun control issue turns out to be. There is only one time that the ACLU ends up in the "law and order" column, and it happens only as the result of political expediency! A nervous expediency at that.

Justice! Justice! But There Is No Justice

When you leave the political anomaly of gun control and return to what true civil libertarians do best (cause the rest of us to think long and hard about our system of justice), the ACLU still can't get it right. Oddly enough, the ACLU's obsession with criminal procedure ends up backfiring against the very ones whose protection is sought: those who are accused of crimes. There are now so many procedural bites at the judicial apple for each criminal defendant that the criminal justice system is in a state of critical meltdown.

What could be more fundamental to civil liberties than the right to a fair trial? But, because of all the motions to suppress and motions to dismiss filed in the name of civil liberties, hardly anyone can find an empty courtroom anymore. (The problem is compounded by complicated minimum sentencing guidelines and use of the criminal justice system for essentially non-criminal matters like environmental protection.) Consequently, instead of getting the fair trial to which they are constitutionally entitled, most criminal defendants find that their only moment of justice is a hasty plea-bargain in the hallway of the courthouse. Thanks in large measure to the ACLU, the right to a fair trial has been sacrificed upon the altar of procedural exactitude.

What the ACLU seemingly lacks is any appreciation for the big picture. The implementation of expansive rules governing police conduct is now so burdensome that the temple of justice is collapsing under its own weight. But that could be only an overture to unthinkable events to come.

If one dares to view society through the widest possible lens, one is likely to see the awful image of Thomas Hobbes' terrible Leviathan. Especially significant for those who believe in social contract theories, it was Hobbes who pointed out that people can tolerate almost anything but chronic insecurity. They crave law and order as much as they need food. When starved for civil order they will sanction virtually anything that promises to provide that order. Enter, stage left, the Leviathan—whoever or whatever it takes to give the people what they most want and need. If the Leviathan had a name, it would be Totalitarianism.

The grandest of all ironies would be an alarming progression from legitimate civil liberties, to hyperextended criminal procedures, to gridlock of the criminal justice system, to widespread lawlessness and anarchy, to a nation so fearful for its personal safety that—in exchange for personal security—it would *beg* to have civil liberties taken away. Such a frightening scenario is not just scaremongering. It has happened before.

London columnist John Keegan reminds us that when ordinary Germans in the 1930s feared the catastrophic collapse of their society, they eagerly turned to Adolph Hitler and his grand scheme of social control. "That included a 'block warden' in every corner house to spy on the neighbors, vigilantism, party police forces, compulsory membership of disciplined youth movements and universal military service at the social level and, at the legal, deprivation of civil rights, forced emigration, arbitrary arrest, imprisonment without trial, judicial murder and, eventually, mass extermination of the enemies of the people." [31]

What looms ominously ahead for any society that values the freedom of criminals above the freedom of ordinary citizens to walk the streets safely is a society that one day will beg for totalitarian protections at the expense of civil liberties. (Does the aftermath of the Oklahoma City bombing tell us anything?)

Note that the proposed progression is not from *freedom* to *totalitarianism,* but from one form of totalitarianism (elitist control over all of society, including a monolithic system of criminal procedure) to another form of totalitarianism (a Hitler-like despotism). They all cry liberty, but there is no liberty. They all cry justice, but there is no justice.

Nothing is more enslaving than an addiction to procedure for its own sake. Explaining this principle to the Pharisaical legalists of his own day, Jesus said, "The Sabbath was made for man; not man for the Sabbath."[32] For today's civil libertarians, the updated message is: "Procedure is made for justice; not justice for procedure." If the multiplicity of procedural rules doesn't work for the good of the people—criminals and law-abiding citizens alike—then of what value is it?

What the ACLU needs to see is that due process—as important as it is—is only a means, not an end in itself. Laws alone cannot guarantee either a just society for those who are accused of crime or a secure society for everyone else. In fact, the paradox is that, the more law there is, the less chance that true justice will ever be achieved.

Grant Gilmore summed it up elegantly in his Yale University lecture on "The Age of Anxiety": "The better the society, the less law there will be....The worse the society, the more law there will be....In Heaven, there will be no law, and the lion will lie down with the lamb....In Hell, there will be nothing but law, and due process will be meticulously observed."[33]

Un-American Civil Liberties

"TRUE PATRIOTISM HATES INJUSTICE IN ITS
OWN LAND MORE THAN ANYWHERE ELSE."

CLARENCE DARROW

B orn of anti-war sentiment in World War I and linked with a fascination for Communism, the ACLU has been haunted throughout its history with the charge of being unpatriotic. Has the leopard changed its spots after 75 years? The ACLU did, in fact, support the country in World War II, but was staunchly anti-war once again during the Vietnam conflict. Likewise, Communist sympathies have been abandoned for years, but there is a lingering love of leftist governments abroad which continues to prompt many of the ACLU's domestic security policies.

Being anti-war can be both religiously motivated and patriotic. But, the ACLU's anti-war stance is mostly a matter of politics, not of religious conscience. Hence, the ACLU risks being seen as unpatriotic. Nor does it help the ACLU's image that it adamantly supports flag burning as a means of political protest. For all the talk about symbolic free speech (an argument which the ACLU would rightly deny to any pro-life supporter who would kill an abortion doctor), the ACLU can hardly claim that flag burning is a symbol of patriotism.

If the ACLU is not itself unpatriotic, it has a consistent record of supporting those who are. Perhaps that could be rationalized as a principled defense of those with whom the ACLU strongly disagrees. Unfortunately, the ACLU has not proceeded solely from civil libertarian concerns, but has taken a political stance consistent with the unpatriotic causes it defends.

CHAPTER   9

Un-American Civil Liberties

I f during its first thirty years the American Civil Liberties Union was the length and shadow of Roger Baldwin, then it is not surprising that even today's ACLU would be defensive of criminal procedure and prisoners' rights. For at one point, Baldwin himself became a convicted criminal and personally experienced incarceration in prison.

Nor, by the same token, is it surprising that today's ACLU should continue to reflect attitudes toward national security and patriotism which were the cause of Roger Baldwin's incarceration. The crime that landed Baldwin behind bars was a refusal to register for the draft during World War I. What, then, might one expect? As was Baldwin, so is today's ACLU—anti–government (except whenever statism is considered to be an ally), anti–war (unless politically expedient to be otherwise), and, in the minds of many, at times even anti–American.

Both Baldwin and the ACLU would undergo significant changes in perspective over the years relative to war, the draft, and the importance of national security, but it is difficult to grow beyond one's roots. A look back at the earliest days of the ACLU reveals much of the thinking which, still today, colors ACLU policy. After examining the roots of the ACLU, one begins to sense the full significance of the fact that the civil liberties movement was born of political dissent and anti–war radicalism.

137

Even the progression of organizational continuity is telling. The progenitor of the American Civil Liberties Union was the National Civil Liberties Bureau (NCLB), which evolved from the earlier Civil Liberties Bureau (CLB), which itself was an offshoot of the American Union Against Militarism (AUAM), founded in 1914 to oppose America's entry into World War I. Roger Baldwin, who joined AUAM in 1916 and established within it the Bureau for Conscientious Objectors, later founded and led the CLB, NCLB, and eventually the ACLU. It is from that anti–war genesis that everything else has followed course.

As wave after wave of patriotism washed over the nation at the beginning of the First World War, it became increasingly clear that dissent would not be tolerated. In the midst of wartime hysteria, the government entered upon an era of unprecedented political repression, targeted primarily at free speech and association. But that simply made the anti–war coalition of anarchists, socialists, German and Irish immigrants, and labor union radicals all the more defiant. The unhappy result was that freedom of association and speech became almost as important a battleground on the home front as the war itself on foreign shores.

It is from this womb of anti–war sentiment that the civil liberties movement took life. Given such beginnings, it would not have been altogether difficult to predict that the ACLU would be associated historically with leftist labor unions, Communists, illegal immigrants, and anti–war protesters. Why, then, has the ACLU seemingly been so shocked when charged with being un–American? Guilt by association is not always legitimate, but it is almost always irresistible.

Un–American, Un–Christian, or Simply Unpopular?

The history of the ACLU could have taken another turn. Conscientious objection to war is not necessarily un–American. In fact, its roots dig far deeper into the fertile soil of religious faith than the rockier soil of political persuasion. Ironically, the ACLU's association with religious pacifists could well have changed the storyline for the ACLU, and its public image both then and now. But it was only a temporary alliance of political convenience that linked the AUAM with the historic peace churches—the Brethren, the Mennonites, and the Quakers. Certainly, there was little natural affinity with the staunchly religious beliefs of a then–little–known sect called the International Bible Students Association (with which the ACLU would have a long association under the group's later and better–known name of Jehovah's Witnesses).

Of course, Baldwin and the AUAM were quite happy to make use of religious rhetoric when convenient to their cause. For example, they claimed at that time what today the ACLU would vehemently disavow—that involuntary military conscription was "contrary to the Christian principles on which American society was based" and in violation of the "sacred liberty of conscience" implicit in the Bill of Rights.[1] In his own trial for violating the draft law, Baldwin would later say that conscription was "a flat contradiction of all our cherished ideals of individual freedom, democratic liberty and Christian teaching."[2]

The fact that "Christian teaching" is listed *following* "individual free-dom" is probably more than mere coincidence. In all likelihood, the religious reference was nothing more than a useful bit of embroidery attached to the true reason for Baldwin's opposition to conscription: individual freedom. Interpreted correctly, his reference to "individual freedom" translates into the type of anarchistic political freedom advocated by the American Socialist Party and the radical Industrial Workers of the World (IWW), his strongest anti–war allies. In fact, it was Eugene Debs of the American Socialist Party whose earlier personal legal defense against an Espionage Act charge provided the model for Baldwin's own political state-ment while pleading guilty to refusal to register.[3]

Despite the rhetoric, it was not religious faith that propelled Baldwin or the AUAM, but political ideology, plain and simple. Had it been the former rather than the latter, the ACLU's anti–religious bent might never have existed. Nor, undoubtedly, its reputation for being un–American. After all, America was formed from the crucible of religious conscience and conscientious objection. It was the AUAM's political opposition to the war, not an individual's religious conscience, that gave rise to the ACLU's early reputation and continues even today to frame the many anti–government, anti–war policies promoted by the ACLU.

Objection of the Elitist Conscience

There is something suspiciously convenient about many of the posi-tions taken by civil libertarians. Whether it be their objection to metal detectors at airports, or their opposition to incarceration for criminals, or their policy against sobriety checkpoints, civil libertarians have the luxury of appearing principled and high–minded—as long as someone else is taking care of business.

It is all the more true of national security interests. As long as someone is out there calling a halt to military aggression, civil libertarians can sit back in comfort and talk all day about freedom. They needn't dirty themselves—or risk their lives—to learn that freedom sometimes comes only a terrifying yard at a time through bloodied barbed wire and the blistering attack of bombs and bullets. Individually, of course, many ACLU members have, in fact, served proudly in the military. It is the ACLU's official policies that appear disturbingly distanced from reality.

As if scripted, Roger Baldwin's own incarceration for refusing the draft was a perfect picture of such iconoclastic luxury. In the twenty days between his arrest and trial, for instance, Baldwin was in the custody of a marshall ("a fine young Yale man," he wrote his mother[4]) with whom he would often dine out at a fine restaurant.

Later, when he was serving his eleven–month sentence, Baldwin called it his "vacation on the government." He spent his time quite happily—reading, writing, and tending the prison garden. In fact, in his second jail (a county penitentiary in Caldwell, New Jersey) his cell door was not locked, and he was permitted to take a walk whenever he pleased. Clearly, it wasn't your basic hard–time incarceration. Baldwin had exchanged one ivory tower for another. This one happened to have bars on the windows, but little else had changed.

The irony was that, like so many who vociferously protest the "immoral" actions of their government in times of war, Baldwin was quite happy to be cut a "special deal" by that same government. The poor souls who submitted to the draft and were dodging bullets in the fox holes on foreign soil were defending the very freedom that Baldwin was experiencing in the middle of a state–side prison. Where else but in America?

Fellow Travellers Under the Red Flag

In the postwar years, terrorist bombings, race riots, and militant union strikes proved to be a lethal cocktail spawning widespread fears of revolution. Nor did it help that the American Communist Party was organized during this time of social foment. For most folks, it all added up to conspiratorial subversion. And who should come to the defense of all these "subversives" but the ACLU?

Viewed from a current perspective of the ACLU, it would not be remarkable that the ACLU would be willing—even eager—to defend political radicals against heavy–handed government repression. As a civil liberties organization, that's its job. But there was more than simply a civil liberties connection in the 1920s and '30s. During that time, the ACLU itself was seduced by the socialist vision and had more than a passing interest in Communism. Revolution, radical social change, and anarchy were never really foreign terms to ACLU lips. Baldwin and the ACLU weren't just *defending* left–wing activists, they *were* left–wing activists.

Little wonder, then, that—whatever the cause, whatever the evidence—the ACLU always sided with the radicals against the government. Undoubtedly, it was that unfailing pattern of support (as well as, perhaps, the political climate of the day) which led a committee of the New York legislature in 1928 to conclude that the ACLU was not just a neutral civil liberties organization, but a fellow traveler:

> The American Civil Liberties Union, in the last analysis, is a supporter of all subversive movements; its propaganda is detrimental to the interest of the State. It attempts not only to protect crime, but to encourage attacks upon our institutions in every form...[Its] main work is to uphold the communists in spreading revolutionary propaganda and inciting revolutionary activities to undermine American institutions and overthrow our Federal Government.[5]

If perhaps the case was overstated, the ACLU was hardly in a position to protest its innocence. ACLU member Harry Ward, for example, chaired both the ACLU and one of the largest Popular Front groups, the American League for Peace and Democracy.[6] Board member Robert W. Dunn made two trips to the Soviet Union to lend assistance to the newly established Communist government.[7] And, of course, Baldwin himself was consumed with admiration for the Russian Revolution, which he called "the greatest and most daring experiment yet undertaken to recreate society in terms of human values."[8]

For Baldwin, it was not just a grand experiment. In 1935, in words he lived to regret, Baldwin made the infamous Harvard class book statement that "Communism is the goal."[9] So besotted was Baldwin, that he was willing to brazenly justify the "temporary" deprivations of civil liberties during the start–up phase of the people's revolution (a concession he was unwilling to make to his own government in a time of national crisis.)

Seeing the Light

Although the ACLU was never a Communist front, it could hardly have been more in sympathy with Communism's socialist ideology. At least initially. But it all began to unravel in the late '30s. There was, first of all, an unexpected disillusionment of the highest order, occasioned by the Hitler–Stalin pact. In the minds of America's idealistic socialists, that pact finally tore down a mythical wall which they had wishfully constructed between Communism and totalitarianism. Baldwin, in particular, was sent into an ideological tail–spin, and by 1943 he was openly anti–Communist.

The second cause for reassessment was the increasing pressure being brought to bear in America against Communist sympathy. It was a matter of simple pragmatism: In order to avoid suspicion, censure, and loss of civil libertarian credibility, the ACLU simply had to move from left to right. And move it did—all the way to the "1940 Resolution" (barring Communists from leadership positions within the ACLU) and the mid-night massacre of Communist board member Elizabeth Gurley Flynn. In an era of "outing" Communists, even Roger Baldwin himself eventually named names to the FBI![10]

In addition to reassessing their views of Communism, Baldwin and the ACLU also saw the Second World War in quite a different light from the First World War. The threat of Hitler, Mussolini, and Japan's Tojo put a dif-ferent perspective on civil libertarian thinking. Even on the issue of conscientious objection, there was no dissent from the ACLU, nor did it support any pacifists who refused to register for the draft.

Long forgotten was Baldwin's statement made before his local draft board that he was "opposed to the use of force to accomplish any ends, however good."[11] "Pacifist" Baldwin had already lent his approval to Americans fighting for the Loyalists during the Spanish civil war, calling it "a police action in aid of a legal government."[12] Now, in the midst of World War II, it was clear that the use of force to accomplish some ends was acceptable after all.

Playing Patriot Games

Since the very moment of its inception, it seems the ACLU has been playing patriot games. On again; off again. Sometimes aiding and abetting the enemy; sometimes snitching on the enemy. Over the 75 years of its exis-tence, the face of the ACLU has been reflected in both the mirror of principle and the mirror of expediency. Pro–Communist in the '20s and '30s; anti–Communist during the '40s and '50s. Apolitical at times; political at other times. Anti–war in World War I; pro–war in World War II. Left here; Right there.

And yet, throughout it all, the ACLU somehow managed to wave enthusiastically the banner of patriotism. ACLU apologist Samuel Walker frankly admits that much of what the world saw was a well–rehearsed show.

> Though Baldwin wore his contempt for the legal process like a badge, he and the others repeatedly invoked the imagery of "old fashioned American liberties." Their tactic of reading the Declaration of Independence, the Constitution, or the Bill of Rights in free speech fights was a calculated appeal to patriotic sentiment. It was an exercise in mythmaking, an effort to capture the symbols of Americanism for the cause of civil liberties. In the long run the strategy worked.[13]

The obvious question is, "Why was it *mythmaking* for the ACLU to recite a litany of the founding documents 'for the cause of civil liberties' if those documents were the obvious bedrock of such liberties?" The answer, surely, is that it was not "the cause of civil liberties" that needed to be bolstered artificially by the Bill of Rights, but rather other political interests not addressed therein. Political interests that were *not*, in fact, patriotic.

Faced with a history of such patriotic mythmaking, one is cautioned to look ever more closely at current ACLU policies dealing with national security which are decoratively packaged in the same flowery language of the founding documents. If it had its own way, the ACLU would forbid spying in peacetime, even for foreign intelligence;[14] prevent press restrictions during a time of war;[15] eliminate the Foreign Agents Registration Act;[16] and continue to permit desecration of the flag as a means of political protest. ("Although we understand the strong patriotic sentiments that inspire such legislation, we believe that flag burning or desecration, like draft card burning, is a form of symbolic speech....").[17]

The problem with each of these policy positions is that they may reflect, not simply a precautionary protection against potential civil liberties abuse, but a much more fundamental disdain of one's government. For a nation trying to assess the allegiance of the ACLU, it has always been difficult to decide which of the two possible interpretations ought to be accepted.

As long as the ACLU limits its policies and activities to strictly civil libertarian concerns, the public is willing to opt for the former, patriotic interpretation. On the other hand, as long as the ACLU insists on aggressively taking radical political positions relative to national security, the public is as entitled to draw unfavorable conclusions regarding the ACLU's loyalty to the country as favorable ones. Unfortunately for the ACLU, nothing about its history does much to invoke any benefit of the doubt in its favor.

To say that the ACLU maintains policies which often border on the unpatriotic is not to imply that patriotism, of itself, has any ethical, moral, or spiritual currency. As G.K. Chesterton put it, "'My country, right or wrong', is a thing that no patriot would think of saying except in a desperate case. It is like saying, 'My mother, drunk or sober'."[18] True patriotism is not blind allegiance to any nation or government, but rather a communitarian commitment to values commonly shared by a nation or people.

But not all values are of equal value. Patriotism thus takes on a moral legitimacy when it recognizes that allegiance to a nation must be prefaced by the nation's own commitment to moral governance. (Who was the true patriot: Heinrich Himmler, who acted legally in the bent cause of Hitler's SS; or Arthur Schindler, who acted treasonably with his sacred list?)

There is, thus, an honorable place for being "unpatriotic" if what that means is not supporting a nation tempted to abandon moral governance. Whether the ACLU may lay claim to true patriotism or, to the contrary, is guilty of betrayal may ultimately depend not upon its anti–war record or its historical flirtation with socialist ideology but upon its commitment to moral governance. Can the ACLU's current commitment to moral radicalism possibly help to dispel its reputation for being un–American? Interestingly, the ACLU may not even care that it is seen to be un–American. For many members, apparently, such a charge merely serves to confirm the ACLU's liberal credentials.

Insecurity About National Security

Despite the great pendulum swing away from open comradeship with Communism in the '40s and '50s, there remains to this day a residual taint from the ACLU's early socialist liaisons. Along the way (in 1976), the "1940 Resolution" was rescinded and Elizabeth Gurley Flynn was "rehabilitated." Speaking more broadly, however, Jeremy Rabkin suggests that "a lingering regard for the revolutionary left—in later decades more sentimental than conspiratorial—has continued to fuel 'civil libertarian' fervor in some quarters...."[19]

It is remarkable, to say the least, that the ACLU maintains a record of opposing foreign aid to certain countries like El Salvador, in the name of human rights, while not generally objecting to foreign aid to Communist countries, past and present, whose history of human rights is equally abysmal. Certainly, the ACLU never voiced concern when aid was being given to the Sandinistas, or when generous credit terms were being given to the former Soviet Union. Coincidence? Oversight? Or, in fact, lingering socialist sympathies?

Although the ACLU has made a determined effort not to get overly entangled in foreign civil liberties issues, it does maintain an interest in foreign affairs through the Center for National Security Studies. The Center's motto is taken from a letter by James Madison to Thomas Jefferson in which Madison said, "Perhaps it is a universal truth that the loss of liberty at home is to be charged to provisions against danger, real or pretended, from abroad."

Sharing that concern, the Center and the ACLU believe that it is in the interest of civil liberties in America to (in the words of Richard and Susan Vigilante) "play down or reinterpret threats from abroad so they will not be used to restrict civil liberties as the ACLU understands them."[20] In thus favoring anti–democratic governments, it appears that the superpatriot's lamentable "My country, right or wrong" is countered by a deplorable "Any country but my own."

Vietnam and a Return to Anti–War Roots

For the ACLU, the Vietnam era was déjà vu. It was like turning back the clock fifty years. Defending anti–war protesters and draft dodgers, and challenging the war's constitutionality was an adrenaline rush for a second generation of civil libertarians birthed in the anti–war tradition. All the old free speech issues came back to life. Did the First Amendment protect the burning of a draft card as a form of symbolic speech? Could a high school student be disciplined for wearing a black arm band in protest of the war?

Even the issue of conscientious objection was revisited. In the 1965 (pre–escalation) *Seeger* case, the Court had already extended the right of conscientious objection to those whose beliefs paralleled those of conventional religion. The ACLU then sought (unsuccessfully) to exclude from the Selective Service Act's reach what was known as "selective objection," whereby one could choose which particular war he might be conscientiously opposed to. (Why would that additional classification be necessary if one's beliefs about a particular war were sensed so strongly that they "paralleled those of conventional religion?" Any lesser motive would be patently political and unworthy of recognition.)

Yet, the bigger issue was always the legitimacy of the war itself (unassociated with conscription levels). On this issue the ACLU actually did a flip–flop. In January of 1966, the ACLU concluded that the war "does not, in and of itself, represent a civil liberties question."[21] But by June of 1970, the influence of older, more moderate members had collapsed, and the ACLU justified opposition to the war on the basis of the civil unrest which it caused back home. Whatever the merits of the war itself, the ACLU declared that the war "fostered an atmosphere of violence which resulted in the slaying of college students and black people, violent attacks on and by demonstrators both for and against the war, and a climate of repression in which attempts have been made to stifle criticism of the war."[22] Cast now in civil libertarian terms, it was the ACLU's own declaration of war against the war.

The importance of the ACLU's opposition to the Vietnam war is not whether that position was either un–American or patriotic, but whether an anti–war stance was consistent with the ACLU's policy of non–partisanship. Clearly it was not, and that produced no end of consternation within the ACLU itself.

Because of one Vietnam era case in particular, the ACLU itself became a house divided. It was the Justice Department's suit against Dr. Benjamin Spock and four other anti–war protesters. Whether the ACLU ought to represent the Boston Five for the purpose of furthering its own anti–war stance became a watershed between activists and moderates in which the activists eventually won out. The internal dispute also led away from the ACLU's exclusive reliance on amicus curiae briefs towards more direct representation. But most important of all, the Spock case was seen by many within the ACLU itself as "the point at which the ACLU abandoned civil liberties for a 'political' agenda."[23]

Quick reflection back on the ACLU's anti–war roots calls to question whether the ACLU was ever truly non–political. From the beginning, it was civil liberties in aid of political action, not political action in aid of civil liberties. And, as the ACLU's opposition to the war in Vietnam reminds us, its political posture has never really changed. The ACLU continues to be what it has always been (with the notable exception of World War II)—anti–war and anti–government.

That said, some things had indeed changed between World War I and the war in Vietnam. First, the ACLU's policies during World War I were distinctly influenced by its love affair with socialism. By the time of Vietnam, anti–war sentiment was influenced, not by idealistic socialism, but by a combination of everything from the high ground of moral repugnance to anti–establishment instincts.

In its cultural context, opposition to the war in Vietnam may have been for some less a matter of social consciousness based upon lofty ideology than a matter of simply asserting one's unfettered individuality. If the rhetoric of anti–war protest was cast in terms of morality, for many protesters the free–love, drug culture climate sometimes associated with anti–war protest ("Make love, not war") betrayed the legitimacy of the rhetoric and distanced it considerably from classic anti–war activism.

Before anyone quite realized what was happening, a younger, post–Watergate, baby–boomer generation was altogether comfortable with draft dodging and flag burning, and harbored a growing suspicion of national security secrets and covert operations. Superpatriotism was considered passe. If over seven decades the ACLU hadn't fundamentally changed its spots, to a large extent the nation had. So much so, that the unthinkable happened: In 1992, America elected a President who himself had avoided the draft during Vietnam. We have now come full circle. If being anti–war was un–American, then after nearly three–quarters of a century from the ACLU's birth, being un–American has somehow become fashionably American.

The ACLU's anti–war involvement demonstrates, not so much that the ACLU is un–American, but that it is both patently political and politically leftist. As with most organizations, the ACLU reflects in its policies the views of its members. Whatever its usual restraints, it would have been hard for the ACLU not to be caught up in the anti–war movement. Anti–war fever was sweeping through all the liberal organizations and motivating new members to join the ACLU.

So why does the ACLU maintain the pretense of being non–political and non–partisan? That war was fought, and lost, long ago.

CHAPTER 10

Religious Persecution with a Twist

PERSECUTION IS NOT AN ORIGINAL FEATURE OF ANY RELIGION; BUT IT IS
ALWAYS THE STRONGLY MARKED FEATURE OF ALL LAW-RELIGIONS.

THOMAS PAINE

The ACLU's boast of being America's foremost protector of religious expression is ludicrous. Apart from cases justified by other peripheral civil libertarian concerns, religious believers cannot count on the ACLU to come to their defense. Never is that more true than when religious exercise intersects with public schools. At that point, the ACLU employs its private interpretation of church-state separation to justify censorship, reduced academic freedom, and limitations on students' rights. Under any other circumstances, the ACLU would be outraged by such threats to civil liberties. The double standard is further proof that the ACLU is not just religiously neutral, but staunchly anti-religious. Particularly, anti-Christian.

If a teacher promotes an immoral lifestyle, the ACLU takes no notice. If anything, it will come to the teacher's defense under its policy of academic freedom. But if a teacher dares allude to a religious belief, then, suddenly, all the talk is of "impressionable young children" who need protecting against subtle indoctrination.

If anyone needs protecting against indoctrination, it is school officials, who for years have been the object of an ACLU propaganda campaign aimed at imposing its own hyper-interpretation of the Establishment Clause. Of one thing you can be sure: The last thing church-state separation was ever meant to be was a license for religious persecution.

Religious Persecution with a Twist

In September of 1986, school teacher Kenneth Roberts sat reading at his desk while his class of fifth-graders at the Berkeley Gardens Elementary School in Denver, Colorado, also sat reading quietly at their own desks. The fifteen-minute "silent reading period" was a daily part of the classroom curriculum in which the students' reading skills were encouraged. Students were permitted to choose their own reading material, either from the school library, the smaller classroom library, or even something brought from home. Roberts always joined the students during their reading time in order to set a good example for them.

The classroom door opened, and Roberts looked up to see his principal, Kathleen Madigan, who had come to make a routine visit. As Madigan made her way around the classroom, she noticed that Roberts was reading a Bible. Roberts kept a copy of it on his desk and would often read it during the silent reading period. Madigan curtly told Roberts that she expected him to keep the Bible off his desk between 8:00 a.m. and 3:30 p.m.

Convinced that his choice of reading material—like that of his students—was a matter of personal preference, Roberts continued from time to time in his reading of it. In November, Madigan once again made a routine visit to the classroom and once again observed Roberts with his opened Bible. Madigan repeated her earlier admonition that he should keep his Bible in his desk during school hours.

The following September, a parent-teacher open house was held at Berkeley Gardens Elementary, during which one of the parents perused Roberts' classroom library, a collection of some 239 books of varying content which he had compiled over 19 years of teaching. When the parent spotted two books, *The Bible in Pictures* and *The Life of Jesus*, a complaint was immediately lodged with Madigan. That same evening, Madigan inspected the two books and, without inquiring how they were used, instructed Roberts then and there to remove them.

Madigan's reason for removing the books? "It's a violation of the separation between church and state," she explained tersely.

Four days following removal of the books, Roberts discussed the matter with Principal Madigan. He questioned the propriety of her directive and asked her for any written school district guidelines or policies that he had violated or that would guide him in choosing what materials he could display in his classroom. Madigan refused his request, stating that common sense and her previous explanations were sufficient.

In another four days, Roberts wrote a memo to Madigan, requesting that she reconsider her directive. After consulting with various school officials, Madigan held firm. The following week, a meeting between Madigan, Roberts, and the head of personnel for the school district, yielded a written directive to Roberts which stated: "The law is clear that religion may not be taught in a public school. To avoid the appearance of teaching religion, I have given you this directive. Failure to comply with this directive will be considered insubordination and could result in disciplinary action."

The matter eventually went to court. At the trial, it was brought out that Roberts displayed a poster in his classroom that read, "You have only to open your eyes to see the hand of God." However, the evidence was undisputed that Roberts never read aloud from the Bible nor proselytized his faith to his students.

Testimony also revealed that, while the school district concurred in the removal of the two books in question, it ignored the presence of books dealing with Greek gods and goddesses and American Indian religions. In fact, Roberts had taught specifically about the Navajo Indian religion, and had sometimes silently read a book dealing with the life of Buddha. Like his Bible, that book had been kept on his desk for some period. Despite this evidence, Madigan testified that she feared Roberts' practice of keeping his Bible on his desk and reading from it frequently during the silent reading period was setting "a Christian tone" in his classroom.

As it turned out, the controversy was not confined to Roberts' classroom. It also emerged that sometime in September 1987, Madigan went to the school library and removed a copy of the Bible from the library shelves. Madigan denied that she had removed the Bible, but stipulated at the trial that the Bible would be replaced and not removed again.

The trial court found that, taken together, Roberts' Bible reading, the poster, and the presence of the two "Christian books" in the classroom library created the appearance that Roberts was seeking to advance his religious views.[1]

Straining at Constitutional Gnats

Unless it were part of a court record, one could hardly imagine that such a travesty of First Amendment protections could happen in America. Kenneth Roberts, joined by a number of students and their parents, appealed the trial court's decision on the basis that their rights of free speech, academic freedom, and access to information had been violated. They also alleged that the school district's actions violated the Establishment Clause by treating Christianity in a non-neutral, disparaging manner.

It should have been a straightforward, slam-dunk case for Roberts. In *Tinker v. Des Moines Independent Community School District* (1969), Justice Abe Fortas held that "it can hardly be argued that either students or teachers shed their constitutional rights to freedom of speech or expression at the schoolhouse gate."[2] (*Tinker* had been brought by the American Civil Liberties Union on behalf of thirteen-year-old junior high student Mary Beth Tinker, who had worn a black armband to school in protest of the Vietnam war.)

In the ACLU's official Briefing Paper on Church and State, the reader is told that "the ACLU has earned a reputation as the nation's foremost protector of the rights of individuals to practice their religion."[3] Given that vaunted claim, one could have expected the ACLU to leap to Robert's defense. Had he been a Hindu reading the Bhagavad-Gita, or a socialist reading Marx's Das Kapital, you can be certain that the ACLU would have been quick to defend.

On the grounds of academic freedom alone, the ACLU should have been a natural ally. ACLU's Policy 62, pertaining to Teacher's Rights in Primary and Secondary Education, says that "the teacher has the right to identify and express his or her own point of view in the classroom as long as it is indicated clearly that it is the teacher's own."[4] Roberts, of course, had not even gone so far as to express his own point of view.

Relevant especially to the two censored books, the ACLU policy further states that, "Within the individual classroom, the teacher should be given reasonable scope in the implementation of the designated objectives, content, and methods of the curriculum, and in the choice of supplementary material other than textbooks."[5] Two out of 239 books surely was a decision within a teacher's "reasonable scope" (particularly when the books were merely excerpted presentations of the complete Bible, which itself is constitutionally permitted to be included in the school library's larger collection).

Additionally, Policy 62 states that, "In general, the rights of teachers in secondary schools are the same as the rights of teachers in colleges and universities...." When you turn to ACLU Policy 60, which addresses Academic Freedom in higher education, you find that, "A teacher should not be dismissed for holding and expressing opinions, religious, political, social or otherwise...."[6] Roberts himself wasn't actually dismissed, but neither, by this policy, could he have been.

Even more telling is this statement that, "The harm done by a few teachers who might, undetected, misuse their positions for political or religious ends is far less than the harm that is done by political screening, which only forces teachers to become less courageous and less independent in the pursuit of truth, more cautious and more subservient."[7] What was more harmful—Roberts silently reading his own Bible in the presence of his students, or students being told through Madigan's actions that the Bible is so threatening that it needs to be censored from their very view?

By now you surely must have guessed that, despite all its rhetoric and bold claims about defending individuals' religious liberties, the American Civil Liberties sided with Madigan and the school district *against* Roberts. If there is anything that the ACLU hates more than censorship, it is any form of public religious expression. When you realize how much the ACLU hates censorship, it tells you more than you really want to know about its anti-religious, and particularly its anti-Christian, bias.

As the case went up on appeal from the District Court to the 10th Circuit, the local chapter of the ACLU in Colorado (joined by the American Jewish Congress and the Anti-Defamation League of B'nai B'rith) submitted an amicus brief on behalf of Madigan and the school district. The appellate court agreed with the ACLU that Roberts' actions had placed indirect coercive pressure upon religious minorities to conform to the prevailing officially approved religion. "Such coercive pressure," said the court, "is surely at its peak when the religious minorities are impressionable children who look to their teacher as a role model."[8]

Was there any evidence that Mr. Roberts' students felt coerced? Or that any religious minorities (as opposed to ultra-sensitive political liberals) actually felt offended? Or even that there *were* religious minorities in his class? The factual assumptions which are made by the courts in such cases are utterly dumbfounding—evidence once again of nothing less than a vicious anti-religious bias on the part of secular activists in the halls of justice.

The court swiftly dismissed the free speech and academic freedom arguments, saying that, "Mr. Roberts' conduct, in the context of a fifth-grade class full of impressionable children, had the purpose and effect of communicating a message of endorsement of religion in a manner that might reasonably be perceived to bear the imprimatur of the school."

Look closely at the court's analysis. Rather than naturally connecting free speech and academic freedom (both pertaining to an individual's rights) with the Free Exercise Clause (also relating to an *individual's* rights), the court forcibly wedged in the Establishment Clause (which pertains to *state* action). Would it have been considered state action if Roberts had been reading *Playboy* instead of the Bible? Is the only difference between the two the fact that in the case of *Playboy* the imprimatur of the school would clearly have nothing to do with religion? If so, does it make sense that *Playboy* should receive greater constitutional protection than the Bible?

What we are witnessing in this almost unbelievable case is the way in which the ACLU's "absolutist" position on free speech is cavalierly abandoned when the particular free speech at risk involves religion. There can be no doubt about it: In the eyes of the American Civil Liberties Union, religious free speech is but a bastard child of the Bill of Rights. The rule in this political card game is that non-religious free speech trumps anything, while religious free speech is a constitutional oxymoron that gets trumped by virtually anything else.

In retrospect, it is easy to see where Kenneth Roberts went wrong. If he was intent upon leaving his Bible on the top of his desk for all his students to see, he should have left it opened to the Song of Solomon, or perhaps Ezekiel, chapter 23. The graphic sexual imagery contained in those writings would have been the kind of language the ACLU could get excited about defending.

A Case of Religious Harassment

In his dissenting opinion in the case, Judge Barrett reminded his fellow jurists that the Supreme Court has made it clear that the Constitution "affirmatively mandates accommodation, not merely tolerance, of all religions, and forbids hostility towards any."[9] In Judge Barrett's view, Robert's actions were passive and *de minimis*, while Madigan's actions against Roberts "were acts of intolerance, lack of accommodation and hostility toward the Christian religion."[10] On its face, it certainly *looks like* Roberts was the target of a personal attack against his religious beliefs. At best, the Establishment angle seems to have been a convenient pretense.

In 1993, a controversy was stirred when the Equal Employment Opportunity Commission proposed guidelines against religious harassment in the workplace.[11] Under the Civil Rights Act of 1964 and a number of court rulings, it was already illegal for employers to demean an employee's religion, or even to allow an employee to abuse a co-worker because of his or her religious belief. So, was there any need for additional government involvement? The EEOC apparently thought so. In three years, complaints had increased from 389 to 587 (which means either that there is more religious harassment than before, or that it is reported more than before, or—more likely—that there is more *legal* harassment than before).

When you look at some of the complaints which were filed, you realize how messy the guidelines would have been for the ACLU. Consider, for example, that one worker was called by fellow employees a "pus-gutted Catholic" for eating fish on Friday. Another worker, a Jew, was taunted by a supervisor as a "Christ killer" and "Jew faggot."[12] It all sounds very much like the genre of "hate speech" that the ACLU has defended under the heading of free speech. But would the ACLU wish to join hands with Jerry Falwell or with Louis Sheldon of the Traditional Values Coalition, who opposed the guidelines?

Falwell and Sheldon argued that the ill-defined subjectivity involved in the proposed guidelines would end up punishing constitutionally protected religious expression. (Considering parallel guidelines regarding sexual harassment, at a minimum such subjectivity could make religious harassment charges easy to allege and difficult to defend.)

In the end, the EEOC voted to drop the proposed guidelines. But the hostility towards religious expression has not subsided. One wonders if even the proposed guidelines would have prevented any future harassment of Roberts by Madigan. Or would Madigan have been able to hide behind the protection of the Establishment Clause to harass Roberts by using "constitutional hate speech" rather than "gutter-talk hate speech?"

At least with ordinary hate speech, there is no active interference with a worker's religious activity. What Madigan did to Roberts was the flat out denial of religious free exercise. And in that, of course, she was aided and abetted by the American Civil Liberties Union, "the nation's foremost protector of the rights of individuals to practice their religion."[13]

Chilling Effect on Religious Freedom

Judge Barrett may very well have been right about the intolerance and hostility demonstrated in the case. Nor should it be surprising. Devout Christians, Jews, and other religious zealots have been persecuted as martyrs throughout recorded history. But it is also possible that Kathleen Madigan suffered from a widely shared church-state paranoia, most easily detected by its symptomatic overinterpretation of the Constitution. Such paranoia is intentionally cultivated through a barrage of menacing letters sent by the ACLU to schools, churches, employers, and government entities, threatening legal action if the ACLU's private interpretation of religious freedoms isn't strictly adhered to.

The result of all this propaganda and intimidation is nothing less than a chilling effect on religious expression. Think long and hard about that—particularly when what is "chilled" is religious free speech. Try "chilling" any other kind of free speech through similar means of intimidation, and you will quickly have the ACLU all over your back. That kind of hypocrisy results largely because of the stereotype that "free thinking" means "battling religious dogma." Unfortunately, the ACLU is so blinded by the stereotype that it has concluded free speech is a one-sided coin: for non-religious speech only.

It's Religious Discrimination, Pure and Simple

Thanks in large measure to the ACLU, the belief that there is a wall of separation between *faith* and state, not just *church* and state, is endemic. (The exercise of religious faith in the public square is not prohibited; only the federal imposition of a particular faith.) Hardly anyone any longer knows the difference. Hardly anyone today understands the specific concerns which led to the Establishment Clause or appreciates the crucial importance of the Free Exercise Clause. With the ACLU and other liberal-Left advocates constantly tossing the two clauses together into a high-speed blender, most Americans are completely oblivious to the subtle metamorphosis that has taken place. What was intended as protection against an official national church (something with which virtually every devout believer today would heartily agree) has become, instead, a supposed constitutional justification for nothing short of religious discrimination.

The irony is that, where persecution of one's faith (if it was deemed to be heresy) once came at the hands of an established church, the perverted interpretation of the Establishment Clause has now made it possible for one's faith to be persecuted by the state instead. Rather than separating church and state, the liberal-Left seeks to substitute a monolithic state for a monolithic church. Predictably, government discrimination is no less oppressive than that of the most dogmatic church. The inquisitors and the heretics may have crossed traditional lines, but rest assured it's business as usual.

If that proposition were ever in doubt, consider the case of Larry Witters, a severely vision-impaired resident of Washington state who was denied educational and vocational rehabilitation benefits to which he was otherwise entitled, simply because he wished to attend a religious college with the intent to pursue a religious vocation.[14]

Then there's the similar case of James Zobrest, a hearing-impaired high school student who was denied his right to a state-paid sign language instructor under both the Disabilities in Education Act and its Arizona counterpart, simply because his parents wanted him to attend a Roman Catholic High School. Although the Supreme Court eventually reversed the lower court's decision upholding the government's denial of Zobrest's rights, it was too late to prevent the religious discrimination which he and his parents had faced throughout his high school education.[15]

Had Witters or Zobrest been denied their statutory benefits on the basis of being black, female, or gay, the ACLU would have rushed to their defense. But the fact that they were denied benefits because of their religious beliefs changed the picture altogether. All other forms of discrimination get the ACLU's immediate attention. Religious discrimination has to take a number and stand in line.

One of the Supreme Court's most recent decisions demonstrates what side of the fence the ACLU is on when it comes to religious discrimination. In the 1995 *Rosenberger* case,[16] the ACLU supported the University of Virginia when it was challenged for denying funds to the student paper, "Wide Awake," simply because it was "too religious." The university gave student-activity money to 118 other groups, including a Muslim publication and a gay and lesbian organization, but argued that it would be a violation of the Establishment Clause to fund a student newspaper having a distinctively Christian perspective. What else could this denial of equal access be if not religious discrimination?

Fortunately, in this case, the Supreme Court upheld "Wide Awake's" right of equal access to university funds, citing the kind of First Amendment concerns that the ACLU normally would have urged, but for the fact that religious free speech was involved. Interestingly, the ACLU's brief was in direct contradiction to its own Policy 71 (regarding student publications) which says that "all student publications...should enjoy full freedom of the press [even when] subsidized...by a tax on student funds."[17]

One can hardly begin to describe the extent to which religious discrimination has become a civil liberties blindspot. If you are not already convinced, consider the experience of Fordham University's campus radio station, WFUV. When it needed a new transmission tower to meet FCC regulations, it applied for a grant from the Commerce Department pursuant to a federal statute. In every other way qualified to receive the grant, WFUV was turned down for the sole reason that it aired a one-hour university chapel worship service each week—a 47-year tradition.[18]

Like seemingly everyone else, the Commerce Department had been brainwashed into thinking that the Establishment Clause was intended, not as a protective shield, but as a sword of hostility against religion. Had Fordham been a state university with a radio station that aired round-the-clock rock and rap filth, it would have gotten its transmitter. What else but religious discrimination accounts for the difference?

Of course, it is not just the denial of equal access to the public coffers that constitutes religious discrimination. Two companion cases, both of which take us back to the halls of public education, illustrate the breadth of religious discrimination even when no public funds are involved. Significantly, the cases likely would have never arisen but for an earlier suit filed by the ACLU which resulted in the school changing its former accommodative policy to one that was seemingly neutral but pointedly anti-religious in intent.[19]

The first case arose in a Southern California high school when Alexander Perumal wanted to distribute flyers advertising his Bible study club meetings at lunch hour on the school lawn. It did not matter that Alex had complied with all the constitutional guidelines as to the time, place, and manner in which students can distribute literature. Despite full compliance, school officials censored Perumal's flyers for the sole reason that it was—you guessed it—religious. Student flyers for virtually any other purpose would have been perfectly acceptable.

The second case involved Russ Read, who was photo editor of his school's yearbook. Staff policy entitled Russ to place a free quarter-page ad in the section where anyone wishing to do so could purchase space. In addition to ads from local businesses, there were often personal messages paid for by students or their families. Every ad and message was gladly accepted, except for young Read's proposed ad: a picture of his school Bible study club, with a message welcoming other students to join them in the fall. Need you ask why? School officials nixed the ad for the sole reason that it had a religious reference. Once again, religion became the victim of public discrimination.

The cases of Alex Perumal and Russ Read were reviewed by two California lower courts, and, in each instance, the court denied their claim that the school district had violated their free speech rights.[20] Neither the California Supreme Court nor the U.S. Supreme Court was willing to grant review.[21] It was the most memorable lesson the school district ever taught to Alex and Russ: that religious speech is not like any other free speech, and that even your local school district can practice religious discrimination and get away with it.

Equal Access: The Antidote to Discrimination

As these cases so clearly demonstrate, religion has been effectively segregated from the public arena by the so-called "wall of separation." But, in the hands of the ACLU and a public saturated with its misguided view of the Establishment Clause, separate is by no means equal. In case after case where there is some public entitlement, religion is singled out for non-entitlement. Religious speech is officially denied; religious faith is officially snubbed.

The strangest thing about religious discrimination is that most people think it is officially sanctioned if not officially mandated. Yet quite the opposite is true. In one case after another, without dissent, the Court has rejected the notion that the Establishment Clause somehow requires discrimination against religious persons or groups who seek to take advantage of that which would otherwise be a generally-available public benefit or privilege.[22] One of the most recent in a long line of such cases is the *Lamb's Chapel* case, in which the Court declared it to be a violation of the Free Speech Clause to exclude the religious community from after-hours use of public school buildings where other community groups expressing other viewpoints are permitted such access.[23]

As in earlier desegregation cases, the Court is saying that religion can no more be the basis for separate, but unequal, treatment than can race.

Period. Unfortunately, however, in other Establishment Clause cases the Court (either by what it has said or, more often, refused to say) has sent out mixed signals, often suggesting that the Establishment Clause and the Free Exercise Clause are in conflict. Naturally, that confusion is all the ACLU needs to justify its own radical separationist view of the Establishment Clause with its inherent potential for religious discrimination.

Perpetuation of the Court's Establishment Clause confusion and the ACLU's strict separationist position combine to be the primary motivating force behind what has now come to be known as the Religious Equality Amendment. Although the exact wording is still taking shape, the language would be very much as follows:

> Neither the United States nor any State shall abridge the right of any person or group, including students in public schools, to engage in prayer or other religious expression in circumstances in which they are permitted to engage in other forms of personal or group expression; nor shall the United States or any State deny benefits to or otherwise discriminate against any person or group on account of the religious character of the speech, ideas, motivations, or identity of such person or group.

The purpose of the proposed constitutional amendment is to clarify the language of the First Amendment once and for all. It would get us back to the point where religious expression has an equal seat at the table, equal access to the marketplace of ideas, and an equal right along with everyone else to share in the public bounty. It would put an end to governmental hostility toward religion and assure the kind of accommodation the Court speaks of, but cannot bring itself to enforce. In short, it would bring about an end to officially imposed religious discrimination.

Passage of such an amendment would mean that Kenneth Roberts still couldn't indoctrinate his fifth-grade students with his personal Christian beliefs, but Kathleen Madigan could no longer violate Roberts' right to read his own Bible in his students' presence. It would mean that the state of Washington still couldn't create a special fund to build a college to be operated by a particular church, but Larry Witters could use money to which he is entitled in order to attend any college he wants, even if it happens to be religious.

The Religious Equality Amendment would mean that the Commerce Department still could not supply funds for radio transmitters only for church-related universities, but Fordham University could have a place in the line if the Commerce Department were passing out transmitters to everyone else on the block. And it would mean that school districts still couldn't force students to attend a Bible study, but Alex and Russ could pass out their flyers inviting their fellow students to join them on a voluntary basis.

It's a level playing field we are asking for here. That's all. It's not special rights we are after, just equal rights. Nor is it *new* rights we are demanding; only the ones we are already guaranteed by the First Amendment. Of all people, the ACLU ought to understand this best. Why in the world would civil libertarians be on the other side of a fight for First Amendment freedom?

Even President Clinton has seen the handwriting on the wall. His administration has now issued guidelines to educate school administrators regarding the freedoms that students currently have while on school campuses. In a speech at Madison High School in Vienna, Virginia, Clinton acknowledged that public schools are not "religion-free zones."[24] For most school administrators, even that minimal concession would be a novel idea.

Although Clinton's much-touted guidelines are a step in the right direction, unfortunately they break no new legal ground. Given the ACLU's determined assault against religious expression in the schools and areas much further afield, free exercise and equal access will not be safe until they are guaranteed by something very much like the Religious Equality Amendment. Will the Clinton Administration be willing to support such an amendment? Is it even remotely possible that the ACLU would join in its passage?

Of this I suspect we can be assured: As long as the devil has a fork in his hands, he's going to use it whenever and wherever he can to provoke discrimination against religious expression. But I'll tell you something about that fork: He certainly didn't get it from the Establishment Clause, and it's high time we knocked that threatening weapon from his hands.

CHAPTER 11

Whatever Happened to Antidisestablish-mentarianism?

"A RULE OF LAW SHOULD NOT BE DRAWN
FROM A FIGURE OF SPEECH."
JUSTICE REED

The ACLU boasts of being America's greatest defender of religious liberty. Nothing could be further from the truth. While on occasion the ACLU has intervened on behalf of individuals and groups whose attempts at exercising religious freedom were being legally challenged, that is not the usual story. Through a persistent campaign of law suits and threatening letters to government officials, the ACLU has almost singlehandedly put a choke-hold on free exercise—particularly in the arena of public education.

Surprisingly, the ACLU justifies this assault against religious expression on the basis of the First Amendment's vaunted Establishment Clause, a clause intended to protect free exercise, not shut it down. Unfortunately, the ACLU's own anti-religious bias has blurred its vision of the plain meaning of the clause. What the Establishment Clause says is that Congress—meaning the federal government—shall not establish any particular denomination or faith as the nation's official church or religion. The Clause does not forbid a *state* from exercising its right of establishment, or, short of that, from promoting religious expression in any manner it wishes, absent coercion.

Certainly, no state today seeks establishment. But, frustrated parents in local school districts everywhere are desperate to have their children taught in an atmosphere which fosters moral and spiritual values. It's time to turn the clock back to when their right to do so was unquestionably established.

Whatever Happened to Antidisestablish-mentarianism?

I f one were to ask what all the fuss is about in issues affecting religious liberty, strangely enough the answer from both camps would be the same: "The Constitution, of course!" Civil libertarians such as the ACLU argue that public-supported religious expression violates the First Amendment. And, with no less assurance, religious activists argue that *prohibiting* public-supported religious expression violates the First Amendment!

In the former case, it is the First Amendment's Establishment Clause that forms the basis for the ACLU's objection. ("Congress shall make no law respecting an establishment of religion....") In the latter case, it is the First Amendment's Free Exercise Clause that undergirds the concern of religious activists. ("...or prohibiting the free exercise thereof....") In terms of rhetoric, it becomes the battle of the clauses: Establishment vs. Exercise; Exercise vs. Establishment.

In actuality, there is no basis for this "battle of the clauses." The two clauses are like two sides of the same coin. They are not in competition; nor can they be isolated as if they have no relevance to each other. As Stephen Carter reminds us, "It is plain that the Founders conceived of these clauses less as distinct entities than as parts of a coherent whole."[1] In order for a person to have complete freedom of religious faith, no one church, denomination, or system of faith can become the official church, denomination, or faith of the nation.

To put it another way, there are two clauses in pursuit of a common purpose. One clause is *proscriptive* (the federal government must not prefer one religion over another); the other is *prescriptive* (every citizen has an affirmative right to exercise the faith of his or her preference).

One might reasonably suppose that the Free Exercise Clause would win the minds of civil libertarians as well as the hearts of religious activists. What could be more libertarian than the right to freely exercise one's religious beliefs? Yet, civil libertarians regularly see the Establishment Clause as trumping the Free Exercise Clause—an argument patently without merit. If, under any circumstances, the Establishment Clause can be interpreted to mean that government can prohibit the free exercise of faith, the very essence of the Free Exercise Clause will be emasculated. Such a result would be complete nonsense.

From a simultaneous consideration of the two clauses, it is clear that the Establishment Clause exists, not in derogation of, but in aid of, free exercise. Whereas non-establishment is the *method*, free exercise is the *goal*. Whereas non-establishment is the *means*, the right to free exercise is the *end*.

Therefore, if the Establishment Clause is permitted in practice to override the Free Exercise Clause, then the First Amendment itself has been turned on its end and free exercise becomes endangered by its own protector. Mark this well: Whenever the Establishment Clause is used as a means of *limiting* the free exercise of religion, as opposed to *facilitating* it, you can be sure that somewhere along the line the Establishment Clause has been grossly misinterpreted.

In light of the many ongoing threats to free exercise, the ACLU's extraordinary focus, instead, on a clearly wrongheaded understanding of the Establishment Clause is a telling commentary on its anti-religious bias. Never in the history of the United States has there been an established national church. Nor is it even remotely conceivable that there could ever be one. Simply compare Britain's governmentally ordained Church of England, and you begin to appreciate how different our nation has been from its inception. Indeed, getting out from under the ecclesiastical thumb of a doctrinally suppressive tax-supported church is what motivated large numbers of believers to join the steady stream westward to the new colonies in America.

This is not to say that America has not been, until late, a "Christian nation." Like all faith, this is by choice. By origin and the voluntarily-expressed preference of a majority, the United States has been intrinsically linked to institutions and practices which are distinctly Christian. On occasion, the Supreme Court has been frank to say so. Writing in the 1892 case of *Church of the Holy Trinity v. U.S.*, for example, Justice Brewer acknowledged with candor that "this is a Christian nation."[2] But being *officially* "Christian" is something altogether different. That we have never been.

The threat we face from government today is not the establishment of an organized, official church, but loss of freedom to exercise individual faith. As a civil liberties organization set for the defense of freedom, the ACLU has unquestionably chosen the wrong side in this battle. Worse yet, it has taken what was meant to be a shield (the Establishment Clause) and made of it a sword to fight against religious liberty.

Federal Versus State Establishment

In the fierce debate over religious liberty, most of us have all but forgotten our eighth-grade American history lessons. To have any informed understanding of the Establishment Clause, it is crucial to flip back through the history books and remember that, as late as the time of the Revolutionary War, at least nine (and possibly as many as twelve) of the thirteen fledgling states had either established churches or established religions. (Because there were differing degrees of establishment at various times, a precise headcount is not always possible.)

The Episcopal Church was the established church in at least five of the former colonies: Maryland, Virginia, North Carolina, South Carolina, and Georgia. In New York and New Jersey, the Episcopal Church received substantial financial support, if not full endorsement. In Massachusetts, New Hampshire and Connecticut, the Congregationalist Church was officially established. And, finally, in Pennsylvania and Delaware, all "Christian sects" were established, with the possible exception of Roman Catholics.

More telling yet, these were the same dissenters who had fled England in protest against an established church. Rather obviously, therefore, it was not establishment, per se, to which they objected. What they found offensive was either the *particular* establishment of the Church of England, or any other establishment of religion in which they had no voice.

If given a voice, however, establishment was not only acceptable but highly desirable as a means of exercising their particular religious beliefs. In terms of church-state relations, our Founders would have identified more closely with the theocracy of ancient Israel than with the strict separation between the secular and the sacred that exists today.

What, then, could be more clear than that the potential establishment of an official *national* religion was of primary concern our Founders? Read again the precise wording of the Establishment Clause: "*Congress* shall make no law respecting an establishment of religion."

It is *Congress*, not the individual states, that the framers of our Constitution had in mind when they penned the Establishment Clause. And there were two reasons for them to fear what a federal legislature might do. First and foremost, they wanted to make sure that there would never be an established *national* church like the one from which they had just escaped in the American Revolution. If they were to be a union of states, they did not want the established church of any one state to become predominant over all the others.

At this crucial juncture in our nation's history, the Establishment Clause was central to the larger debate over federalism. In the words of a recent Harvard Law Review note, the Clause was "adopted to assuage the fear of centralized power."[3] Without a guarantee to the states that the federal government would not establish one church to the exclusion of all others, the Constitution likely would never have been adopted.

Seemingly lost on the ACLU is the fact that the Establishment Clause was never intended to confer civil rights of any kind apart from each citizen's inferred right to be free of a nationally established church or religion. (Even the promotion and encouragement of religion in general, when nondiscriminatory toward all religions and sects, gives no personal standing to complain.) At the state level, it is even more clear that nothing in the Establishment Clause gives any individual citizen or group of citizens the right to complain of anyone else's free exercise, or to invoke governmental action to limit that free exercise in any way. If perhaps the Free Exercise Clause grants individual standing where state action becomes coercive, the Establishment Clause was intended for an altogether different purpose.

What, then, is the purpose of the Establishment Clause? As originally conceived, it was one among a number of political devices set in place to curb the powers of the federal government—certainly not a weapon to be used by partisans in a cultural war. Like the Tenth Amendment, the Establishment Clause is a constitutional device reserving power to the states, but in a specific area of concern: religious liberty. Seen in that light, it creates *state* rights, not individual rights.

Scaling Jefferson's Proverbial "Wall"

One of the most fascinating historical footnotes to our current religious liberties debate is the origin of the much-disputed (and enormously misleading) phrase, "wall of separation." This unfortunate metaphor, first used by Thomas Jefferson, was officially adopted by the Supreme Court in *Everson v. Board of Education*[4], almost completely out of the blue and with virtually no reference to the Amendment's obvious history and intent. Generally invoked uncritically ever since, the graphic figure of speech has given rise to a cottage industry of cases and arguments pertaining to the so-called "separation of church and state."

Having grossly misapplied and misinterpreted Jefferson's metaphorical "wall," the Court has been forced ever since to invent an entirely new lexicon of church-state terminology. Words like "excessive government entanglement," "secular legislative purpose," and "accommodation"—especially when applied to the states—are totally irrelevant to the Establishment Clause. It hardly seems to matter that Jefferson's metaphor has been ripped out of its historical context and elevated to a status higher than the Establishment Clause itself.

One jurist who would never have had any part in this linguistic hijacking is Benjamin Cardozo. Said Cardozo, "[Metaphors] in law are to be narrowly watched, for starting as devices to liberate thought, they end often by enslaving it."[5]

In this case, the hijacking has its origin, not in any statutory or constitutional language, but in a private letter from Thomas Jefferson to members of the Danbury Baptist Association who, in 1801, were trying to enlist Jefferson's support for their efforts to dislodge the Congregationalists in Connecticut. From the 1790s onward, the Danbury Baptist Association was one of the religious groups that had been partially successful in disestablishing the Connecticut establishment. But, because Danbury was still a Congregationalist stronghold, they wanted to get Jefferson's name behind the movement and put an end to the established church once and for all. (Some also have suggested that the Baptists had heard a rumor that a particular denomination was about to be named as the nation's official denomination, a proposition to which they quite understandably would have been opposed.)

Getting Jefferson's support was not terribly difficult for the Baptists, because Jefferson was personally opposed to establishment. His response to the Baptists on January 1, 1802, therefore, is hardly surprising:

> Believing with you that religion is a matter which lies solely
> between man and his God; that he owes account to none other
> for his faith or his worship...I contemplate with sovereign rev-
> erence that act of the whole American people which declared

that their Legislature should "make no law respecting an establishment of religion or prohibiting the free exercise thereof," thus building a wall of separation between Church and State.[6]

If that seems to be a straightforward confirmation of how the phrase "wall of separation" is employed in religious liberties arguments today, a closer look is warranted. It is important to note, first of all, that the phrase "wall of separation," was used by Jefferson with reference to the *federal* government. (The "Legislature" of "the whole American people.")

Second, there is no attempt on Jefferson's part to make a case for the proposition that the Establishment Clause automatically invalidated the Congregationalists' establishment in Connecticut. What Jefferson is doing is voicing his personal opinion that the same principle of non-establishment embodied in the First Amendment *should* be at work in Connecticut. But by no means was that the import of the First Amendment itself. Jefferson's personal opinion was clearly not the law of the land; otherwise, he undoubtedly would have appealed to its authority.

While confirming that an official "wall of separation" was mandated with reference to *federal* establishment, not once did Jefferson hint that *state* establishment was in any way a violation of the First Amendment. Therefore, any use of the phrase to construct a free-standing, wide-reaching barrier to the establishment or promotion of religion at the state level is a patent perversion of the historical context in which Jefferson's metaphor was employed.

This distinction between a state-established religion and a federally-established religion takes on increased significance considering that Jefferson, along with James Madison, had earlier been instrumental in disestablishing the Episcopal church in Virginia. (Jefferson's Bill for Establishing Religious Freedom was passed by the Virginia Legislature in November, 1785.) Even so, instead of telling the Baptists that the Congregationalists were *constitutionally* out-of-bounds to maintain an established church in Connecticut, Jefferson simply expressed sympathy with the position taken by the Baptists in their own efforts at disestablishment. At the state level, he had been down that road himself, successfully.

If Jefferson hoped that eventually the "wall of separation" would extend not only to the *federal government* but also to *government in general* (i.e., the states), his own words confirm that *government in general* was not contemplated by the First Amendment. The significance of the distinction is that, by virtue of the First Amendment, individual states were left with the option of deciding whether to have an established state church or religion, and, if so, which one it would be.

Despite his own preference to the contrary, this is precisely how Thomas Jefferson viewed the constitutional relationship between the federal government and the states relative to religious belief and practice. Consider, for example, his Second Inaugural Address (some fourteen years after the First Amendment was adopted). In the address, Jefferson responds to criticism which had been leveled against him for refusing to proclaim special religious occasions of national fasting or thanksgiving:

> In matters of religion I have considered that its free exercise is placed by the Constitution independent of the powers of the General [federal] Government. I have therefore undertaken on no occasion to prescribe the religious exercises suited to it, but have left them, as the Constitution has found them, under the direction and discipline of *the church or state authorities acknowledged by the religious societies* [emphasis added].[7]

What we see here is Jefferson's keen recognition that there are actually *two* distinct "walls of separation" contemplated by the First Amendment. The first was erected to prevent the federal government from dictating religious belief or practice on a national level. ("I have therefore undertaken on no occasion to prescribe the religious exercises suited to [free exercise of religion].") The second was erected to prevent the federal government from interfering with whatever religious exercises the individual states might choose to endorse. ("[These are matters for] the church or state authorities acknowledged by the religious societies.")

It is true, of course, that Jefferson had a stricter view of church-state separation on the national level than his predecessors. Jefferson was reluctant to promote religion even generally at the national level, which explains his opposition to issuing religious proclamations. But even Jefferson's refusal to issue a Thanksgiving Proclamation tells us something important about how he viewed promotion of religion at the federal level to be different from that which could be done at the state level. As *President* Jefferson, he refused to do what he had done earlier as *Governor* Jefferson.[8] Whatever he may have felt to be the appropriate distance to be maintained between the federal government and religion generally, it is clear that he put that issue in a completely different ballpark from what the states might legitimately do in the promotion of religion.

Tracking Jefferson's own thinking, therefore, it is proper to speak of "church-state separation" when reference is being made to the federal government's separation from any particular church or religion, but improper and meaningless when intended for any broader, more generic application. Nothing in either Jefferson's metaphor or the First Amendment would require a "church-state separation" at the state level. In fact, the very lack of church-state separation in the individual states at the time of the First Amendment's passage and even afterwards is the best evidence yet of how completely distorted the phrase is used by the ACLU and courts today.

What we need instead of more loose talk about some all-inclusive "separation of church and state" is a careful separation of Jefferson's two walls. Having indiscriminately bricked the two walls together, from *Everson* onward, the courts have reduced the entire religious freedom discussion to a hopeless muddle. What "church-state" really stands for today is summed up in a single word: incoherence.

The Great Incorporation Fallacy

In the wake of the Civil War, the Fourteenth Amendment was passed to insure that both equal protection and due process would apply to all of America's citizens, regardless of race or any other factor. But the amendment itself stirred even further controversy, known as the "incorporation" debate. The question was: "Should the rights guaranteed in the Bill of Rights be incorporated into the Fourteenth Amendment so as to make those rights applicable to the states?" The idea of "total incorporation" (incorporating all of them in one fell swoop) was rejected; but one by one, through a process of "selective incorporation," almost all of the rights guaranteed in the first ten amendments were eventually incorporated.

Without any clear analysis, and for no greater reason than that it was somehow related to the Free Exercise Clause, the Establishment Clause was forcibly wedged into the Fourteenth Amendment and made applicable to the states. But it was like putting a square peg into a round hole. Hardly anyone at the time stopped to realize that it simply didn't fit.

Perhaps a case could be made for, say, incorporating the Free Speech Clause into the Fourteenth Amendment, and thus making that guarantee applicable to the states. For that matter, even the Free Exercise Clause. But the same could never be said of the Establishment Clause. The very purpose of the Establishment Clause was to prevent the federalization of any single rule of faith that would have the effect of precluding local option by the individual states.

Far from demanding uniformity among the states, the Establishment Clause was meant to jealously guard against federally-mandated religious uniformity. Again, church-state separation is a proper concept when applied to the federal government, but it has no application whatsoever to the individual states.

Anyone inclined to do so should be careful not to dismiss this argument as the product of some bizarre, self-serving analysis dreamed up by the religious-Right. Articles and notes in one respected law review after another are making the same point.[9] "The Clause's incorporation is logically incoherent," says the Harvard Law Review note previously referenced.[10] And Yale professor Akhil Reed Amar could hardly agree more forcefully: "...to apply the clause against a state government is precisely to eliminate its right to choose whether to establish a religion—a right explicitly confirmed by the establishment clause itself!"[11]

Respected jurists have also lent their voices to the growing chorus of those who see incorporation of the Establishment Clause to be a glaring violation of both history and logic. It's time well spent to read then-Justice Rehnquist's dissenting opinion in *Wallace v. Jaffree*[12] (the Alabama minute-of-silence case). "Without rejecting incorporation *per se*, he recognized the tension inherent in current doctrines and provided historical analysis which gave credence to a lower court claim that the establishment clause was wrongly incorporated."[14] That lower court claim was the carefully researched opinion of federal district judge Brevard Hand in *Jaffree v. Board of School Commissioners*, whose bold analysis makes shambles of conventional wisdom regarding the Establishment Clause and its incorporation.

If the Court wants a way out of the morass of church-state cases, there is a clear path. It must simply go back to square one, and frankly acknowledge that the incorporation of the Establishment Clause was a terrible call. Unfortunately, anything short of that will leave the Court forever lost in the wilderness.

The Fear of Disestablishment

As best indicated by the words, "*respecting an establishment of religion,*" the second thing the states wanted to insure was that Congress would not pass any law *disestablishing* their *already-established* state churches or religion. Even Harvard's Laurence Tribe grudgingly acknowledges that a main purpose of the Establishment Clause was "to protect state religious establishments from national displacement."[15] As a practical matter (given the religious pluralism among the various Christian sects), the states were probably less concerned about the federal government establishing some national church than about the possibility that the federal government would interfere with existing state establishments.[16]

With so much historical water under the bridge, we tend to forget that disestablishment in the individual states came, not by the First Amendment or by an act of Congress, but by acts of the individual states themselves. Of their own free will. In their own timing. For their own reasons. (Massachusetts, the last state to disestablish completely, did not do so until 1833.)

What happened in virtually every case was that the states became more and more religiously diverse, to the point where an established church no longer made sense. (In Virginia, for example, the minority religious groups such as Presbyterians, Lutherans, Quakers, and Baptists gained such strength that the "established" Episcopalians actually became a minority.) So, one by one, they dumped the state churches through their respective political processes.

Yet, even that is not the end of the establishment story. Except in a few persistent states (perhaps four to six), the process of disestablishing particular denominations generally had been completed by the time the Constitution and the First Amendment were adopted. What will stagger many modern minds, is the fact that, although official state *churches* were mostly disestablished, the Christian religion remained the officially established *religion* in virtually all of the states.

Typical of individual state constitutions at the time of the Constitution's adoption is this wording from Part 1, Article III of the Massachusetts state constitution:

> And every denomination of Christians, demeaning themselves peaceably, and as good subjects of the commonwealth, shall be equally under the protection of the law: and no subordination of any sect or denomination to another shall ever be established by law.[17]

And from Article XXXVIII of South Carolina's state constitution comes similar wording:

> That all denominations of Christian[s]...in this State, demeaning themselves peaceably and faithfully, shall enjoy equal religious and civil privileges.[18]

If at the time of the Constitution's adoption only a handful of states retained established denominations, virtually all states had an officially established religion—namely, Christianity. To most people's ears today, such official endorsement of the Christian faith seems surprising, if not downright un-American! But, unless we are willing to re-write history, state establishment of religion, even after the adoption of the First Amendment and its Establishment Clause, is an incontrovertible fact.

In truth, up until Jefferson's "wall of separation" metaphor was inflated to constitutional proportions in the *Everson* case in 1947, it was perfectly clear to everyone as a matter of law that the Establishment Clause did not restrain the states from promoting religion or even establishing one.[19] That common understanding is confirmed by Justice Stewart, when he wrote that, "The Establishment Clause was primarily an attempt to insure that Congress not only would be powerless to establish a national church, but would also be unable to interfere with existing state establishment. Each state was left free to go its own way and pursue its own policy with respect to religion."[20]

Justice Stewart went on to note that "it is not without irony that a constitutional provision evidently designed to leave the States free to go their own way should now have become a restriction upon their autonomy."[21] Ironic, indeed! And all the more so, one would think, in the eyes of a civil liberties organization dedicated to the defense of the Constitution. A court injunction of the type the ACLU regularly seeks against state action in the realm of religious expression is exactly the kind of frustration which the Establishment Clause attempted to preclude.[22] Far from being a noble defense of the Constitution, the ACLU's position in most of its religious liberty cases is both anti-constitutional and anti-civil libertarian.

Updated Concerns Regarding Disestablishment

Should anyone think that the foregoing discussion about establishment and disestablishment is just ancient history, stay tuned. The implications for our own generation are abundantly clear (though perhaps shocking to most): If the states could *disestablish* an official church or religion, they could once again *establish* an official church or religion, should they so choose.

Naturally, that is not likely to happen. (I, for one, certainly would never want it to happen.) For the same reason that official state churches were disestablished (the rise of religious pluralism), it is inconceivable that any state in the Union today would establish an official church or religion—not even the Mormons in Utah. But the point remains: Constitutionally, the individual states retain the hypothetical right to establish an official church or religion or, short of that, *to maintain whatever religious stance they wish.* Translated into the language of the Court, it means that states can do whatever they want, short of impinging on free exercise, in order to acknowledge, accommodate, or even promote religion. They need not be neutral toward religion nor "strictly separated" from it. Only a constitutional interpretation which ignores original intent (or blindly follows the misguided precedent of a long line of cases which have done just that) could reach any other conclusion.

There is more than one way to run afoul of the Establishment Clause. By mandating national standards regarding the exercise of religious belief, the Supreme Court itself has broken down Jefferson's "wall of separation" and has done that which Congress could not do in passing laws respecting the establishment of religion. By some grand stroke of irony, every decision of the Supreme Court which invokes the Establishment Clause to invalidate some state (as opposed to federal) action is itself in violation of the spirit of Establishment Clause!

Power to the People!

If anyone dares think that all of the above is nothing more than some tired and overworn states-rights argument, think again. As Justice Clarence Thomas has reminded us in his "first principles" dissent in the 1995 congressional term limit case, "The ultimate source of the Constitution's authority is the consent of the people of each individual state."[23] At stake here is not some unrealistic romantic notion of a loose confederation of sovereign governmental entities. At stake here is nothing less than the power of the American people to decide for themselves the limits of their religious expression, as grandly and boldly articulated by the Constitution before it fell victim to liberal-Left makeover artists.

Re-empowerment of the people is the burning issue. At the local level, it is about the right of individual parents and local school boards to make important decisions about religious beliefs that will significantly affect their children and the children of other parents, whatever their beliefs. The experience of the last quarter century has shown that *someone* will make those decisions, whether for good or for ill. (Government neutrality is itself a decision having its own set of necessarily-discriminatory consequences.) So, the only issue is: who will make those crucial decisions?

Will it be the national *establishment* of the ersatz religion of secularism? (Even a non-religious establishment which actively promotes laws impinging on free exercise violates the First Amendment.) Or, will it be parents and teachers at the grass roots level?

Given the heavy-handedness of the federal government in matters of strictly local concern, the Establishment Clause should more correctly be referred to as the Disestablishment Clause. *Disestablishment* is what the First Amendment itself mandates be done to the officious intermeddlers who have dared to tell the rest of us how we will, or will not, practice our religious faith.

ACLU propaganda to the contrary notwithstanding, the ACLU's nationally-enforced secularist faith—not locally sanctioned school prayer, or the teaching of creation, or display of the Ten Commandments—is the only establishment today which violates the First Amendment. Hiding behind a mythical wall it has labored hard to construct, the ACLU promotes a kind of separation between church and state which wholly ignores the Establishment Clause's concern for religious expression and necessarily favors the values of anyone whose world view can be described as irreligious.[24]

If one wonders why such hot-button classroom issues as school prayer, creation and evolution, the "rainbow curriculum," and condom give-aways engender so much emotion on the part of parents, it is partially due to the same fear that prompted the adoption of the First Amendment—the fear of disestablishment. Today's religiously-motivated parents are concerned that, for all intents and purposes, secularism has been established as the nation's official religion, and that it now threatens at the local level (principally through the schools) to disestablish all other religious belief.

What parents passionately seek is the kind of "wall of separation" to which Jefferson alluded in his Second Inaugural Address—a wall which fences the federal government out, while parents, through their local school districts and state boards of education, determine how best to implement their constitutional right to free exercise of religion. In its revisionist abuse of Jefferson's "wall of separation," the Court—prompted and prodded by the ACLU—has perpetuated a myth of church-state separation which speaks of neutrality, but in the end is built upon hostility.

It is just such hostility that puts most Americans at odds with the ACLU. Most parents believe that the educational process cannot, with impunity, be divorced from the divine process. Yet, secularist to the core, the ACLU couldn't be more strongly opposed. And that is where the real battle lies.

It is not a battle of the clauses, for they do not war against each other. It is not a battle of semantics, for the wording is plain to any honest reader. And it is not a battle of history, for there is no reasonable cause for historical debate. The battle is spiritual, between religion and irreligion. Between belief and the forces of nonbelief. Between the ACLU's secularism and our nation's faith.

When the devil repeatedly tempted the Lord on the pinnacle of the temple, the Lord appealed time and again to the Founding Document, saying, "It is written....It is written...." But the devil didn't want to hear what was written, for that would have put an end to the issue. Some twenty centuries removed, nothing really has changed. The devil's contempt for what is written is as manifest as ever. But this time he is trying even harder to win. This time, he's taking his case to court.

So far, he's winning.

CHAPTER 12

When Liberty Hasn't Got a Prayer

"EDUCATION WITHOUT RELIGION, AS USEFUL AS IT IS,
SEEMS RATHER TO MAKE MAN A MORE CLEVER DEVIL."
C. S. LEWIS

It is understandable that a secularist organization like the ACLU would have little interest in promoting prayer in the classroom. Even religious folks are more hesitant these days to have their children led in prayer by teachers who are themselves increasingly secularist. But it's time to be clear about who should make such decisions and precisely what the Constitution has to say about it.

Listen to the ACLU, and you'll be told that the Establishment Clause absolutely forbids prayer in public classrooms. As seen in the previous chapter, that simply cannot be the case. The only legitimate concern is the possibility of coercion, which would be a violation of the Free Exercise Clause. But First Amendment clauses are not interchangeable. As long as individual conscience is honored in matters of religious expression, there is nothing in the Establishment Clause which forbids a state or local school district from promoting moral values—even, if deemed suitable—by introducing students to such spiritual exercises as prayer.

School prayer may not be the answer, but it has become symbolic of the struggle of parents everywhere who want their children to have a value-oriented education and to learn that all rights and responsibilities begin and end with God. As long as the ACLU objects to school prayer (particularly on a bogus constitutional basis), it confirms that civil libertarianism has become both anti-family and anti-faith.

When Liberty Hasn't Got a Prayer

I f you want to find out what the religious liberties controversy is all about, simply double-click on the school prayer icon. Hardly anything could be more symbolic of the struggle between the ACLU and the religious-Right. What an irony! Two benign, even lofty words—*school* and *prayer*—when combined, are guaranteed fighting words! If not as emotive as the single word *abortion*, nevertheless the issue of school prayer has become a Gettysburg-like battle in a larger cultural war.

The irony continues when one considers that the American Civil Liberties Union—proud defender of free speech (not to mention the professed defender of religious liberty) opposes school prayer with a fervor nothing short of religious. Naturally, hate speech and kiddy porn get the ACLU's highest protection, but school prayer gets a complete thumbs down. For the ACLU, there is no room for compromise: under no circumstances can pornography be abridged; under no circumstances can school-organized prayer in public education be permitted.

One can only be mystified at the incongruity. Not, of course, that there are no legitimate grounds for concern about school prayer. Surely, for example, dictating what actual prayer public school children shall pray is by no means to be taken lightly. If for no other reason, the wording of school prayers is not as easily predictable as it once might have been. In an increasingly multi-cultural, pluralistic society, you can be sure that Christian parents would be no more comfortable with a prayer in the name of some New Age earth goddess than Jewish parents would be comfortable with prayer in the name of Jesus, or Muslim parents with prayer in the name of anyone but Mohammed.

Nor is it right that any individual student be *required* to pray. Nothing could be more fundamental to our nation than freedom of conscience. Indeed, it is the very bedrock of American liberty. Therefore, no student will be forced, in violation of conscience, to salute the flag, or to vow allegiance to the government, or to pray to a God in whom he or she does not believe. Toward that vigilance, religious believers gladly join hands with civil libertarians.

The issue of school prayer thus narrows to the question of whether opportunity may be provided by a public school for its students to pray in some formal, organized way, which neither forces students to participate, nor cavalierly determines the content of what they shall pray without being sensitive to pluralistic beliefs. The key words are "formal and organized," as opposed to individual, personal prayers, which the school could no more prohibit than it could mandate. These "unorganized prayers" would include personal prayers at mealtimes, or outside of class—even in groups, if the students so chose.

But the more difficult question remains: In what "formal and organized" manner may students be given the opportunity to pray? It is at this point that religious believers and civil libertarians unclasp hands and put on the boxing gloves.

The School Prayer Decisions

A review of the principal school prayer decisions demonstrates just how far removed from the Constitution the ACLU and the courts have been in recent years. For its part, the ACLU launched the anti-prayer movement by objecting to New York's schools using the "Lord's Prayer." When New York responded with a non-denominational prayer, the ACLU once again moved to block its use. As a matter of strategy, the national ACLU was against filing a suit, fearing that the Court might set a national standard approving school prayer. Therefore, the New York chapter filed suit of its own.[1] Naturally, the national ACLU was delighted with the surprise decision in the 1962 landmark case of *Engel v. Vitale*.[2]

Tracking the ACLU's argument, the Supreme Court mutilated the clear intent of the Establishment Clause beyond all recognition. For starters, the decision glossed over the obvious constitutional distinction between federal and state action. Justice Hugo Black's majority opinion speaks generically of "government," as if it were all of one kind. ("It is no part of the business of *government* to compose official prayers for any group of the American people to recite as a part of a religious program carried on by *government* [emphasis added].")

Justice Black surely knew better than to blithely mix together all government, acknowledging at one point that "the First Amendment was added to the Constitution to stand as a guarantee that neither the power nor the prestige of the *Federal Government* would be used to...influence the kinds of prayer the American people can say."

Having just acknowledged that crucial distinction, Black unfortunately once again proceeded to toss both federal and state government into one undifferentiated heap: "Under [the First] Amendment's prohibition against governmental establishment of religion, as reinforced by the provisions of the Fourteenth Amendment, *government* in this country, *be it state or federal*, is without power to prescribe by law any particular form of prayer.... [emphasis added]"

Like Justice Black, the ACLU still fails to grasp that the very purpose of the Establishment Clause was such as to remove it from the scope of the Fourteenth Amendment. How can you enforce a national standard on the states through the Fourteenth Amendment, when establishing that national standard is itself a violation of the Constitution?

The Nonsense of Policy Arguments

Unless and until this fundamental misunderstanding of the Establishment Clause is properly sorted out, it is futile to put forward competing arguments, one way or the other, regarding school prayer. If the Establishment Clause is, in fact, applicable to the states, then the federal government can rule, on the basis of social policy, if it so wishes, regarding what does or does not constitute excessive state government entanglement in religion. If, on the other hand, the Establishment Clause is *not* applicable to the states, then neither the Congress nor, by extension, the Court can make any judgment whatsoever about the desirability of state school-prayer legislation, apart from any coercive element that would violate the right of free exercise.

Conveniently, Justice Black cruised right by the decisive federal-state issue and headed straight for pragmatic policy arguments. School prayer, he opined, would "destroy government and degrade religion." Maybe he was right. Maybe he was wrong. Many of us who are believers would agree that faith is invariably compromised when the church (as opposed to individual believers themselves) becomes entangled in politics. But it is not for the Supreme Court to supplant the wisdom of parents and local school boards with its own opinions as to what might be beneficial or detrimental to either church or state. (With regard to the best interests of the church, many jurists would be the last to know.)

To justify his own wisdom on the matter of school prayer, Justice Black boldly sallied forth into a full-blown discussion of the Church of England's Book of Common Prayer, and how divisive and coercive its adoption had become. Amazingly, even John Bunyan's persecution by the established Church of England is dredged up in support of opposition to school prayer—as if there were even the slightest correlation.

We must not forget that church-state separation in England, had it happened, would have meant something fundamentally different from the same act of disestablishment in the *United States*. The political division of a nation by states has significant ramifications for both the political process and state-by-state religious expression, which must never be overlooked or taken for granted.

But pragmatic arguments are as useless as they are irrelevant to the discussion. If Justice Black's concern about potential divisiveness is the reason for prohibiting school prayer, what could be more divisive than the federal government telling parents and local school boards how to educate their children? Has the Court's ban on school prayer effectively brought about national consensus and harmony?

How Less Threatening Can Free Exercise Get?

The surprising thing about the *Engel* decision is how utterly benign the state's legislation was, and how carefully and sensitively it had been thought out. The Board of Education of New Hyde Park, New York, had composed and recommended a prayer which was both simple and non-sectarian: "Almighty God, we acknowledge our dependence upon Thee, and we beg Thy blessings upon us, our parents, our teachers and our country."

The wording of the prayer could have come straight out of any Presidential inaugural address, from Washington to Jefferson to Lincoln; from

Roosevelt to Kennedy to Clinton. Or from the lips of any Senate Chaplin over the past 200 years. Or, even, from the Supreme Court itself. At the opening of each day's Session, the Justices and all who are in the court-room stand while the Crier says, "God save the United States and this Honorable Court."

To make an argument with which the ACLU probably would agree (for quite different reasons), just how greatly distanced is such language from the words "In God We Trust" on our coins, or the reverential "one nation *under God*" in our pledge of allegiance? Many Americans are probably unaware of the following deity-filled stanza of our national anthem:

> O, thus be it ever when freemen shall stand
> Between their lov'd home and the war's desolation!
> Blest with vict'ry and peace may the heav'n rescued land
> Praise the power that hath made and preserved us a nation!
> Then conquer we must when our cause it is just,
> and this be our motto—"In God is our trust."
> And the Star-Spangled Banner in triumph shall wave
> O'er the land of the free and the home of the brave.

As Justice Stewart noted in his dissent to *Engel*, there is little here of "official religion" and much of "highly cherished spiritual traditions of our Nation—traditions which come down to us from those who almost two hundred years ago vowed [in the Declaration of Independence] their 'firm Reliance on the Protection of divine Providence' when they proclaimed the freedom and independence of this brave new world."

Unable to fault the New York prayer's actual wording, Justice Black had to content himself with stating the obvious, that the prayer was a "religious activity." Yet, how that particular form of religious activity is qual-itatively different from students reading the Declaration of Independence, or pledging allegiance, or singing the national anthem—all having explicit ref-erences to God—was hardly addressed. Black apparently felt no threat from a kind of civil religion expressed only on "patriotic or ceremonial occasions" which "bears no true resemblance to the unquestioned religious exercise" of school prayer.

So now, children, this is the lesson of the day: As long as school prayer is merely ceremonial, euphemistic, and pallid, it is constitutional. When it becomes anything like serious, genuine gratitude for divine care and provi-dence, it instantly becomes unconstitutional.

Curious Options for Opting Out

As for Justice Black's concern about potential coercion, the New York legislation could also not have been more cautious or sensitive. In his concurring opinion, Justice Douglas had absolutely no quarrel with the provisions which had been made for non-participation:

> The prayer is said upon the commencement of the school day, immediately following the pledge of allegiance to the flag. The prayer is said aloud in the presence of a teacher, who either leads the recitation or selects a student to do so. No student, however, is compelled to take part. The respondents have adopted a regulation which provides that "Neither teachers nor any school authority shall comment on participation or non-participation...nor suggest or request that any posture or language be used or dress be worn or be not used or not worn."
>
> Provision is also made for excusing children, upon written request of a parent or guardian, from the saying of the prayer or from the room in which the prayer is said. A letter implementing and explaining this regulation has been sent to each taxpayer and parent in the school district. As I read this regulation, a child is free to stand or not stand, to recite or not recite, without fear of reprisal or even comment by the teacher or any other school official.
>
> In short, the only one who need utter the prayer is the teacher; and no teacher is complaining of it. Students can stand mute or even leave the classroom, if they desire.

As Justice Douglas confirmed, no stone had been unturned in an effort to respect conscientious objection to participation. Yet, for the majority in *Engel*, that effort counted for nothing. "Neither [the prayer's content] nor the fact that its observance on the part of the students is voluntary can serve to free it from the limitations of the Establishment Clause." How, asked the Court, can we overlook the embarrassment, pressure, and potential for stigma when students choose not to participate?

By that reasoning, of course, the Court would also have to prohibit public schools from having their students salute the flag or say the pledge of allegiance or sing the national anthem. (As Justice Douglas noted, the prayer in question followed immediately after the pledge of allegiance.) Any number of students—principally those whose parents are Jehovah's Witnesses—are conscientiously unable to participate in either the pledge or the national anthem. Does their potential embarrassment or stigmatization give cause for the Court to prohibit the patriotic exercises? And, if not, in what way is voluntary prayer any more coercive?

Besides, it is little more than speculation to say that school kids are traumatized by their opting out of voluntary religious or patriotic exercises. When I think back to my own school days, I remember with fondness when my conscientious omission of a certain phrase in the prescribed prayer was not a reason for embarrassment, but reason for proud distinction. Yea, even a daily verification of righteous superiority! Nor was I offended that the class was engaging in a prayer with which I did not wholly agree. Although still a youngster, I appreciated the value of prayer in general, even if the specific prayer was not one to which my parents and I could completely subscribe.

Furthermore, there would be those from minority groups who would applaud a sense of culture and attention to spiritual values even if not precisely their own. One thinks, for example, of columnist Barbara Amiel who reflected on her childhood as a young Jewish girl growing up in British schools:

> Why are we unable to view ourselves as a given culture, with or without a predominant religion, to which law-abiding people from all over the globe are welcomed and free to practice privately whatever religious or cultural manifestation they wish, and maintain a separate group identity for themselves if they choose, but without altering the notion that this is an existing culture? As a child from a minority culture, I found it perfectly in order to be excused from Christian prayers at school."[3]

When the Court abandons sound legal precedent for the murky waters of subjective policy arguments, one person's opinion might be just as sound as the next. If perhaps some students might be embarrassed by opting out, other students may well appreciate that their minority status contributes to a strong cultural identity which they might not otherwise have.

Debatable policy arguments aside, if the objection to school prayer is one of coercion, the case for either direct or indirect coercion simply wasn't proved in *Engel*. Should such coercion ever be proved (as it was in *McCollum v. Board of Education*[4]), then the Free Exercise Clause itself would nullify the offending guidelines. (One person's free exercise cannot preclude another's free exercise.)

This is precisely the point at which the Court's inquiry must end. Moving even the tiniest of steps beyond the legitimate issue of coercion takes the Court into what has become the explosive minefield of the Establishment Clause, where the Court erroneously feels that the public square must be sanitized of even the slightest reference to religion. The talk quickly turns from *enablement* (a legitimate concern emanating from free exercise) to an unfounded paranoia about *endorsement* (a bogus concept leading down the path to religious discrimination and—to complete the cycle—the endorsement of secularism instead).

Once the Court abandoned coercion as the standard by which to judge governmental action in school prayer cases, then inevitable references to the Establishment Clause became nothing more than frustrating efforts at further building and buttressing Jefferson's misconstrued "wall." Hence the confusing and exasperating "church-state" thicket from which the Court seemingly cannot extricate itself. Hence, too, the ACLU's use of that judicially-maintained "wall"[5] to justify its hostility toward religion.

Playing the Indoctrination Game

If perhaps the ACLU is concerned with coercion in the form of embarrassment and stigmatization, the ACLU's primary objection to school prayers takes a somewhat different slant. For the ACLU, it is the potential for indoctrination that offends. According to ACLU Policy 81, "The ACLU believes that any program of religious indoctrination—direct or indirect—in the public schools or by use of public resources is a violation of the constitutional principle of separation of church and state and must be opposed."

Included among the six items particularly opposed by the ACLU under that rationale is sub-section 2: "The practice of regular Bible reading and organized prayers represents a form of indoctrination which is barred."[6]

Interestingly, in the *Engel* case, Justice Douglas specifically found that New York's set prayer was not a vehicle for indoctrination. "There is," said Douglas, "no effort at indoctrination and no attempt at exposition." What's more, Douglas stated that, "New York's prayer is of a character that does not involve any element of proselytizing as in the *McCollum* case."

If any organization is intent on classroom indoctrination, it is the American Civil Liberties Union. Under Policy 81, the ACLU opposes "the inculcation of religious doctrines even if they are presented as alternatives to scientific theories"—a thinly veiled rule against the teaching of anything but naturalistic evolution. By eliminating all alternative origin-of-life theories, the ACLU insures the exclusive indoctrination of its own secularist faith.

It is perhaps one of the more brazen of all its hypocrisies. In the guise of attacking religious indoctrination and defending pluralism, what the ACLU really wants is to advance a climate of agnosticism and religious skepticism.[7] Skepticism, that is, of all but its own secular humanist religion. (Like the proverbial rose, religion by any other name is still religion.)

That the ACLU further betrays its professed concern for indoctrination and coercion in public schools is best demonstrated in ACLU Policy 86, which addresses the circumstances under which a student may be excused from classes on the basis of conscientious objection. The preamble says that "the Union opposes measures whereby public school pupils may be excused from certain courses for religious reasons: for example, Christian Scientists who wish to be excused from hygiene courses." (Translate "hygiene courses" into "sex-education" courses, and you begin to get a hint of what the ACLU is up to.)

Why must students not be permitted to opt out of classes on the basis of religious conscience? Because, says the ACLU incredibly, "such measures set a bad precedent for the indirect control of the public school curriculum by religious bodies." Wow! What can one say? Rarely has the Establishment Clause been so overinflated, nor the Free Exercise Clause so devalued.

The ACLU's various policies regarding religious freedom in public schools are a revealing collection of anti-religious bias. When school prayer is at issue, provisions for opting out count for nothing. Under no circumstances are students permitted to say even the most nonsectarian of prayers (or even to engage in a moment of silence). School prayer is constitutionally dead, period. But, when it comes to explaining abortion and condoms to students, there can be no opt-out provisions on the basis of religious conscience!

At every turn, ACLU policy makes a sham of free exercise. It gets worse with every paragraph. "Freedom of religion," continues Policy 86, "does not extend so far that parents may withdraw children from classes which they feel conflict with their religious principles, even when they cannot practically avail themselves of the right to send their children to private schools." (And, naturally, the ACLU opposes voucher plans and tax credits just to make sure that parents cannot, in fact, afford private schools.[8])

We've come a long way from the First Amendment, not to mention even the most basic appreciation for spiritual values. Voluntary school prayer? No. Involuntary sex-education? Yes. The anti-religious bias of the ACLU is so glaring that, surely, even the Prince of Darkness is slightly embarrassed.

Considering the ACLU's blatant opposition to free exercise in public schools, it's time for some truth in advertising. Once again, the ACLU's claim to be "the nation's foremost protector of the rights of individuals to practice their religion"[9] is not just preposterous. It is nothing short of outrageous.

Student Rights for Everything but Prayer

You can tell where the ACLU's heart really is when you see how fervently it supports student rights of every possible kind—particularly with regard to free speech—except, of course, when students demand the right to participate in student-initiated, student-led prayers. At this point, we are no longer talking about school-sponsored prayers, like in the New York *Engel* case. We are not even talking about the *Lee v. Weisman* case, in which the principal of a public middle school invited a rabbi to lead a nonsectarian prayer at a graduation ceremony.[10] (Following in the steps of *Engel*, the Court, not unexpectedly, found the clergy-led prayer to be a First Amendment violation.)

What we are talking about here is the right for then-18-year-old Jennifer Griffin to invoke God's guidance during her graduation speech at Forest Hills High School in Marshville, North Carolina. When principal Barry Aycock announced months before graduation that, based upon recent court rulings, prayers would no longer be allowed, students protested. They enlisted the aid of the American Center for Law and Justice, and an agreement was reached that permitted the students to make overt appeals to God, as they desired.[11]

Naturally, that didn't stop the ACLU from sending letters to other schools warning against student-led prayers. This letter, for example, warned that, "Student-led prayer is unconstitutional....[school boards should] reject organized efforts to include prayers in graduation ceremonies, whether such efforts come from students or any other group."[12]

The ACLU agrees that individual student speakers can mention their religious views, but when school officials put the issue of student-led graduation prayers to a vote, or encourage students "with a wink or a nod," the ACLU believes it still smacks of government endorsement. Of student-initiated, student-led prayers, ACLU legal director Steve Shapiro says, "I don't think the issue is resolved at all."[13]

In 1995, the Supreme Court vacated an Appeals Court ruling that student-led prayer at a public school graduation is unconstitutional. However, the Court did not itself specifically decide the issue, leaving the issue in more fog than either side would wish.[14]

Someone who would agree whole-heartedly with the fact that the issue is not resolved is A. Dewayne Oldham, Principal of Westmoreland (Tennessee) High School. Like hundreds of other school principals, Oldham received one of the ACLU's threatening letters. When he told his graduating students that, because of the letter, he could not give them permission to pray, the students took it upon themselves at the ceremony to recite the Lord's Prayer.

Oldham, having being caught in the middle of the fray, filed suit for a declaratory judgment, claiming that the ACLU was violating his students' First Amendment right to free speech by trying to stop their prayers. What an irony, the great defender of free speech having to defend itself for threatening to shut down free speech! And, to compound the felony, the ACLU had the gall to go into court and argue that the suit was not ripe for litigation because, after all, it had not actually filed suit, but merely exercised its right of free speech to *threaten* suit![15]

Meanwhile, it was business as usual for the ACLU in southern California. The ACLU was rushing to the rescue of 14-year-old John Spindler who had decided to challenge the Simi Valley Unified School District's new dress code. The code, adopted in an effort to stem gang violence, banned shirts adorned with any writing or pictures, except school emblems. Defying the code, Spindler came to school wearing a T-shirt emblazoned with the American flag and the bald eagle.

How did the ACLU see the issue? "We are talking about a school trying to ban expression of its students," said ACLU attorney Robin Toma. Elizabeth Schroeder, associate director of the ACLU of Southern California, agreed, saying, "The 1st Amendment does not stop at the school house doors."[16]

Who can make any sense of it? A public school student has the First Amendment free-speech right to defy a school-initiated dress code, but not a First Amendment free-speech right to voluntarily participate in a school-initiated prayer. One form of free speech (non-religious) gets the ACLU all worked up over student rights; another form of free speech (religious) finds the ACLU jumping in with all fours on the other side.

One wonders what position the ACLU would have taken if John Spindler's T-shirt had been emblazoned with the Lord's Prayer. If the school *prohibited* his wearing it, would that be a violation of Spindler's student rights to free speech? If, on the other hand, the school *permitted* his wearing it, would that be a violation of the Establishment Clause as a school-condoned, indirect form of religious indoctrination?

After awhile, it all gets a bit much. Just how far does the ACLU think it can twist the wax nose of the First Amendment back and forth to meet its own anti-religious agenda without the nose breaking completely off?

In 1981, the ACLU showed its true anti-religious colors when it produced and distributed a poster showing a militant evangelical believer charging out on a horse. One could hardly miss the biting sarcasm: "If the Moral Majority gets its way, you better start praying."[17] The real truth, of course, is just the opposite. As seen so clearly in its vitriolic opposition to school prayer, the poster should have read: "When the ACLU gets its way, you no longer have the *right* to pray." (At least, not as a class or student body whenever the school provides a specific opportunity for students to pray.)

Can an Amendment Make Amends?

School prayer proponents have been so marginalized by *Engel* and its progeny, it appears that nothing short of a constitutional amendment can rectify the Court's intransigence on the subject. Indeed, the broader scope of religious liberty begs a better resolution. Lest it be forgotten, there are any number of thorny religious liberty issues in addition to school prayer. These include "release time" for religious education; school vouchers and tax credits for parents wishing to send their children to private schools; the expenditure of public funds for textbooks or busing for parochial school children; use of public school facilities by religious organizations; observance of religious holidays; posting of religious symbols, such as the Ten Commandments; and so forth seemingly forever. Nor does this listing even begin to address the innumerable other religious liberty issues which are wholly unassociated with public schools.

So what is the answer? How can America resolve this long-running and deep-seated family feud? Gary Bauer, of the Family Research Council, gives us some idea of the complexity of the challenge when he says, "If you get ten legal scholars in a room to talk about this, you get eleven different opinions."[18] And, given the potential implications for both sides, few have any desire to rush the process. Says Jay Sekulow of the American Center for Law and Justice, "It's not that the issue [of school prayer] is in trouble, it's that this is an amendment to the Constitution and it needs to be done properly."[19]

We have already discussed briefly the Religious Equality Amendment which appears to be the current consensus approach to resolving the religious liberties dilemma. But perhaps another way to get out of the muddle is to carefully retrace our steps to the point where we got into the muddle in the first place. Why not go all the way back to Jefferson and the Framers, and clarify what should have been obvious all along, that there are two distinct "walls of separation": the one, between church and government on the federal level; the other, between the federal government and state action relative to religious expression.

Perhaps what we need is an uncluttered amendment which makes no specific reference to school prayer (which, after all, is only one among many religious liberty issues), and which makes clear who it is that will decide all such issues. Will it be the federal government, or will it be state legislatures and local school boards?

Perhaps something like the following wording could move the discussion in the right direction: "Nothing in the First Amendment shall be construed to imply that individual states are prohibited from enabling religious expression as determined by its citizens in pursuit of the free exercise of religion."

Naturally, such an amendment would not put an end to the debate. (Indeed, it probably would stir it up!) But it would put the shoe on the right foot. It would restore the original intent of the framers of the Constitution. It would empower the people to determine for themselves at a local level what is best for their communities. And it would express trust in the democratic process and in the sense of fair play and tolerance that people of all faiths (and non-faith) so desperately seek.

Most of all, such an amendment would once and for all disestablish the secular religion of the ACLU and compel it, along with every other special interest group in America, to participate in the debate at the local level.

Perhaps, at the end of the 20th Century, states should no longer retain even the hypothetical power of establishment, since both state-established churches and state-established religion have long ago disappeared. But, if so, that relinquished power must be resurrected in some fashion so as to provide an equivalent modern empowerment which captures the spirit of the original First Amendment guarantees. If that takes a constitutional amendment, then we have no option but to seek such an amendment, whether it be the one I have proposed here or the Religious Equality Amendment which is already on the table. Either approach would emancipate us from the hostility toward religion engendered by misguided Establishment Clause analysis, and serve to open a desperately needed dialogue.

Who knows what might result? The outcome of the dialogue between civil libertarians and religious activists is by no means a foregone conclusion. Religious activists might well decide that any prayer which would be so nonsectarian and pluralistic as to win public approval would, in fact, end up trivializing prayer, thereby rendering the exercise meaningless. Religious activists might also decide that there are other channels into which they can more fruitfully pour their energies, like proposing ways in which basic moral values can more directly be inculcated into the educational process. Would not a morally-based curriculum be the greater victory, even if the symbolism of school prayer had to be sacrificed for the cause?

It is equally possible that dedicated civil libertarians might one day decide there is less to fear about school prayer than they have previously believed—that, in a time of social decline, it might just be the right moment to reexamine communitarian values and their relation to spiritual verities. Would it not be a great civil libertarian victory if the symbolism of school prayer contributed in some small way to the freedom from fear which now haunts schoolchildren on the playground and even in their classrooms?

Again, who knows? At this point, we certainly don't seem to be making much headway fighting the same old battles over and over again in the federal courts. As is, the problem seems insoluble. So, maybe bringing the religious liberties discussion back to our local communities is worth a try. Maybe it's even something worth praying about.

CHAPTER 13

Monkey Trials and Evolving Classrooms

"WHAT BEGAN WITH DARWIN AS EVOLUTION HAS BECOME
EVOLUTIONISM, THE EFFORT TO INTERPRET MAN AND
HIS UNIVERSE IN EVOLUTIONARY CONCEPTS."
PHILIP SCHARPER

For militant secularists like the ACLU, school prayer has never been anything more than a skirmish. The ultimate goal has always been to get God himself out of the classroom. To do that, you ban Bible reading, strip the walls of the Ten Commandments, and forbid student prayers. Most importantly, you censor any serious reference to the Creator and, instead, present students with the only possible alternative: chance existence resulting from purposeless evolution.

To justify such censorship, the ACLU frantically waives the Establishment Clause, as if mention of a Grand Designer heralds the appointment of the Pope as America's spiritual leader. Hardly anyone notices that, quite to the contrary, censorship of Creation teaching facilitates the establishment of the ACLU's own secular humanist faith, no less a religion than any other.

On shaky constitutional ground, the ACLU parades before the courts popstar evolutionists who make supercilious references to Creation-thinking as "shoddy science." It hardly matters that the experts vehemently disagree among themselves as to the mechanics of how chance origins could yield such an intelligently functioning universe. Or of what use half a wing would be to a bird. Or how asexual creatures learned about sex in one crucial generation. Does not "freedom to learn" include the right to challenge conventional wisdom? Not, apparently, if there is any chance that hard questions might end up pointing heavenward.

Monkey Trials and Evolving Classrooms

I t began as a test case for the ACLU. Then as a clever Chamber of Commerce ploy. Then as a battle of egos. Then as a media circus. In the end, it heralded the most crucial, though perhaps least understood, battle for the control of America's spiritual mind. More than any other single case, the sensational 1925 Scopes "monkey trial" in Tennessee changed the philosophical landscape in America, paving the way, not only for significant change in public education, but, more importantly, for unprecedented implementation of the liberal-Left agenda.

One could view the *Scopes* trial as a pivotal case in church-state constitutionalism, and certainly it was that, despite the fact that the Establishment Clause aspect was never tested in the Supreme Court. One wishing to do so could also see it as a significant milestone in the march toward academic freedom. But, unless one sees the *Scopes* trial as a watershed in America's most fundamental values, then its full impact has been grossly underestimated.

Dayton, Tennessee, businessman George Rappelyea could hardly have guessed the historical and social reverberations which would result from his brainstorm to give the local economy a boost. It was he who persuaded a young science teacher, John Thomas Scopes, to violate the newly-enacted Tennessee law which prohibited public school teachers from teaching "any theory that denies the story of the Divine Creation of man as taught in the Bible." Rappelyea's idea was to promote Dayton by creating a huge media event, pitting two celebrity advocates against each other in a battle over the Bible. In fundamentalist Tennessee, it was a marketing scheme which guaranteed success.

If perhaps George Rappelyea was unaware of the full implications of the "monkey trial," Roger Baldwin and the ACLU in New York were all too aware of what was at stake. Their interest had been stirred by an article about the Tennessee law which caught the eye of ACLU secretary Lucille Milner. Milner, while clipping news articles relevant to civil liberties, handed the article to Roger Baldwin. She said, "Here's something that ought to have our attention." Baldwin immediately recognized the full scope of libertarian concerns, and hurried into print a newspaper article offering ACLU assistance to any person willing to violate the law.[1]

It was a hoped-for test case that the ACLU eagerly relished. What could possibly be sweeter? It would pit Bible-belt fundamentalists against the northeastern liberal establishment, the Bible versus science, religion versus secularism, and Christian dominance versus cultural pluralism. It was all there in one delicious setting worthy of a Hollywood production. Indeed, the trial turned out to be so colorful that it inspired the 1955 play *Inherit the Wind* and its more famous film version in 1960.

What was needed for this drama to unfold in real life was the perfect cast of characters. As it turned out, the leading roles could not have been better typecast. Three-time Democratic presidential candidate and the pre-eminent fundamentalist of his day, William Jennings Bryan, was brought in to prosecute the case. The defense featured the flamboyant, avowed atheist and defender of unpopular causes, Clarence Darrow, whose offer of assistance was accepted.

If that match-up was perfect for the slick marketers and clamoring media, it was not at all what the ACLU wanted. The "unrespectable" Darrow was seen as too much of a risk when what lay at stake for the ACLU was, not just publicity, but crucial civil libertarian issues. Over lunch in New York, ACLU's Walter Nelles and Felix Frankfurter tried passionately to persuade Scopes to replace Darrow with someone more suitable. Unmoved, Scopes said defiantly, "I want Darrow."[2]

With that, the stage was set for the rancorous eight-day trial in which Darrow boldly framed the issue in terms of pluralism and tolerance: "If today you can take a thing like evolution and make it a crime to teach it in the public school, tomorrow you can make it a crime to teach it in the private school....At the next session you may ban books and the newspapers. Soon you may set Catholic against Protestant and Protestant against Protestant, and try to foist your own religion upon the minds of men."[3]

One wonders what Darrow might have thought had he been able to foresee the time when it would be impermissible by law to teach creation. Would his civil libertarian instincts have been honest enough to say, "If today you can take a thing like creation and make it impermissible to teach it in the public school, tomorrow you may try to foist your own anti-creationist secularism upon the minds of men"? Did academic freedom run only one way for Baldwin and the ACLU—*their* way?

For his part, William Jennings Bryan successfully convinced Judge John Raulston that the sole question was whether the legislature had the right to determine public school curricula. With that restrictive ruling, the ACLU's case was left in shambles. The ACLU's carefully orchestrated lineup of defense witnesses—renowned scientists and liberal theologians—were left cooling their heels in the courthouse hallway.

It was left to Darrow's streetfighter instincts to save the day. Through a crafty bit of maneuvering (which even the ACLU found appalling[4]), Darrow played on Bryan's ego and coaxed Bryan into taking the witness stand himself in defense of Fundamentalism. Under Darrow's fierce examination, Bryan quickly became muddled, and, to the gasps of his literalist supporters, even stated that the six days of the creation account in Genesis were not literal, twenty-four hour days.

That exchange quickly brought to an end what the Tennessee Supreme Court later characterized as "this bizarre case."[5] Not at all enticed by Darrow's appeal to a broader concern regarding human freedom, the jury deliberated for only nine minutes and returned the obvious verdict: "Guilty." The grand irony is that, after all the stir, Judge Raulston made an error in instructing the jury about the $100 fine which was imposed (the jury should have set it, not the judge), resulting in Scopes' conviction being overturned on appeal. And, in a rather more immediate and tragic postscript, William Jennings Bryan died a week after the trial.

Emergence of the New Fundamentalists

Although the prosecution emerged victorious, if greatly embarrassed, the long-range victory went to the ACLU and the broader liberal cause. Over the next two years, anti-evolution legislation was defeated in twenty-two states. (That said, a 1941 survey found that evolution was being taught by only half the nation's science teachers. It took the Soviet's "sputnik" and a renewed interest in teaching hard science in the 1960s to radically shift the balance.[6])

On the religious front, *Scopes* proved to be the catalyst in a widening rift between mainstream Protestant denominations and fundamentalist churches. Thanks to *Scopes*, the more liberal churches discovered that they had more in common with libertarian secularists than with believers whose biblical fundamentals stood in the way of a liberating social gospel.

Undoubtedly, the most important spinoff from *Scopes* was a growing disapproval of any group of people imposing their religious views on others. This new spirit of social tolerance would outdistance merely the imposition of specific religious dogma by one group on another. Its true fruit would be borne half a century later in our current culture's pluralistic, individualistic, relativistic non-judgmentalism.

Those nouveau-libertarian beliefs form the core doctrine of what has become the *New Fundamentalism*, a fundamentalism which—through the power of political correctness—is being evangelistically imposed by an elitist minority of Leftists on a majority of mainstream Americans with a fervor more intense than any ever mustered by Bible-belt fundamentalists. Now the tables have completely turned. Now, it is the New Fundamentalists who are practicing intellectual bigotry. Although their dogma is at the opposite end of the spectrum, their nationwide Leftist-inspired legislation takes virtually the same path as its Tennessee predecessor—prohibiting public school teachers from teaching any theory that *affirms* creation.

The Scope of Liberal Bigotry

Samuel Walker says that, "The sensational Scopes 'monkey trial' thrust the ACLU into the national spotlight as the defender of the freedom to learn."[7] But in practice, this translates into the freedom to learn only whatever is consistent with the liberal-Left agenda. If a local school board or a given state wishes to permit the teaching of creation along with the teaching of evolution, then the ACLU quickly becomes mute about the "freedom to learn."

Of course, church-state separation is the immediate constitutional rhetoric one hears from the ACLU. But a fair and balanced approach to the subject could hardly constitute the kind of governmental indoctrination forbidden by the Courts. Governmental indoctrination is a term far more suited to the intentional censorship of one side of an argument—never better illustrated than where evolution alone is allowed to be taught. And, despite its billing, evolution is only an argument. Lest we forget, even its most ardent supporters still call it the *theory* of evolution.

When after years of local skirmishes the evolution issue eventually reached the Supreme Court in 1968 in the case of *Epperson v. Arkansas*, the pro-civil libertarian Warren Court declared a 1928 Arkansas anti-evolution statute unconstitutional.[8] Naturally, there was no mention of the ACLU's vaunted "freedom to learn," only the liberal-Left's pet issue of establishment. Given this judicial green light, public schools all over America even more boldly indoctrinated their students with an uncontradicted evolutionary tour de force.

It was this blatantly one-sided presentation of a liberal-Left world view that prompted a spate of legislation in twenty-three states in the early 1980s mandating "balanced treatment" of both evolution and creation. The ease with which the laws were passed in nearly half the States points to mainstream America's repulsion at liberal censorship. Arkansas' statute, for example, passed in the state senate by a vote of 16 to 2 after only 15 minutes of debate. In each of the twenty-three states, the legislation would mean that "creation-science" would be taught alongside "evolution-science." Seem fair enough? Not for the ACLU.

Upon learning of the Arkansas legislation, ACLU's then-elder-statesman Roger Baldwin (five months from death), called Ira Glasser and—fearful of losing ground gained in the *Scopes* episode fifty-six years earlier—demanded to know: "Did you read about that Arkansas law? What are you going to do about it?"[9] What Glasser and the ACLU did about it was to organize twenty-three plaintiffs, including parents, teachers, and clergy, and to line up such expert witnesses as Harvard paleontologist Stephen Jay Gould and Cornell's celebrated Carl Sagan.

The trial was hardly the media circus *Scopes* had been, but in the end both the trial and appellate courts ruled the Arkansas law to be unconstitutional. The courts agreed with the ACLU's argument that, "It was simply and purely an effort to introduce the biblical version of creation into the public school curricula."[10]

It was a closer call but with the same result when Louisiana passed a more tempered piece of "balanced treatment" legislation. Even without any reference to the biblical account of Creation, Louisiana's law was struck down by the Rehnquist Court in 1987 by a 7-to-2 margin. Writing for the majority in the case of *Edwards v. Aguillard*, Justice William Brennan held that the law's "preeminent purpose was clearly to advance the religious viewpoint that a supernatural being created humankind."[11]   Coming as it did from a more conservative Court, *Edwards* became yet another example of the ACLU's successful repackaging of the First Amendment's quite-differently-intended Establishment Clause.

It surely cuts little ice with the liberal-Left, but it just has to be said again that, if there *were* a legitimate establishment issue, the shoe would be on the other foot. Today, it is the anti-religious religion of secularism that is being imposed by pro-evolution legislation. Call your sacred beliefs *science* or *philosophy*, rather than *religion*, and you can have the best of both worlds constitutionally. In a single stroke, you can both censor another's religion and promote your own.

This brings us back to chapter two and the continuing litany of hypocrisy practiced by the ACLU. Rarely does it get any more breathtaking than when you compare the ACLU's outrage against the "balanced treatment" legislation on one hand, with, on the other, the ACLU's contradictory position when Tennessee parents sued to remove secular humanist books from the Hawkins County schools.

The parents complained that exposing their children to secular humanist literature violated their right to free exercise of religion. Despite support from ACLU board member Nadine Strossen, who argued that the students should be permitted an alternative reading program, the ACLU's full board decided that "mere exposure" to different points of view did not constitute indoctrination or forced participation in a religious exercise.[12]

In that light, try to explain how exposing students to different points of view about the origins of the universe constitutes indoctrination or forced participation in a religious exercise! Simultaneously, the ACLU has not just one, but two clauses of the First Amendment all in a twist. It simply can't be clearer: the ACLU is not only hopelessly biased against religion, but hypocritically guilty of violating its own policies regarding censorship, academic freedom, and freedom of expression.

The Great Coverup

Does no one in the ACLU stop to ask what simply has to be the obvious question? In a world of theoretical possibilities, either our universe did in fact result from chance evolutionary forces or did in fact result from purposeful design. If the theory of evolution is so scientifically secure, what does it have to fear from cross-examination? The answer to that question, of course, is *almost everything!* That is why all the big guns of science are hastily assembled at the mere mention of the "C" word. But can even the big guns withstand vigorous examination?

Let the ACLU bring in Stephen Jay Gould, for example. When he has finished testifying about how unscientific creation is, pull out his book, *Wonderful Life*, based upon the Burgess Shale findings, and ask him whether Charles Darwin got it right in theorizing about "survival of the fittest." What you will hear Gould say is that the human race did not result from the survival of the *fittest*, but of the *luckiest*. "Replay the tape a million times from a Burgess beginning," he says, "and I doubt that anything like Homo sapiens would ever evolve again."[13]

Not only are there enormous gaps in the fossil record (which one would not expect to encounter if there had been a steady progression from amoeba to man), but in the supposedly 530-million-year-old Burgess Shale there is a disparity in anatomical design far exceeding the modern range throughout the world (calling into question what, until recently, has been the sacred dogma of upwardly ascending multiplication of life forms.)

Next, question Gould concerning Darwin's observations about the slow progression of a bird's wing as it selectively mutated and adapted to meet its need to fly. Gould, as well as most other evolutionists today, will tell you that Darwin was wrong about that, too. At last, the leading lights among evolutionists are admitting what should have been obvious all along—that only half a wing would have been absolutely useless to an evolving bird. With only half a wing, the slowly evolving "pre-bird" in the struggle for survival would never have developed fully enough to have the benefit of wings.

In an act of desperation, evolutionists like Gould have come up with some ingenuous rescue theories, like so-called "punctuated equilibrium," in which evolution oxymoronically occurred by "great leaps." No wings one day; wings the next. (Well, sort of.) Can this make any more sense than the old theory? Or even as much?

The point is this: By no means is there unanimity among evolutionists themselves about which is *the* theory of evolution. If we cannot yet be assured of the *right* theory, then how can we have any assurance that evolution by any theory is a valid explanation of human origin? As long as that doubt exists, what danger is there in presenting a competing "design" theory that one could reasonably and logically accept even without the slightest resort to the Bible? (After all, in every other context, it is reasonable and logical to believe that order and intelligibility are the result of intelligent design.)

The danger of presenting the competing theory is obvious: A "design" theory presupposes a Grand Designer, which, for many people, gets disturbingly close to the idea of God—especially a God who is in control of the universe and who may make demands upon us that we would rather be free to ignore.

We see the problem vividly illustrated in the case of Orange County, California, high school biology teacher John Peloza who insisted on teaching his students both evolution and creation. When parents complained, Peloza was reprimanded by the school district. "I never quote Genesis in my classroom," he said. "When I give my presentation, I give two sides, one that we are here by chance and the other that we are here by design."[14] At the mere mention of the word "design," an attorney for the school district shot back, "Creationism is not a scientific theory, it is a religious belief."[15]

Interesting, isn't it, that what many take to be a fact—*creation*—is almost invariably referred to by opponents as *"creationism."* That subtle change alone puts creation into the category of beliefs, and—by only the slightest extension—into the category of religious beliefs which are off-limits in the classroom. It hardly seems to matter that "evolutionism," should one choose to call it that, is no less a belief, and one which, because it asks the rational mind to believe that a vast and orderly universe resulted from sheer chance, is no less a leap of faith and therefore not unlike religious faith.

Might Schools At Least Challenge?

For more than 125 years, the evolutionary origin of humankind has been convincingly embedded in the modern mind through scientific and educational propaganda which has reached brainwashing proportions. Most people today have bought the theory—lock, stock, and barrel—without once questioning the implications of even the highly publicized search for the "missing link." (As if there would be just one intermediate set of bones out there somewhere....)

The ongoing, feverish search is prompted by the thought that, if man really did evolve from lower primates, surely there ought to be some evidence of it. (Quite a good point, actually.) So, more than a century after Darwin first proposed the theory, the search goes on. Every year or so, of course, we read of yet another spectacular discovery of *the* "missing link"— only to hear rival paleontologists dispute the claims and then proceed to dig further into their own vivid imaginations.

One might suppose that with all this uncertainty about evolutionary theory junior high and high school textbooks would be filled with—if not the creation alternative—at least the kind of hard questions that legitimate science ought to be asking. But, no, that might expose the weak underbelly of conventional wisdom about our origins.

Who, for example, would dare ask about the *true* missing link: the *sex link*? In the supposed evolution from asexual life forms to sexual life forms (necessary to the general theory of progression from one species to another), there is an evidentiary gap you could drive an 18-wheeler through. You find that gap when you slow down the blur of millions of years that evolutionists like to dazzle us with. Rewind the evolutionary tape ever so slowly and inevitably you come to a freeze-frame moment where there would have been no sexual organisms whatsoever. Now, play the tape forward again, and all of a sudden you see millions of sexual creatures. Between the two readings on the tape is, if you will, an 18 1/2-minute gap that even Richard Nixon would have been proud of— and causing just about as much stonewalling among the scientific community in an attempted coverup.

The questions are self-evident. Given evolution's necessity of long periods of time and countless minor mutations, how could any single asexual organism have survived long enough to develop the male sexual organ which would be needed in order to mate with a potential female so as to produce offspring for the next generation of sexual creatures? (Try to imagine what it would take to develop from scratch complex organs like the male penis or the female vagina.) And what are the odds that the first male and first female independently developed their sexual organs exactly to match? And at precisely the same time? And in the same place? And actually *liked each other* well enough to mate!

It is not enough merely to cite the existence of hermaphroditic life forms such as planaria, the New Zealand snail (potamopyrgus antipodarum), coral reef fish, or East Coast oysters. These organisms (which reproduce in strange ways, sometimes male, sometimes female; or perhaps sometimes sexually, sometimes asexually) only further beg the question of how they could have evolved their own bizarre hermaphroditic reproductive capacities. *Observation* is no substitute for *explanation*. Nor do they suggest how higher life forms might have moved from asexual to sexual reproduction.

One need not go so far as to wonder about the origin of penises and vaginas. There is also difficulty with the origin of the stamen and pistil.

Even chromosomes have beginnings mysterious enough to warrant high school students asking about the whole system of X chromosomes and Y chromosomes. They learn that amoebae and paramecia contain all their genes on one type of strand, so where, all of a sudden, did a male bug and a female bug come from?

One can only wonder whether these tough questions are included as part of a student's "freedom to learn" or "right to know." Are high school students in St. Louis, Seattle, and Sheboygan ever told that there are serious problems with evolution theory? Have they been informed about the dearth of evidence in the fossil record? Or the difficulties with methods of scientific dating? Or the uselessness of half a wing?

As for the missing sex link, are America's students ever introduced to articles like David Crews' *Scientific American* piece (January, 1994) entitled "Animal Sexuality"? Crews attempts an altogether fascinating explanation for the missing sex link, but acknowledges right up front: "Amazingly enough, scientists cannot conclusively say why sex exists." Recent work in animal studies, he says, provides "a *glimpse* [emphasis added] at how sex evolved"—hardly the scientific certainty smugly suggested by those who would insist that evolution theory has filled in all the blanks beyond a reasonable doubt.[16]

Perhaps this very line of thought suggests a possible resolution of the impasse between creationists and evolutionists. Would the ACLU accept robust cross-examination of evolution in the nation's schools? Would the line of church-state separation be crossed if students were presented with evolution's major evidentiary difficulties?

Taking it a significant step further, would it violate the Establishment Clause to suggest to students that, even if they accept biological evolution as the scientifically correct explanation of human origin, they still have to come up with scores of other independent theories to explain the origins of light, gravity, air, energy, water—the sun, the moon, and the stars? And that each of those various theories must somehow coordinate precisely with every other theory in order to fully explain why our vast, mysterious universe operates as it does?

Or do we realize all too well that such a universal explanation is beyond scientific ken. And does that embarrassing black hole of scientific insight—particularly in the face of creation's universal explanation of the genesis of all things—explain why creation must be censored from the inquisitive minds of America's young people?

When Liberals Condescend

Perhaps it is the arrogance of the liberal-Left that most offends. In his call for wider tolerance for faith in America, Yale's Stephen Carter cites a number of examples of slurs against creationists. There was, for instance, the *Omni* magazine article that appeared during the court battle over Louisiana's "balanced treatment" statute. In it, the author complained that "intolerance has raised its pea-brained head," then ironically displayed her own intolerance by characterizing a belief in creation as "the latest surreal joke in a deranged world."[17]

Literary critic Harold Bloom also stuck it to creation supporters by quoting H.L.Mencken: "They are everywhere where learning is too heavy a burden for mortal minds to carry."[18] And likely speaking on behalf of most members of the scientific community, renowned anthropologist Richard Leakey said of the "balanced treatment" approach that it was—not to put too fine a point on it—"utterly stupid."[19]

"All of this," says Carter, "adds up to a perception of creationists as backward, irrational, illiberal fanatics—not too smart and not too deserving of respect."[20] Unfortunately, Carter himself hastens to add: "I should make clear that I am no creationist—not, at least, in the popular sense. So-called scientific creationism...seems to me shoddy science, not science at all, really."[21]

At least Carter is honest enough to admit that, if creation-thinking is as mindless as its detractors believe, then tens of millions of Americans have lost their minds. Carter points to two major surveys which tell us that 82-87 percent of adults in America believe that God created human beings—whether the process was spontaneous, as in the Genesis account (44-47 percent), or gradual, with God guiding the process over great expanses of time (38-40 percent).[22] Carter wryly observes that the numbers "suggest that an attack on creationists as a minority trying to foist its views of science on an oppressed majority are a little bit overdrawn."[23] Indeed!

Sure, Creationists Believe in Evolution

Apart from snobbish swipes at fundamentalist Bible-thumpers, the best way to muddle the issue and make creationists look like country bumpkins is to conveniently confuse the two kinds of evolution at issue in all the debates.

The truth of the matter is that no serious thinker among creationists denies the process of *micro*evolution (adaptation *within* species,) which is easily provable. However, it is a quite different proposition to support *macro*evolution (classic, Darwinian-type evolution from *one* species to *another*), a speculative theory yet to be proven. Creationists do not deny observable, "lower-case" evolution, if you will; only the projected, as-yet-unconfirmed "capitalized" Evolution.

It is not a terribly sophisticated illustration, but it may help to clarify the point. Suppose you have a visitor from another country who is completely unfamiliar with the game of football. Take him to the local stadium and, beginning at one of the goal lines, walk him through each yard line up to the fifty. At each yard line, as appropriate, tell him that it's the ten-, twenty-, thirty-, forty-, and fifty-yard line. Now take him to the next yard line and ask him what it is. The answer you would likely get is "the sixty."

On the basis of the progression which the visitor has observed, his answer would be rational enough, but wrong. Rational-but-wrong can also be true in the world of science. What Darwin and other evolutionists have done is to take observable evolution *within species* and extrapolate that observation into a theory about evolution *from one species into another* which is neither observable nor, so far, proven.

Creationists understand completely what science is talking about up to the fifty-yard line, as it were. What they dispute is (in the case of macroevolution) the quantum leap conclusion which is made from that point forward. Given the vagaries of available evidence and the level of speculation necessary to support so grand a scientific paradigm as amoeba-to-man evolution, those who object to it didn't just fall off the turnip truck.

Do creationists believe in evolution? Sure they do. Just not the kind that has man's mutant predecessor washing up on the shores of some mythical primeval sea as a glob of greenish goo.

A Short Course in Coherence

In a purposely created universe, science and faith are cohesive. They both derive from the same Grand Designer. Creationists are not schizophrenics, living in a rational world for all but their view of life's origins. Indeed, creationists respond that it is the evolutionist who divorces science from faith, the physical from the metaphysical, the secular from the spiritual—and thereby is robbed of coherence. For the evolutionist, it was a false start all along. What hope of coherence can there realistically be when Chance is the First Cause?

It is the creationist's quest for rational coherence, as much as his allegiance to spiritual authority, that explains why the teaching of evolution is met with such resistance. As Professor Carter correctly observes, the rejection of "balanced treatment" laws "represents a humiliating constitutional slap in the faces of millions of Americans who are unwilling to make the separation of faith and self that secular political and legal culture often demand."[24]

Let no one miss the point: The incoherent attempt to separate the secular realm from the spiritual—not the First Amendment's Establishment Clause—is what "separation of church and state" is all about in the eyes of the American Civil Liberties Union.

For the ACLU, libertarianism both proceeds from and manifests itself in incoherence. Fundamental philosophical incoherence goes a long way toward explaining the ACLU's striking inconsistencies—indeed, its many hypocrisies. Void of coherent philosophical absolutes, the ACLU is forced into creating its own set of arbitrary absolutes—such as its absolutist position on free speech—which provides a comforting appearance of coherence, yet is only maintained at the high cost of having to defend unworthy causes like kiddy porn.

Ideas have consequences. Ideas about life's origins have the most profound and far-reaching consequences of all. In the following chapter, the full implications of evolution thinking will be scrutinized in greater detail. But there's no need to hold you in suspense. The surprise victim of the survival of the fittest turns out to be none other than civil liberty itself.

CHAPTER 14

Survival of the Unfittest Liberties

"IF THERE IS NO GOD, EVERYTHING IS PERMITTED."
FYODOR DOSTOYEVSKY

Creation versus Evolution is no abstract debate. The ACLU knows all too well that what school children are taught about human origins is a high-stakes struggle. Nothing is more fundamental to social issues than where we came from, why we are here, and where we are going. What people believe about hot-button issues like abortion, euthanasia, and gay rights almost inevitably comes down to how they view human origins. For the ACLU, especially, creation teaching threatens the moral legitimacy of its neo-civil libertarian agenda and its support of immoral political causes.

What the ACLU fails to understand is that, if we owe our existence to survival of the fittest, the very idea of human rights is baseless, and civil liberties are reduced to nothing more than codified platitudes, easily repealed. The Founders who first gave us the Bill of Rights would be dumbfounded to learn that schoolchildren could not be taught about the Creator. They fully understood that only by the literal fact of creation are we endowed with certain inalienable rights. In the jungle, there is neither equal protection, due process, nor right to life.

The ACLU is naive to believe that it can deny the fact of purposeful creation, yet maintain that civil liberties are inviolable. Facts cannot so easily be divorced from values. When schoolchildren are taught that they evolved from monkeys, can we blame them if they act like animals?

Survival of the Unfittest Liberties

R emember Clarence Darrow's argument in the *Scopes* trial? With all his rhetorical skills in high gear, Darrow warned of a creationist slippery slope, saying, "If today you can take a thing like evolution and make it a crime to teach it in the public school, tomorrow you can make it a crime to teach it in the private school..." and so on.[1]

Darrow was right about that slippery slope. As it turned out, however, he was wrong about which side of the controversy would be sliding down that slope. The sinister deed of moving from the public school to the private school in order to push its own ideology was left to none other than the American Civil Liberties Union itself.

It happened in 1983-84, when the ACLU of Virginia aggressively sought to punish students at Jerry Falwell's Liberty Baptist College. The ACLU unsuccessfully tried to convince the Virginia State Board of Education to deny accreditation to the biology education program, which would have meant that Liberty Baptist graduates could not have been hired as biology teachers by Virginia public school districts or by public schools in any other state.

Why this interference with a private school's academic accreditation? Surely you can guess. Liberty Baptist biology students were being taught creation, and, therefore, allowing them to teach in public schools would be tantamount to an establishment of religion.

Virginia ACLU Executive Director Chan Kedrick explained (presumably with a straight face) the three reasons for the ACLU's opposition to accreditation: 1) That in his (off-campus) sermons, college founder Jerry Falwell had preached against evolution and said that students at the college should study evolution only in order to refute it; 2) that Liberty College faculty were required to affirm their belief in the literal truth of the Bible; and 3) that the college had been accredited by an association of fundamentalist colleges, which itself endorsed creation.[2]

The civil liberties implications are outrageous. As Richard and Susan Vigilante explain, "The ACLU's position presumes without evidence that fundamentalists would violate state law and sneak creationism into the schools. It seeks, therefore, to punish fundamentalists not for any wrongdoing but for their privately held religious beliefs."[3] Incredibly, the beliefs being punished would not even have been those of the graduates themselves, but rather the beliefs of the Liberty Baptist faculty who alone were required to affirm creation.

Now what was that about the American Civil Liberties Union being the defender of our rights to freedom of belief, freedom of religion, and freedom of expression? Did somebody also say that the ACLU was not anti-religious?

How in the name of liberty could the ACLU discard its most fundamental civil libertarian principles to go after a private school that chose to affirm and teach creation? Simple. The moral implications of creation teaching strike at the very core of neo-civil libertarianism, threatening to destroy its liberal-Leftist political agenda. Like a noxious weed, creation must be stamped out whenever and wherever it raises its ugly head—even, apparently, if it requires violating civil liberties in the process.

This example demonstrates how far we have come from the understanding of our Founders, who would not have felt threatened in the least by the teaching of creation. In fact, these original civil libertarians would be dumbstruck to learn that the ACLU was so paranoid about creation. Quite to the contrary, they understood all too well the crucial link between a factual—dare we say *literal*—creation and our most precious liberties.

Declaration of Creation

Most of us assume that fundamental human rights—like the rights to life, liberty, and the pursuit of happiness—are linked to our Constitution and its near-sacred Bill of Rights. But where do *those* rights come from? At the end of the day, it is not the Constitution which ultimately guarantees our rights, but the principles of higher law stated in that other hallowed American document, the Declaration of Independence.

Someone once provided this illuminated version: *"We hold these truths to be self-evident"*—that is, so plain that their truth is recognized upon their mere statement—*"that all men are created equal"*—so that no person can claim superior entitlement; *"that they are endowed"*—not by edicts of emperors, or decrees of Parliament or acts of Congress, but *"by their Creator"*—in whose image they are made—*"with certain inalienable rights"*—that is, rights which cannot be bartered away, or given away, or taken away except in punishment of crime—*"and that among these are life, liberty, and the pursuit of happiness, and to secure these"*—not grant them but secure them—*"governments are instituted among men, deriving their just powers from the consent of the governed."*

Nice words, but do they really mean anything? In light of the previous chapter, it is the word *Creator* that most ought to pique our interest. Did Thomas Jefferson, who wrote these words, really believe in a Creator? Do the familiar phrases "created equal" and "endowed by their Creator" actually mean *so made by their Creator* or are they meaningless euphemisms?

Of course, we hear many references to "a Higher Power," or "Our Maker," or "The Almighty." Printed on our money are the words, "In God we trust;" in our pledge of allegiance, "One nation under God;" and in courtroom oaths, "so help me God." But do we really believe in a Creator who is the ultimate source of the basic human rights which we have come to expect and which the American Civil Liberties Union is committed to defend?

The Declaration's reference to a Creator could be, of course, just a catch-all expression for the generic deity of America's non-sectarian civil religion. On the other hand, it is also possible that the Founders actually meant what they said—that, indeed, our fundamental human rights exist only by virtue of a supernatural act of creation.

For Founders, Creation Was the Key

Jefferson himself was a deist. Deists were rationalists, believing in the ultimate rule of Reason and the scientific advances of Enlightenment Europe. For deists, God was a benevolent deity whose essential characteristic was *order*. It was the vast orderliness of the universe which compelled deists, through their reasoning processes, to believe in a God sufficiently powerful and intelligent enough to bring that order into existence.

But the God of the deists closed up shop after creation and went home. He no longer intervened in the affairs of humankind whom he had created. Nor did he reveal himself through divine revelation. What deists believed did not emanate from the Bible or any other sacred writing.

As ought to be evident, Jefferson was not a Christian by any traditional definition. He would never have described himself as a Southern Baptist fundamentalist or as a member of the late Moral Majority. Deists like Jefferson and Thomas Paine (whose writings played a significant role in the founding of our nation) were often bitterly outspoken against the authority of the Bible. In fact, there could hardly be a more caustic rejection of Christianity than this, contained in Paine's *The Age of Reason:*

> It is certain that what is called the Christian system of faith, including in it the whimsical account of the creation; the strange story of Eve, the snake, and the apple; the amphibious idea of a man-god; the corporeal idea of the death of a god; the mythological idea of a family of gods, and the Christian system of arithmetic that three are one and one is three, are all irreconcilable, not only to the divine gift of reason that God has given to man, but to the knowledge that man gains of the power and wisdom of God by the aid of the sciences, and by studying the structure of the universe that God has made.

A Jerry Falwell, Pat Robertson, or Billy Graham he was not! Yet Paine's categorical rejection of Christianity and biblical revelation must not cloud the force of his underlying belief in creation. It was not the fact of creation that Paine questioned, but what he took to be a "whimsical account" of that creation. By use of "the divine gift of reason that God has given to man," Paine had no doubt but that we are all part of a "universe that God has made."

It is possible, of course, that Charles Darwin might have changed Paine's mind 65 years later, when he published *Origin of Species.* Darwin's scientific bent certainly would have coincided with Paine's own deist perspective. It is even possible that Darwinism might be the reason we no longer see many deists around. (Darwin's personal ambivalence about God ultimately yielded to a confirmed agnosticism.) But Paine's Darwinian conversion is not altogether a foregone conclusion. Paine was fiercely convinced of an intelligent, purposeful First Cause, who had brought order and meaning into existence by his eternal power:

> Everything we behold carries in itself the internal evidence that it did not make itself. Every man is an evidence to himself that

he did not make himself; neither could his father make himself, nor his grandfather, nor any of his race; neither could any tree, plant, or animal make itself; and it is the conviction arising from this evidence that carries us on, as it were, by necessity, to the belief of a first cause eternally existing, of a nature totally different to any material existence we know of, and by the power of which all things exist; and this first cause, man calls God.[4]

Creation is Not Just Bible-thumping

Of one thing we can be certain. Paine would not have looked kindly upon efforts by the American Civil Liberties Union to exclude any mention in public schools of the Creator to whom he and Jefferson attributed the very source of civil liberties. (Should we expect the Declaration of Independence to be the next target for exclusion from the classroom?)

One can almost see Paine's look of incredulity if he were to read the following statement from People for the American Way's spokesman, Michael Hudson, in a *Los Angeles Times* article. "Science is science and faith is faith," says Hudson superciliously,[5] as if to suggest that creation can only be accepted by blind religious faith. As if to suggest that only mindless Bible-thumpers could possibly object to evolution.

Unfortunately, Justice Brennan's opinion in *Edwards v. Aguillard* makes the same mistake, wrongly attributing creation exclusively to a *"religious viewpoint* [my emphasis] that a supernatural being created humankind." It is the same story from the federal judge who struck down Arkansas' "equal treatment" statute. "The facts that creation science is inspired by the Book of Genesis and that [the words of the statute are] consistent with a literal interpretation of Genesis leave no doubt that a major effect of the Act is the advancement of particular religious beliefs," said the judge.[6]

How shallow (or patently anti-religious) can it get? Neither the backers' motives nor any parallel references in someone's sacred scriptures ought to be relevant. Employing the same logic the judge used would mean the invalidation of all murder laws, because many, if not most, of the legislators who passed the laws were religious folk, and the statutory prohibitions coincide neatly with the Bible's "Thou shalt not kill."[7]

It is also worth mentioning that "the advancement of particular religious beliefs," to use the judge's phrase, is not limited to the Christian faith, as he apparently assumes. Creation thinking and its potential contribution to the advancement of religion could apply just as well to the Jewish and

Muslim faiths, which draw from common textual roots including the Book of Genesis. In fact, Genesis was the first book of the Jewish Pentateuch centuries before it became a part of the "Christian" Bible.

Giving emphasis to the previous chapter, the most pernicious fallacy of the judge's ruling—and indeed of the liberal-Left's anti-creation position in general—is the notion that creation is inspired only by the Book of Genesis, without which no one would ever have conjured up such a wild idea. With that foolish notion, certainly Jefferson and Paine would have sharply disagreed.

Not at all a believer in divine revelation, much less in the opening chapters of Genesis, Thomas Paine nevertheless adamantly insisted that creation was the only reasonable conclusion a person could draw regarding the origin of the universe. From reading Paine's works, you get the feeling that he would find Stephen Jay Gould's "lottery theory" to be just so much scientific sophistry. Paine more likely would agree with Einstein's elegant statement that "the most incomprehensible thing about the universe is that it is comprehensible." The God of deism was a God of order, not of chaos.

Given their rationalistic perspective, the jury is still out on whether Darwin might have convinced Paine and Jefferson to throw away their reasoned conviction that our universe, together with immutable principles of morality and justice which give rise to human rights, is the result of a purposeful, intelligent Creator. What we hear from Thomas Paine is nothing but derision at the suggestion by today's secularists that the *Creator* referred to in the Declaration of Independence is merely a euphemism:

> Do we not see a fair creation prepared to receive us the instant we were born—a world furnished to our hands that cost us nothing? Is it we that light up the sun, that pour down the rain, and fill the earth with abundance? Whether we sleep or wake, the vast machinery of the universe still goes on. Are these things, and the blessings which they indicate in future, nothing to us?...Or is the gloomy pride of man become so intolerable that nothing can flatter it but a sacrifice of the Creator?[8]

What a telling indictment: Intellectual pride that demands the death of a Creator in order to keep itself alive!

Today's intellectual elite who believe with such condescending self-assurance that the very idea of creation is unworthy of a reasoned mind would do well to listen again closely to a fellow civil libertarian. In the middle of his famed treatise, the *Age of Reason*—a classic defense of Enlightenment's scientific rationalism—Paine pauses to insert Addison's famous verse:

> The spacious firmament on high,
> With all the blue ethereal sky,
> And spangled heavens, a shining frame,
> Their great original proclaim.
> The unwearied sun, from day to day,
> Does his Creator's power display,
> And publishes to every land
> The work of an Almighty hand.
>
> Soon as the evening shades prevail
> The moon takes up the wondrous tale,
> And nightly to the listening earth
> Repeats the story of her birth;
> Whilst all the stars that round her burn,
> And all the planets in their turn,
> Confirm the tidings as they roll
> And spread the truth from pole to pole.
>
> What though in solemn silence all
> Move round the dark terrestrial ball?
> What though nor real voice, nor sound,
> Amidst their radiant orbs be found?
> In reason's ear they all rejoice,
> And utter forth a glorious voice;
> Forever singing as they shine,
> THE HAND THAT MADE US IS DIVINE.

"What more does man want to know" asks Paine, "than that the hand or power that made these things is divine, is omnipotent? Let him believe this with the force it is impossible to repel, if he permits his reason to act, and his rule of moral life will follow course."[9]

No Civil Liberties in the Jungle

It is not only morality that is inextricably tied to one's view of origins. Compare also the civil libertarian implications that suggest themselves respectively from Jefferson's *"created equally"* and Darwin's *"survival of the fittest."* Which suggests a greater commitment to human rights? Which do we know had greater appeal to Adolf Hitler?

If you remain unconvinced about the tie between the Creator and our basic human rights, no better case has been made than in an article by Anselm Atkins ("Human Rights Are Cultural Artifacts") in The *Humanist*:

> Those of us who deny that we were created by any creator are drawn ineluctably to the conclusion that no naturally endowed rights exist.
>
> It is curious that Ayn Rand, a committed atheist, did in fact believe in natural rights—such as the "right to life." In this, she was inconsistent. Perhaps her trouble was that, like so many other philosophers, she failed to take seriously the implications of our evolved biological condition: that, at first, there was mute mud and nothing else; then our species, among others; and, last of all, the things we invented (the totality of culture).
>
> Like any educated person...Rand "believed in evolution," but it hardly influenced her thinking....If, on the other hand, Rand had made evolutionary biology the cornerstone of her philosophical anthropology, she might have avoided this contradictory position.[10]

Atkins rightly points us to the philosophical dilemma in which we have indulged for over a century. We want all the natural human rights which we have come to enjoy, without acknowledging the Creator by whom they are bestowed.

Again, Atkins brings us to the harsh reality of what happens to justice and morality when we divorce ourselves from the notion of a Creator:

> Rights make no sense in nature. There are simply biological entities doing what they must do, wanting what they must want, and getting what they can get—living by hook or by crook and then dying. Humanity is part of this.[11]

Where there is a fundamental belief in chance origins, we may *choose* to act more nobly than Atkins pictures us acting (especially in a society which maintains a Judeo-Christian, Creator-affirming framework), but we are not inherently *encouraged* to live nobly. Nor, more importantly, can we demand our "rights"—whether it be the "right to life" or the "right to reproductive choice." Without a Creator, there are no rights.

If Anselm Atkins is right, that "we add 'rights' to our social expectations as new desires are felt and better goals envisioned," then he is also right in recognizing that "The guarantor of our social rights is the society in which we happen to live."[12] No better proof of this can be found than in *Roe v. Wade*, in which an entirely new "right" was invented, and in the subsequent *Webster* decision, in which that "right" was then limited. The Court gives, and the Court takes away. If a Court is all there is, then we all have a right to be worried.

The Morals of Monkeys?

Why was it so important for Paine and Jefferson to recite their personal belief in creation? Why did they feel compelled to join together, rather than separate, faith and state by explicitly referring to the Creator in the Declaration of Independence? As Paine saw it, our rule of moral life flows as a matter of course from how we view our origins.

If he was right about that, it is not just a coincidence that the ACLU, which has been chiefly responsible for the censorship of creation teaching in our public schools, has also associated itself with prostitution, homosexual behavior, drug use, pornography, and abortion—definitive immorality which the Founders would have found repulsive.

Nor can the ACLU absolve itself from this unholy alliance by treating such evils merely as abstract civil libertarian issues. Facilitating immoral causes is not the same as saying, for instance, that you personally disagree with Communism, but will defend another's right to express a belief in it. That is true civil libertarianism. Whatever else you might think about Communism, it is not inherently immoral. By contrast, nothing in civil libertarianism compels the defense of immorality—only a *betrayal* of genuine libertarianism by liberal-Leftist politics masquerading as the genuine article.

The tie between one's position on various moral issues and his or her view of origins is, if not directly causal, at the very least highly suspicious. In my Law and Morality seminar each year, for example, a survey of upper-class law students has consistently shown an almost perfect correlation between how a student feels about various "hot button" moral issues (like abortion, prostitution, and pornography) and the student's belief in either evolution or creation.

On one moral issue after another, those students who believe in creation are polls apart in the extreme from those who believe in evolution.

(Interestingly, those students who indicate a belief in "theistic evolution"—that shadowy halfway house between evolution and creation—are more ambivalent in their responses to moral issues as well.)[13]

Perhaps more graphic proof of the evolution-morals linkage is supplied to us by the growing field of evolutionary psychology. In his recent *Time* article, "Our Cheating Hearts,"[14] Robert Wright reports that evidence of pair-bonding among human beings has been called into question due to recent studies which show that, contrary to conventional wisdom, most bird species are not truly monogamous. The point? "According to evolutionary psychology, it is 'natural' for both men and women—at some times, under some circumstances—to commit adultery...." Our daily, ever shifting attitudes toward a spouse "are the handiwork of natural selection that remain with us today because in the past they led to behaviors that helped spread genes."

What else is one to conclude from this evolution-based study of marital morality, but that "lifelong monogamous devotion just isn't natural...." Lacking any higher view of moral predicates, evolutionary psychologists can only suggest that the natural tendency to marital unfaithfulness might be decreased if there is income redistribution. That's right—*income redistribution*. When one observes the sex lives of apes and understands the dynamics of hunter-gatherer villages, it becomes clear that economic disparity, not lust, is at the heart of marital infidelity!

Call it the New Morality. Seen in the squinting prehistoric light of an evolutionary mist, we humans can be excused for having the morals of a chimp.

Given this alarming connection between evolutionary thinking and current discussions of morality, one is prompted to temper even William Bennett's good advice regarding the inculcation of values in America's younger students. As a part of his commendable efforts to instill a sense of virtue in the young, Bennett wants to make sure that they learn about such basic values as honesty, courtesy, respect, courage, and persistence. With that goal in mind, Bennett suggests that, "We need not get into issues like nuclear war, abortion, creationism, or euthanasia."[15]

Bennett is right, of course, that children can be taught values at a very early age without understanding the theoretical framework from which those values are derived. But it is surprising how early they begin to formulate their own personal paradigm, including notions about God and even afterlife. For that reason, the idea of creation is in a different category from such controversial issues as abortion, euthanasia, and nuclear war. In contrast to those specific moral questions, a child's elementary understanding of origins becomes the foundational blackboard on which all other lessons are learned.

Encouraging fundamental moral values without overly taxing formative minds with some of the more frustratingly nuanced moral issues of the day is certainly wise. But hardly anything could be more palatably introduced to young children than the story of Creation. Naturally, that thought sends cold chills down the spines of those who reject creation. What they conveniently forget, of course, is that, from the earliest children's books onward, *evolution* is being indelibly impressed upon children's minds.

The question, then, is not whether school children should be taught about origins. They already are. The only question is whether they will be presented with an origins framework that encourages the learning of moral values, or whether the framework they are being presented with is actually inimical to good morals.

The Better Days of Civil Rights

The ACLU has not always indulged in morally-debased policies. Perhaps its finest hour was its leadership of the movement for racial equality. In that hour, it proudly aligned itself with black churches and religious leaders who fully understood that racial equality stems directly from the hand of a Creator who has made all mankind equal, regardless of color.

That is precisely why the civil rights movement in the fifties and sixties was blessed with such obvious legitimacy. It resonated with a moral justification that transcended any compelling force which could have been mustered by merely secular egalitarianism. It recognized, without the slightest hint of embarrassment, a hierarchy of moral authority seated at the throne of a Creator God. Indeed, its spiritual predicate was that God purposely created us—every one of us, whatever our pigmentation—and that, therefore, we are compelled to do the work of God in the matter of racial justice.

Martin Luther King's appeal in his famous "I Have a Dream" speech was to an equality based upon the literal fact that, as the Creator's offspring, we are all "God's children." Don't think for even a moment that his reference to our being "God's children" was merely religious window dressing for an otherwise secular message. King knew all too well that, without the moral high ground of Creation assumptions, the campaign against racial discrimination would be reduced to nothing more than majority vote. In such a contest, there are no prizes for guessing who would have lost.

Minority rights are not born of democratic goodwill; nor some kind of imagined "social contract;" nor, certainly, of evolution's survival of the fittest. Rather, minority rights are compelled by an acknowledgement that, even if we are in the majority, we are still our brother's keeper.[16]

The ACLU cannot continue to discriminate wrongly between the sacred and the secular without almost certainly failing to distinguish correctly between moral and amoral campaigns against discrimination. Segregating the secular from the sacred in a political sense is as misguided as segregating the races. Sadly, it is a downward path that quickly leads from the high ground of racial justice to the gutter of gay rights legislation, where it ends up defending nothing more noble than the repugnant practice of sexual perversion.

Not Just a Classroom Controversy

Beginning with the *Scopes* trial in the previous chapter, we have traced the wider implications of creation and evolution thinking, particularly as it influences issues of morality and civil libertarianism. Jefferson and Paine would remind their fellow civil libertarians even today that the orderliness in the vast expanse of the universe fairly shouts of a Creator—a Creator whose moral order is equally as evident. It is to that very moral order that the American Civil Liberties Union has made its most noble appeals.

Why then does the ACLU fight against its nobler instincts? Why does it choose to debase its commitment to human rights by undermining the very Source of those rights? And why is it so intent on censoring legitimate dialogue regarding origins?

When you think about the moral and civil libertarian repercussions, one could well conclude that the ACLU's liberal-Leftist politics these days have not evolved just from a monkey, but from a serpent.

III

Getting to the Heart of the Cultural War

CHAPTER 15

The Schizophrenic Morality of Civil Liberties

"THE DEVIL MAY ALSO MAKE USE OF MORALITY."
KARL BARTH

The ACLU's finest hour was its role in the crusade for racial equality in the civil rights '60s. It did what the conservative/religious Right should have done, but didn't. It appealed to moral authority and to overtly-religious references in order to bring America's collective conscience to account. Whether or not the ACLU would be willing to admit it, civil rights legislation also dramatically demonstrated that—contrary to rumor—morality can indeed be legislated. When it came to racial justice, the ACLU had no hesitancy in imposing its morality on many who violently opposed integration.

Unfortunately, the ACLU lives in a world of moral schizophrenia. For example, at one extreme it insists that society has no right to impose moral standards upon those who would engage in homosexual activity. Yet, at the opposite extreme, it makes moral demands upon society not to discriminate against homosexuals. Morality is a friend when it aids the cause, an enemy when it gets in the way. But, the ACLU can't have it both ways. If society has the moral force to impose its will with regard to racial equality, then it has the moral force to criminalize sodomy, ban abortions, or prosecute for pornography.

Morality, like truth, demands consistency. If the ACLU continues to indulge in moral schizophrenia, it cannot help but forfeit the moral force with which it defends civil liberties.

The Schizophrenic Morality of Civil Liberties

T here are times when the ACLU will actually deign to use the word *morality*. Hardly ever does the ACLU wish to dignify something so principled as civil liberties with something so relative (for them) as morality, but there are times when morality is thought to be helpful to the cause and given temporary license.

The prime example, of course, was when civil libertarians made overt appeals to moral authority during the civil rights movement for racial equality. If the moral dimension was left in the dust as quickly as the ACLU thought it safe to do so, it nevertheless served a good purpose. When Martin Luther King, Jr. rested his case for desegregation on a firm moral base, there was nothing but "amen" from the ACLU chorus.

It should not be forgotten what King said in his stirring "Letter from Birmingham City Jail"—that "a just law is a man-made code that squares with the moral law or the law of God."[1] Whether the ACLU believed in the same "law of God" as Martin Luther King—or even fully appreciated what King meant by the phrase—the ACLU unquestionably understood what it meant to "have God on its side" during a battle for America's minds on so divisive a social issue. The ACLU's role in achieving integration was its finest hour, precisely because the ACLU was not ashamed in that instance to make a straightforward appeal to a higher law.

Anything short of an appeal to higher law likely would have failed. Especially in the South, integration was clearly not the will of the majority. In order to win the day against overwhelming odds, therefore, the ACLU had a timely, if anomalous, conversion to moral absolutes. From the moment of their conversion (however superficial), they ascended the mountain of righteousness from which their call for racial justice simply could not be denied.

Someone might cynically suggest that there was no "conversion" at all—not even temporarily—but that the movement's prophetic call for civic righteousness was merely a convenient vehicle for egalitarian secular ideology. Even so, says Yale's Stephen Carter, it "does not alter the plain historical truth that the movement itself represented a massive infusion of religious rhetoric into the public square."[2]

Ironically, the ACLU's victory over racial injustice was not a natural victory for an organization whose secularist philosophy was antagonistic to its claimed mission of moral uprightness. The victory over racial injustice would more naturally have belonged to those on the conservative-Right who lay claim to transcendent moral values based upon God, Creation, and divine revelation. But on the issue of race, those who by rights should have taken the moral high ground did not, and thereby forfeited any bragging rights—not to mention moral legitimacy—when they left it to secularist civil libertarians to lead the way.

This embarrassing episode probably explains more than anything else why there are many people today who no longer trust conservatives or, more especially, the religious-Right. If nothing else, the mere appearance of a moral lapse opened the door for the liberal-Left to justify current racial policies (like affirmative action) which do not necessarily proceed from the same moral mountain top as desegregation itself. Consider, for example, President Clinton's response when asked about conservative legal activist Clint Bolick's criticisms of Deval Patrick, who had been nominated to head the Justice Department's civil rights division:

> I think this nomination may be about those groups and whether they're proceeding in good faith. And the truth is, a lot of those people are going to be exposed because they never believed in the civil rights laws, they never believed in equal opportunity, they never lifted a finger to give anybody of a

minority race a chance in this country.

If they attack his record, it means just exactly what we've all suspected all along—they don't give a riff about civil rights.[3]

Whether Clinton was right about Clint Bolick personally (and the evidence is that he was not), still, the conservative-Right became vulnerable when, in the civil rights '60s, it did not show the kind of moral leadership which would have been expected from people boldly proclaiming morality-based convictions.

That aside, Stephen Carter points us to two important comparisons between the ACLU-blessed civil rights movement and any number of ACLU-denounced positions taken today by the religious-Right. To set the scene, Carter observes that "there is little about the civil rights movement, other than the vital distinction in the ends that it sought, that makes it very different from the right-wing religious movements of the present day."[4] Furthermore, the leaders of the civil rights movement "spoke openly of the commands of God as a crucial basis for their public activism. They made no effort to disguise their true intention: to impose their religious morality on others."[5]

The first point, then, is that—as demonstrated by the civil rights movement itself—morality can be legislated. No, the law cannot force one to be a morally good person against his will, but it can punish him when he is morally bad. Or, as Martin Luther King put it, "The law could not make people love their neighbors, but it could stop their lynching them."[6]

Secondly, there is simply no question but that, as a leading force in the civil rights movement, the ACLU intentionally, forthrightly, and unashamedly imposed its own moral convictions about racial justice on those who strongly, and sometimes even violently, disagreed.

What the ACLU cannot seem to appreciate is that what it did in the civil rights movement is precisely what it condemns the religious-Right for trying to do in the pro-life movement: bringing moral force to bear on an issue of great social concern. In fact, Stephen Carter takes us back to King's statement about the primacy of moral law and reminds us that such classic natural law "could have been lifted, word for word, from the more recent pastoral letter of Roman Catholic bishops on abortion."[7]

Playing the Morality Trump Card

The civil rights movement is not the only occasion when the ACLU has dared to mention the word *morality*. You also see it crop up from time to time in the ACLU's Policy Guide. There is, for example, ACLU Policy 41 with its discussion of the circumstances under which the ACLU will represent those who might be arrested for acts of civil disobedience. "It should be understood," says the policy, "that nothing in this statement is intended to change the ACLU practice *on moral grounds* [emphasis added]...of urging authorities to extend leniency...."[8]

Morality is offered as the rationale for yet another policy (Policy 54), this time regarding labor unions: "*The principal moral justification* [emphasis added] of unions is that they introduce an element of democracy into the government of industry...."[9] This translates to say that the American Civil Liberties Union, as a union itself, owes its very existence to a moral right.

One of the most intriguing references to morality comes in ACLU Policy 123, regarding the war in Southeast Asia. In voicing its opposition to an officially undeclared war, the statement says that, "The ACLU recognizes that even a declaration of war would leave unresolved *moral* [emphasis added] and civil liberties questions inherent in this or any other war."[10] Note carefully that a distinction is made here between *civil liberties questions* and apparently quite separate moral questions—*moral questions* which are *inherent* in any war. In case there was ever any doubt about the ACLU's definition of "morality," its use of the word *inherent* certainly appears to indicate something more than mere "social-contract morality" and refer to that which legitimately could be construed as a universal higher law.

The appeal to moral grounds in these and other ACLU policies might lead one to believe that the ACLU would have much in common with moral appeals made by conservatives and the religious-Right. But nothing could be further from the truth, as we are reminded by ACLU biographer Samuel Walker. Referring to the conservative coalition, Walker says, "Televangelists led by Jerry Falwell carried their moralistic, anti-civil libertarian message into millions of homes every week."[11]

What are we being told here? That moral appeals are necessarily "anti-civil libertarian?" Or that the ACLU's anti-war, anti-racist policies are *not* "moralistic?"

What we are really being told is that civil libertarians can play the morality trump card whenever they feel a need to, but if anyone else dares to play it, they are threatening civil liberties, violating church-state separation, and generally acting in poor taste.

The Two Faces of Civil Libertarian Morality

By official ACLU policy, issues like war, racial justice, civil disobedience, and unions are very much within the province of overriding moral concerns—so much so that moral law (apparently easily recognized in each case) ought to be the controlling factor. In stark contrast, however, is the language of the ACLU's policy on abortion (Policy 263): "The Union itself offers no comment on the wisdom or the moral implications of abortion, believing that such judgments belong solely in the province of individual conscience and religion."[12]

It is here that the ACLU's attitude toward abortion and racial discrimination is most revealing. In the *Dredd Scott* case of 1857, African-Americans, like today's unborn, had been officially declared to be "non-persons," and therefore could be bought and sold as slaves. Equality and protection under law mean nothing when personhood itself is denied. Where would we be today if the ACLU had taken the same view of racial justice that it has regarding abortion, and blithely affirmed that discrimination belonged "solely in the province of individual conscience and religion?"

When individual conscience is allowed to be the test of personhood, discrimination and even death are no longer evil. At that point, it matters not whether it becomes officially sanctioned slavery or officially sanctioned abortion, or even—as in Nazi Germany—officially sanctioned ethnic cleansing.

The difference between racial discrimination and abortion is, of course, that combatting racial discrimination fits comfortably with the ACLU's egalitarian philosophy, whereas abortion pits the disenfranchised unborn child against the egalitarian feminist "rights" of the mother. In that pairing of interests, who will win is never in doubt.

Given the supremacy of egalitarian philosophy over any kind of higher-law morality, it is easy to see how playing the morality trump card is helpful to the cause of civil rights. When it comes to abortion, however, you can be sure that the morality trump card is stealthily kept in the hand as if it—like the unborn child—never existed.

It is here that we see the two faces of civil libertarian morality. One face (racial justice) is the face of absolute morality; the other (pro-choice abortion), the face of moral relativism. In the former case, legislation against the wishes of the majority is morally mandated. In the latter case, "We maintain that the penal sanctions of the state have no proper application to such matters."[13]

Would it help to resolve the inconsistency if all aborted babies were black? Would abortion then become a moral concern for the ACLU and thereby a civil liberties concern? (Many otherwise-pro-choice feminists have raised as a compelling moral concern the use of abortion for gender selection, particularly when little girl babies are typically being aborted in favor of little boy babies.)

Egalitarian morality is schizophrenic to the extreme—in fact, to *two* extremes: simultaneously *restrictive* of individual liberty (under penalty of law, you must not discriminate), and jealously *protective* of individual liberty (you have a "right to be let alone" when it comes to other moral behavior). Or, put another way: at one and the same time, there is both extreme moralism and extreme moral relativism.

Judge Robert Bork reckons that, "If one had to choose one organization to illustrate this feature of modern left-liberal culture, it would be the American Civil Liberties Union."[14] Why? Because "the ACLU favors intrusive governmental action in the service of morality in some areas but insists that the Constitution mandates moral relativism in others."[15]

> As a friend of mine put it, "Whether the issue be racial balance in schools, seat belts on autos, or the rules for women's basketball in Iowa, the desires of the people to be affected are given little or no weight by the intellectual class."
>
> These are clearly coercions of individuals in order to implement a particular morality. Yet this same segment of our culture emphatically denies the right of majorities to regulate abortion, homosexual conduct, pornography, or even the use of narcotics in the home. On the one hand, there appears to be a degree of morality so severe that it amounts to moralism, and, on the other, a hostility to morality so strong that it amounts to moral relativism."[16]

When the ACLU seems to act inconsistently regarding the weight to be given to morality, it merely reflects the ACLU's commitment, not to morality, but first and foremost to egalitarianism. Since egalitarianism *is* the ACLU's morality, the obvious corollary is that "Law may not be used...to enforce moral standards that are not egalitarian."[17] By current civil libertarian definition, *that* would be immoral!

The problem facing an egalitarian organization like the ACLU is how it can expect to maintain two mutually-contradictory positions regarding morality. If moral relativity reigns supreme, how can one ever legitimately invoke the power of moral authority? Each time the ACLU and the liberal-Left condemn the "moralistic" religious-Right, they take another step down from the moral high ground on any issue about which they feel strongly enough to demand coercive laws.

If, as a matter of civil libertarian morality, the government cannot prohibit private homosexual conduct, for example, by what moral authority may the government prohibit discrimination against practicing homosexuals? Moral relativism in the first instance (homosexual conduct) must undergo a rather daunting metamorphosis in order to have any moral force at all in the second instance (discrimination based on sexual orientation).

An organization that seeks implementation of righteous social policies, yet facilitates unrighteous private morality, undermines any hope it might have of achieving the former. Morality is a seamless garment. Pull one thread, and the whole garment falls apart.

The ACLU's hypocrisy regarding the morality issue is never more evident than when one considers the ACLU's schizophrenic abortion policy. The woman's right to choose an abortion—being a question of private morals—is a matter of relative morality for her alone to decide. But when it comes to forcing society to accept, condone, and, in some instances, even pay for the abortion the woman has chosen, then social policy becomes a matter of absolute morality not to be questioned. Talk about having your cake and eating it too....

If someone were to suggest that there is a distinction to be drawn between social policy and private morality, there is nevertheless a persistent problem. With moral relativism inevitably comes the dethroning of moral authority, leaving only the autonomous, unaccountable Self in its wake. With the enthronement of the autonomous Self inevitably comes the collective society of autonomous Selves—or, ultimately, moral anarchy. When there is free rein in the realm of private morality, who, or what, is left to establish the moral order for society at large? (The answer, in case you missed it, is either a dictator or a totalitarian state.)

This is not to say that all private morality is necessarily of interest to the state. (A state may choose not to criminalize adultery, or private homosexual behavior, for example.) What it does mean, however, is that if the state is *forbidden* to impose a particular morality in the realm of private morals, then by the same token the state would be forbidden to impose a particular morality in the realm of public policy. (Morality itself demands equal protection.) Or, to turn it around, if the state is permitted to impose a particular (liberal) morality in the realm of public policy, then by the same token the state has an equal right to impose a particular (conservative) morality in the realm of private morals.

Relative Morality is No Morality

Despite the occasional appeal to moral authority, the truth is that, except where convenient or necessary, transcendent morality is an anathema to many of today's civil libertarians. In fact, in the textbooks of the liberal-Left, there is no basis for even saying that "the truth is...." At least, not capital-T, absolute Truth.

Certainly, one dare not introduce any silly notions of transcendent truth in the public classroom. That would violate ACLU Policy 60, dealing with academic freedom: "In the classroom, a teacher should promote an atmosphere of free inquiry. This should include discussion of controversial issues without the assumption that they are settled in advance or that there is only one 'right' answer in matters of dispute."[18]

Don't expect the intent of this policy to include a free-wheeling discussion of both evolution and creation. That kind of intellectual honesty would suggest that there is serious debate over which of the two explanations is the "right" answer. Rather, limit discussion to only one of those two alternatives (evolution), as if the question of origins were so settled in advance that it is no longer a controversial issue, and you can avoid a search for the truth altogether.

That done, what the ACLU demands in the classroom is that—apart from elementary math—there is no such thing as only one "right" answer. Hung on the classroom wall where the Ten Commandments used to be are now the "Ten Suggestions of Moral Relativism." For a generation now, truth has been deposited in the waste can of a vacuous educational theory called "values clarification."

Relative truth, like relative morality, should not be of concern simply to the conservative-Right. The easy dismissal of absolute, ultimate truth has always been risky business for civil libertarians committed to the defense of "rights." After all, "rights" must be founded upon some kind of universal assumption; otherwise there is no compelling argument other than a frightening "might makes right." (Or, as nineteenth century philosopher Friedrich Nietzsche put it, "the will to power.")

By contrast, when the Declaration of Independence spoke of rights, it laid down the indispensable predicate that "We hold these *truths* to be self-evident." What could be more fundamental to civil libertarianism than that truth and freedom are inseparable Siamese twins? (This, incidentally, is the *real* reason why the Founders insisted upon guaranteeing free speech. It was not so that we might have some sacred right to peddle smut, but that we could openly pursue truth in the maintenance of freedom.)

In the words of Pope John Paul II (from his recent encyclical *Veritatis Splendor*), "Authentic freedom is ordered to truth"—as in, "You shall know the truth, and the truth will make you free."[19] But here, all of a sudden, we have confirmed the worst fears of secularist civil libertarians. In one sentence, we have introduced, not only the words of a leading religious figure, but also the words of holy Scripture—both taboo in today's social discourse whenever any connection, however tenuous, can be made with governmental action.

If we must talk about values and morality, says the liberal-Left, let it be free of religious influence—particularly in the halls of government, the media, and the public classroom. But as British columnist Clifford Longley points out, "We are about to discover that you cannot just pluck values from thin air. The very idea of a value, hanging there isolated from any foundation in philosophy or theology, is problematical or just ridiculous. There is almost nowhere else to look for such things than in religious tradition."[20] In short, sustained social morality apart from acknowledgement of religion is mere wishful thinking.

A perfect example comes from our British neighbors across the Atlantic. In the wake of a recent series of scandals by public leaders in Britain who had engaged in extra-marital affairs, *Sunday Times* journalist Janet Daley asked, "Why are we so confused about adultery?" Her answer calls for some serious soul-searching: "We want fixed moral points, but we have dismantled the dominion of religion and historical tradition. You cannot get sanctity into the social code by wishing for it."[21]

As Britain's sex scandals remind us, there is often a very practical tie between private morality and public policy. The British are still reeling from revelations of sexual impropriety on the part of one governmental official after another. Because of persistent private immorality, public confidence in the democratic process has steadily eroded. Even where the "indiscretion" is private, when it finally becomes public, whole nations can be caught in a compromising position.

The reality of that truth, along with mounting evidence of widespread social decay, is causing many in Britain to question the wisdom of a whole generation which was almost consciously reared to reject the strictures of formal religion. It is instructive to note, in this regard, that the current reassessment of private and public values is taking place without pressure from anything closely akin to America's religious-Right. In fact, it is the traditional left-wing Labour Party itself that has now taken up the banner of family values and personal responsibility.

Back in the States, Brigitte and Peter Berger see the problem in terms of an inexorable degeneration of morality where there is a decline of faith— that without a religious foundation, "morality is bound to lapse into implausibility."[22] That is because only religion deals with the kind of transcendent higher law that can provide the basis for any universally recognizable standard to which one might wish to appeal.

The Luxury of Being Liberal

We have seen it before. As long as religious influence continues, the liberal-Left has the luxury of dismissing any such faith-based nonsense. But it is all the difference between a generation consciously rooted in truth claims and moral premises, and a later generation which believes that it can remain morally viable without any attachment to outdated truth assumptions. Such a "cut-flower generation" (to use Elton Trueblood's elegant phrase) cannot long survive apart from its roots.

Theologian and social critic Richard John Neuhaus, author of *The Naked Public Square*, underscores this special luxury afforded only to the liberal set: "To be progressive was to rebel against an assumed moral establishment, while continuing to assume that that establishment would provide the habits of virtue that would prevent liberation from turning into libertinism."[23] As he reminds us, the progressive thinkers of the 1960s were people who were "born into a very Protestant society and spent a lifetime drawing on its taken-for-granted moral capital."[24]

The philosophical luxury of which Neuhaus speaks is very much like the ACLU's altogether convenient policy against airport searches. While nobody likes to get frisked, even by an impersonal machine, few people in today's climate of terrorist atrocities would be eager to see airport screening eliminated. (If you're lucky, the passenger sitting next to you is an ACLU lawyer working on a brief demanding greater civil liberties. If you're not, you may be seated next to a crazed suicide bomber.)

As long as the rest of society wisely refuses to accept the ACLU's policy against airport security screening, then the ACLU can safely pontificate to its heart's content about the dangers of infringing on civil liberties in airports. Likewise, as long as the rest of society wisely refuses to go along with the ACLU's liberal-Left amoral philosophy, then the ACLU can safely pontificate about the dangers of traditional family values, morality-based legislation, and seeping gaps in the "wall of separation." But take away traditional family values, morality-based legislation, and the influence of organized religion, and what you will have is a societal Lockerbie disaster waiting to happen.

Which brings us back to the ACLU lawyer busily at work next to you on the plane. You might just want to lean over and suggest to your fellow passenger that 37,000 feet up would be a very good place to re-draft the ACLU's airport screening policy, along with any number of other equally wrong-headed ACLU policies. Because they fail to recognize the compelling moral issues involved, many ACLU policies promise on a broader scope to be equally disastrous.

CHAPTER 16

Speaking Frankly About Religious Faith

"THE BIBLE IS NOTHING BUT A SUCCESSION OF CIVIL RIGHTS STRUGGLES
BY THE JEWISH PEOPLE AGAINST THEIR OPPRESSORS."

JESSE JACKSON

For an organization like the ACLU to be seen as a secularist organization means that its members are, by and large, secularists. It doesn't mean that they don't attend church or synagogue, or are lacking in personal morals. Nor does it necessarily mean that individual members would think of themselves, or refer to themselves, as secularists. They may even see themselves as Christians or Jews. What it does mean, is that in many important ways they think differently and have markedly different world views from those who are not secularists. Generally speaking, members of the ACLU operate on different cultural and philosophical assumptions than do, for example, supporters of the Christian Coalition.

If we are ever going to understand each other, we must speak more frankly about our religious beliefs, or perhaps our non-religious beliefs. It is no coincidence that there are few practicing Catholics or fewer still (if any) fundamentalist Christians in the ACLU. The culture wars are mostly wars between the devoutly religious Right and the secular religious Left. Until we understand the battle between the secular and the sacred, debates over civil liberties are exercises in futility.

The defense of civil liberties is unquestionably a righteous cause. Justice was God's idea. But secularist Christians and Jews in today's ACLU have too often reduced God's justice to a moral abomination. The time has come to go back up the mountain.

Speaking Frankly About Religious Faith

W e come now to an area of the social psyche which is almost forbidden to touch. It's too controversial and too sensitive. Though it
needn't be the case—and certainly shouldn't be—it bears all the
hallmarks of group slander. So we tend to avoid it, as if the Emperor were
truly *not* naked.

Personal religious beliefs are the issue here. On one hand, certainly,
there is no secret about *who* is *who* and *what* is *what,* religiously-speaking.
But, on the other hand, there is an unwritten rule that one should not delve
too deeply into the connection between a person's religious beliefs and his
or her sense of morals, or perhaps between a *lack* of religious conviction and
how that might affect one's judgment on various moral issues.

ACLU biographer Samuel Walker issues an intriguing invitation to
take a closer look at such connections when he includes religious beliefs in
his encyclopedic history of the ACLU. He tells us, for example, that the
ACLU's predecessor—the National Civil Liberties Bureau—had an executive
committee composed of three groups: social reformers, conservative
lawyers, and "Protestant clergy, inspired by the reform ideas of the social
gospel."[1] Among those in the last category were: Presbyterian Norman
Thomas, Unitarian John Haynes Holmes, and Union Theological Seminary
professor Harry F. Ward. Of these, Walker says:

The wartime crisis shattered their old faith and pushed them toward a secular, civil libertarian outlook: Thomas abandoned religion for the Socialist party. Holmes severed his formal ties with Unitarianism, renamed his church the Community church, and transformed it into a nonsectarian community center. Ward eventually became a Marxist.[2]

Look at the juxtaposition between their "old faith" and their new "secular, civil libertarian outlook." Even what might be considered more liberal religious beliefs are significantly distanced from secular libertarian beliefs. Religious faith and secularist philosophy are simply not a natural mix.

This explains in great measure the ACLU's mostly anti-religious stance and its obsession with the Establishment Clause. "Much of the left-liberal elite," says William Bennett, "despise traditional religious beliefs (although they can be very sympathetic to religion when left-wing groups, such as the National Council of Churches, speak for it). The elite generally take a religious position seriously only when it accords with their ideology—for example, promoting 'liberation theology.' But in general they are profoundly uncomfortable with religious institutions and the traditional values they embody."[3]

The natural antagonism between religion and secularism also undoubtedly explains why there were no practicing Catholics on the ACLU's board or staff in the 1950s when the church-state controversy focused primarily on the Roman Catholic church relative to parochial schools, censorship, and abortion.[4]

It further explains why issues like abortion and pornography continue to be hot-button issues for the ACLU. Not only are such issues of intrinsic interest to the ACLU for what they will or will not permit, but they are also highly symbolic of the greater spiritual battle between religion and non-religion; or, if you prefer, between the sacred and the secular.

When a new wave of civil libertarians came onto the scene in the late '50s and early '60s, their secularist attack focused on issues like public school prayers and Bible readings, marking a shift in which the antagonists were no longer primarily Roman Catholics, but fundamentalist Protestants. Yet, little had changed in essence. The issue was still faith versus non-faith, or, to be more precise, faith in transcendent higher-law morality versus faith in a secularist moral relativity.

On one level, the culture war is being fought, not between religion and non-religion, but—as surely as it ever was in Northern Ireland, or Pakistan, or the Sudan—between one religion and another. For all the discomfort elitist civil libertarians typically feel for religion, civil libertarianism itself becomes for them a kind of substitute religion.

It is not simply James M. Barrie's observation that "one's religion is whatever he is most interested in."[5] It goes much deeper, to the level of philosophical commitment and evangelistic fervor. As an insider, Samuel Walker explains it this way:

> The sheer excitement of being on the frontier of social change, combating intolerance, fighting for ideals, and eventually creating new law was one of the keys to the ACLU's longevity and its ability to attract new talent with each passing generation. For many, civil liberties became the equivalent of a secular religion—a set of core principles that gave meaning to their lives.[6]

For many of the older members of the First Church of Civil Liberties, the civil rights movement was the baptism of their new found faith. Says Charles Sykes, "The movement would be the defining moment in their lives, indelibly shaping their view of morality and justice because it provided *something* to believe in."[7]

Born-again civil libertarians do not *disbelieve*. Everyone believes in something, and that becomes their faith. But the secularist dogma believed by most of today's civil libertarians couldn't be further removed from traditional Judeo-Christian doctrine, nor could their moral creed be more distinct. (That's *moral creed*—not to be confused with *personal moral standards*, which, as explained previously by the phrase "cut-flower generation," may be entirely consistent with the prevailing moral values of a predominantly Judeo-Christian culture.)

Is There a Judeo-Christian Morality?

At this point the discussion gets extremely sensitive. One can safely speak all day about the connection between political conservatives and "Bible-belt fundamentalists," but the mere mention of the liberal-Left and a "Jewish connection" has many folks diving for cover. So perhaps the best way to broach the subject is to let Stephen Carter comment on the phrase "Judeo-Christian." In as artful a way as the ticklish Jewish-Christian issue has ever been explored, Carter first takes his readers (in *The Culture of Disbelief*, pp. 85-90) to Mississippi Governor Kirk Fordice's controversial statement that "America is a 'Christian nation'"—spoken to a conference shortly after the stormy 1992 Republican presidential convention.

That the statement should be the least bit controversial to begin with is amazing enough, given the historical usage of that phrase and its affirmation in one legal case after another, all the way up to the Supreme Court. To say that America is a Christian nation is not simply to count heads, nor to exclude other faiths of any stripe which are adhered to by millions of Americans. It is merely a recognition of a cultural heritage (from Christmas to the Pilgrim fathers) which is uniquely Christian.

Theologically, says Carter, it is both right and wrong to speak of a combined Judeo-Christian heritage. Coming from shared historical roots and common Scriptures (at least in part), there are clearly many similarities between Jewish and Christian dogma. But one would be foolish to suggest that Jews and Christians have precisely the same view of the nature of God, or even come anywhere close in their understanding of the Messiah—that central point of contention which most divides the two religions.

These obvious differences undoubtedly prompted sociology professor John Murray Cuddihy to dismiss the idea of a comprehensively shared tradition, saying, "The more orthodox a Jew is and the more orthodox a Christian is, the more likely they are to say, 'To hell with the Judeo-Christian tradition.'"[8]

Talmudic scholar Jacob Neusner agrees. Reflecting back on Governor Fordice's supposed gaffe, Professor Neusner told *Newsweek* that, "Fordice erred politically by failing to send out the proper signal....But theologically and historically, there is no such thing as the Judeo-Christian tradition. It's a secular myth favored by people who are not really believers themselves."[9]

Keep carefully in mind Cuddihy's use of the word *orthodox* relative to both Christians and Jews; and revisit Neusner's comment that the Judeo-Christian tradition is a *secular myth* perpetuated by those who are *not really believers themselves*. Appreciating what lies behind those two observations is imperative to understanding why it is that, even when we move from complex theology to the more basic moral assumptions, there is still no necessary cohesion between Jewish and Christian perspectives.

In fact, as Stephen Carter points out, "On many of the nation's most searing contemporary moral disputes, the gap between Jewish Americans and white Protestant evangelicals...is quite striking."[10] (He goes on to cite, by way of example, significant statistical disparity on the issues of gender roles and abortion.)

How do Jews and Christians move from a shared reverence for the Ten Commandments to a wide disparity on many of today's hot-button moral issues? The clue provided by Cuddihy and Neusner is that we are no longer talking about orthodox Jews and Christians, but secular non-believers who, for a variety of reasons (mostly cultural), nevertheless identify themselves as either Jewish or Christian.

Perhaps Jonathan Miller's wry comment is instructive: "I'm not really a Jew; just Jew-ish, not the whole hog."[11] As Miller's flippant self-analysis suggests in a more serious vein, there is as much distance between a cultural Jew and a religious Jew as there is between a nominal Christian and a devout Christian. And, if a religious Jew and a devout Christian indeed have much in common morally speaking, so, too, do nominal Christians and cultural Jews. What separates cultural Jews and Christians from devout Jews and Christians is not theology, but the theology-free secular mindset which also forms the core doctrine of liberal-Left civil libertarianism.

At stake in the cultural war, then, are two views of the moral order—each worlds apart. Depending upon how it might be defined or understood, each view could be described as "Judeo-Christian." As traditionally defined and understood, the inclusive phrase "Judeo-Christian" refers to a heritage recognizing a Creator God who has established a universal, transcendent moral order in the world, to which each man and woman will be held accountable in the Final Judgment. By contrast, a more modern usage of "Judeo-Christian" may be nothing more than a catch-phrase for a naturalistic secularism that scarcely gives credence to notions of God, universal moral order, and Final Judgment.

Today's civil libertarian secularists include cultural Jews who have moved so far away from a kosher faith that they can no longer distinguish *clean* from *unclean*, free speech from pornography, or free exercise from establishment. Also included are secular Christians who wouldn't know the cross of Christ from a plank in a political platform, nor original intent from the latest political correctness, nor an unborn child created in the image of God from what is tragically referred to as nothing more than "the product of conception."

The ACLU's Jewish Connection

In the history of the ACLU, Jews have not always fared well. When asked why there were so few Jews on the first ACLU Board, Roger Baldwin said, "Because the Jews behaved badly....I mean, they were all for the war. And what's more, they were not pro-labor either."[12] That was in the 1920s.

Even by 1950, when it came time to appoint Roger Baldwin's successor as head of the ACLU, the not-so-subtle message went out: no Jews need apply.[13] At that time, and on through the early 1960s, corporate and academic America was predominately WASPish, with not one Jew being appointed head of a major university or dean of a major law school. The ACLU—already under attack for being anti-democratic and anti-American— did not want to offend the establishment any more than necessary.

Despite the snubbing, one of the ACLU's earliest allies on any number of civil libertarian issues—particularly church-state separation—was the American Jewish Congress, whose staff member Leo Pfeffer became one of the foremost authorities on church and state. ACLU cases were often joined as well by the American Jewish Committee and the Anti-Defamation League.

If ACLU national leadership was still WASPish in the sixties, that was not at all true of the rank and file, particularly in the affiliates. As early as 1960, when the New York Civil Liberties Union—eager not to appear anti-Christian in the landmark school prayer case of *Engel v. Vitale*[14]—insisted that both plaintiff and lead attorney be non-Jews, the case was assigned to *the only non-Jew* on the Union's lawyer committee.[15]

What brought about the significant infusion is unclear, but by the late '60s there was a dramatic rise in the percentage of Jewish members of the ACLU. Perhaps what brought them in by the droves (along with thousands of others) was the anti-Vietnam War campaign and the Nixon impeachment case. Since each cause had been cast in civil libertarian terms, ACLU membership swelled. Among the ACLU's new members, apparently, was an unusually high percentage of Jews.

In a way, it was not surprising. Interviewed as associate director of the ACLU, Alan Reitman explained that, "We have no way of knowing how many members of the ACLU are Jewish. But it's fair to say that given the general liberal tradition of the Jewish community that a large number of Jewish people belong to the ACLU."[16] In fact, as ACLU observer William Donohue confirms, "It is no secret that Jews have supported the ACLU more than has any other ethnic group."[17]

That support dropped almost instantly, of course, in the wake of the ACLU's decision to support free speech rights in the explosive Skokie case. In 1977, the heavily Jewish Chicago suburb of Skokie, Illinois, tried to ban a Nazi demonstration. By the time the furor had abated, the ACLU had lost at least 70,000 members—mostly Jewish. Samuel Walker also points out that, while the ACLU supported affirmative action in the *Bakke* case, "All of the Jewish groups opposed it." As Walker explains, "Affirmative action was a sore point among many Jews who had traditionally been victims of restrictive quotas."[18] (It should be noted, however, that Jews did not speak with one voice on the issue of affirmative action. Many did, in fact, support the policy.)

But if there was a temporary separation, there was never going to be a divorce. The Skokie defection had been no more than a blip on the screen, caused when Jewish identity itself was threatened. From a survey conducted by the American Jewish Community, it was clear that American Jews were still far more liberal than the general population and exceptionally committed to civil liberties.[19]

In the early 1980s, the ACLU's membership had not only recovered from the Skokie losses, it had actually doubled. In response to the increasingly assertive religious-Right on issues like abortion and the nomination of Judge Robert Bork, thousands of Jews returned to the civil libertarian fold. In heart and mind, it had been their comfort zone all along.

In Search of Deeper Civil Libertarian Roots

This brief historical detour brings us back to the point of departure: without any question today, there is indeed a "Jewish connection" strongly evident in the ACLU, from top leadership positions on down. (Consider, for example, executive directors Aryeh Neier and Ira Glasser, and President Nadine Strossen.) This connection to the Jewish community helps to explain much about current civil liberties goals and programs.

One would be on safe ground to assume that the large number of Jews within the ACLU are not religious in any orthodox sense, but cultural Jews with a secularist mindset. (It could be said with equal force that there are likely few evangelical Christians—and probably no fundamentalist Christians at all—in the ACLU.) This alone explains much of the tension between the ACLU and the religious-Right. It has nothing to do with either side being personally anti-Christian or anti-semitic. The tension results from what we have seen earlier in the chapter: an inherent conflict between a religious perspective and a secular world view.

But it was not always so, especially for Jews. Lest we forget, Jews are not the Johnnie-come-latelies of civil liberties, but the ones who started the ball rolling in the first place. Whatever mainline liberal Protestants know about civil liberties, they learned from Jews. Or should have.

If secular Jews have forgotten their roots, their more devout neighbors could remind them that it was Moses and the prophets of Israel who first said over and over, "Do justice! Do justice!" Coming down from Mt. Sinai, Moses articulated the very laws of God from which we learn of fairness and justice:

Do not pervert justice; do not show partiality to the poor or
favoritism to the great, but judge your neighbor fairly.
(Leviticus 19:15)
One witness is not enough to convict a man accused of any
crime or offense he may have committed. A matter must be
established by the testimony of two or three witnesses.
(Deuteronomy 19:15)

Centuries later, the prophet Amos issued this cry against the injustice
which had become rampant in Israel and Judah during the time of the
divided kingdom:

> You oppress the righteous and take bribes
>   and you deprive the poor of justice in the courts.
>
> Hate evil, love good;
>   maintain justice in the courts.
> Perhaps the Lord God Almighty will have mercy
>   on the remnant of Joseph. (Amos 5:12,15)

Isaiah, too, joined in the crusade against the many social injustices
being committed by the people of Judah:

> Woe to those who make unjust laws,
>   to those who issue oppressive decrees,
> to deprive the poor of their rights and
>   withhold justice from the oppressed of my people....
> (Isaiah 10:1,2)

When the Jews thought they were honoring God by their many rituals
and pious fasting, Isaiah brought this stern message from God in response:

> Is not this the kind of fasting I have chosen:
> to loose the chains of injustice
>   and untie the cords of the yoke,
> to set the oppressed free
>   and break every yoke?
> Is it not to share your food with the hungry
>   and to provide the poor wanderer with shelter—
> when you see the naked, to clothe him,
>   and not turn away from your own flesh and blood?
> Then your light will break forth like the dawn,

and your healing will quickly appear;
then your righteousness will go before you,
and the glory of the Lord will be your rear guard.
Then you will call, and the Lord will answer;
you will cry for help, and he will say: Here am I.
(Isaiah 58:6-9)

For Jewish members of the ACLU, the roots of genuine civil libertarian concern go back much further than the Constitution and the Bill of Rights. Much further even than the common law. For Jews today, the civil libertarian tradition goes back to the very dawn of history—to a time when the Jewish sense of morality was a ray of hope in a darkened world of pagan ignorance and injustice.

But there is a catch. That rich civil liberties heritage is inextricably tied to the righteousness of the holy God of the universe, and to the higher-law moral order which he established with each stroke of his divine Creation. True civil libertarians must acknowledge the whole package—not just the bits that may seem more appealing (or perhaps less demanding). Civil liberties divorced from divine law are but empty euphemisms and moral pretense which a person or a society may take or leave.

Worse still are the implications for what causes become just or unjust, moral or immoral. Under the laws of Moses, prostitution and homosexual behavior were not civil liberties, but sins. Considering how sin has gone out of style lately, we've truly come a long way. Yet, don't overestimate the distance we've travelled: the road from sin to civil liberties (and back to sin again) is ever so short. When we abandon the religious foundations, moral authority is quickly set adrift. Let moral authority go adrift, and the cause of civil liberty hasn't a hope of remaining righteous.

If civil libertarian morality is schizophrenic, it only mirrors the philosophical duality of its secular Jewish and Christian members. Those who are Jews are justly proud of their Jewish heritage, but in their secular world view they no longer honor the transcendent religious and moral authority of the God of Abraham, Isaac, and Jacob. Drawn naturally—almost by birthright—to a principled defense of civil liberties, they nevertheless reject the spiritual underpinnings of social justice, and thereby leave themselves vulnerable to the ebb and flow of moral relativity. It is, for them, a fact-value separation (between a particular heritage and the values that ought to inhere in that heritage) which leads people who are hereditarily blessed with genuine civil libertarian values to abandon those values for lesser causes unworthy of their righteous roots.

To be a Jew spiritually is to be an advocate for social justice, not an amoral political activist or, worse yet, a defender of evil. To be nothing more than ethnically and culturally *Jew*-ish is to be circumcised from the very essence of one's Jewish spiritual heritage. As it was in centuries past, so it is today: Not all Israel is Israel. (Nor are all "Christians" Christian.) The true sons and daughters of Abraham are the spiritual offspring of Moses, Elijah, and the prophets—not the secularist progeny of Neier, Glasser, and Strossen. The former went up the mountain of truth and received justice from the hand of God. The latter, by rejecting the preeminence of divine law, have fallen from the mountain and broken anew the commandments written in stone.

Is There a Christian Connection?

If secular Jews are in a moral muddle, so too are secular Christians. It's the same story, repeated: from good roots have come unworthy fruits. At first blush, their civil libertarian heritage would seem directly traceable to Jesus of Nazareth. Soon after the beginning of his ministry, Jesus was unceremoniously run out of his own home town for daring to claim that he was the One sent from God (as Isaiah had prophesied) to preach good news to the poor, to proclaim freedom for the prisoners, and to release the oppressed.[20]

Given the revolutionary message of freedom that he preached, Jesus, the promised Messiah, could easily be viewed as the greatest liberator of all time. And certainly that is what his contemporaries hoped him to be—a political Messiah who would overthrow Roman rule and reestablish the nation of Israel. Radical and anti-establishment, Jesus seemingly embodied the very best of civil libertarian tradition.

From that picture of Christ, secular "Christians" in the ACLU have all the right instincts regarding the need for vigilance in the cause of social justice. However, Jesus' own libertarian instincts were far more profound than that which might be suggested by the Bill of Rights or dictated by current civil libertarian ideology. The good news of Jesus was not the reductionist social gospel of political liberalism. Nor, by any stretch, was it so-called "liberation theology." Jesus was neither a socialist nor a Marxist.

It is true that Jesus overturned the tables of corruption and called his followers to new heights of ethical conduct, nevertheless he did not come into the world to lobby for greater civil rights. In fact, strident demands for civil rights couldn't be further afield from what Jesus taught about suffering loss for the sake of the kingdom:

> But I tell you, Do not resist an evil person. If someone strikes you on the right cheek, turn to him the other also. And if someone wants to sue you and take your tunic, let him have your cloak as well. If someone forces you to go one mile, go with him two miles.[21]

In the gospel of Christ, forbearance counts for more than assertiveness; suffering, for more than self-realization. Above all, Jesus did not give his life simply to secure "individual rights and liberties," as we would know them today.

Nor was Jesus' mission focused on governmental reform or political activism. (And who would have had more cause for political protest than Jesus, a member of an oppressed ethnic minority who was ultimately sentenced to death despite a sham trial lacking any present-day notions of due process?) Rather, his divine mission was the emancipation of mankind from sin so that life beyond this life could be could be snatched from the jaws of hopeless death. "For God so loved the world that he gave his one and only Son, that whoever believes in him shall not perish but have eternal life."[22]

Anyone claiming to be a Christian must surely understand that a concern for civil liberties unconnected with a concern for eternal life misses altogether the kingdom of Christ. His is not a political kingdom, nor egalitarian philosophy, nor secular social reform—and certainly it is not a kingdom which condones, supports, and facilitates unrighteous acts. His is a transcendent, righteous kingdom in which ethical social action flows from the spiritual freedom that one has when liberated from the self-seeking shackles of sin.

When asked by Pilate whether he was a king, Jesus answered, "You are right in saying I am a king," but "my kingdom is not of this world."[23] One wonders whether the National Council of Churches and other mainline Christian denominations which have taken up the banner of pro-feminist and pro-gay theology have carefully considered just what Jesus meant by that statement. Their support of the ACLU in these and other liberal policies should not be interpreted as a divine stamp of approval.

Of one thing you can be certain: Jesus' reference to his spiritual kingdom was not intended to perpetuate any twisted notions of church-state separation. It begs incredulity to believe that Jesus would have favored a policy which would forbid a public school teacher from reading his own

Bible in the classroom; or prohibit a church from dismissing an openly-gay organist; or prevent students from praying together on a school campus.

When asked by his detractors whether it was right to pay taxes, Jesus amazed them with his response—that one should "render to Caesar the things that are Caesar's, and to God the things that are God's." If the secularist Christian finds comfort in Jesus' distinction between God's jurisdiction and Caesar's, he misses Jesus' point altogether. To the secular-thinking religious establishment of his own day, Jesus said plainly: Give the government what is due, but don't forget that, whereas civil government may be the duly constituted authority in the land, even so, God and his spiritual kingdom remain supremely Sovereign.

Secular Christians who have traded divine Truth for the shallow substitute of moral relativism have betrayed both the kingdom and its King. Let no one be fooled: those who have aided and abetted unrighteous acts in the cause of civil liberties are preaching a gospel other than the gospel of Christ. And in their antihistorical, misguided notions of church-state separation, which serve only to thwart the kingdom of God on earth, they not only dishonor the sanctified name they wear, but crucify Christ anew.

Whether for Christian or Jew, the noble ideals of true civil libertarian concern are lost along the way in the hurried flight from the mountain of religious faith to the wilderness of secular belief. Many people of faith have begun that journey with all the right intentions. (Social justice is a righteous cause.) But somewhere along the way, the devil has changed the signposts, and there are those who have taken the wrong path at the fork of the road.

Only one question remains: Will ideological secularism forever banish the ACLU to the devil's kingdom, or will its dogged commitment to principle give it a second chance to seek the kingdom of God and his righteousness?

CHAPTER 17

Is There Any Common Ground?

"THE GREATEST LESSON THAT WESTERN SOCIETY HAS TO LEARN IS TO TAKE NOTE OF MODERATE OPINION."

SIR COLIN SPEDDING

Perhaps it is naive to think that there could ever be any common ground between the ACLU and those who fundamentally disagree with their liberal-Left policies. Perhaps a fight to the death is inevitable. Culture wars need not be bloody, but sometimes they simply need to be fought. Yet, one can always hope that, despite the great cultural divide between the religious Right and the secular Left, between the politically conservative and the radically liberal, there is *some* room for common ground, *some* place for a peace table. Truly, a house divided against itself cannot long stand. Too much is at stake for future generations for us not to make every effort to explore those values which are shared between us.

Common ground might possibly be found in our shared commitments to choice, to freedom of speech, and, most of all, to life. The conservative/religious Right is not against choice per se. Choice is exactly what it wants when it comes to school vouchers. Nor are they against free speech. In fact, that is what they so desperately want when it comes to religious speech. Nor, on the other hand, is the ACLU untouched by an appeal to the value of human life. Whatever else may be the basis for its policy against capital punishment, on that issue the ACLU is squarely in the right-to-life camp.

Is it not possible, then, to show the white flag long enough to explore each other's commitments? All wars eventually end.

Is There Any Common Ground?

The membership recruitment letter from Ira Glasser began with dire warnings of impending disaster for America's civil liberties:

Dear Friend:

Not until after the summer of 1992, when the Republican National Convention featured these hateful speeches of Pat Robertson and Pat Buchanan did the media begin to pay attention to the re-emergence of a massively funded and dangerous political force. A force that is now threatening civil liberties in virtually every community in America and will *continue* to do so—with *even greater intensity* at the local level now that the White House opposes their agenda.

Quotes from the "hateful speeches" to which Glasser referred were featured in bold print at the top of the letter:

"[Unless America returns to] her Christian roots...she will continue to legalize sodomy, slaughter innocent babies, destroy the minds of her children, squander her resources, and sink into oblivion."

— Rev. Pat Robertson

"There is a religious war going on....We must take back our cities, and take back our culture, and take back our country!"
— Patrick J. Buchanan

Over the next eight pages, the letter continued—with apocalyptic urgency—a barrage of warnings against the religious-Right:

Here at the American Civil Liberties Union we had *already* been watching for some time—and with growing alarm.

Their method? To prey upon the fears of millions of people who are all too willing to believe that sacrificing personal liberty will help solve our nation's problems.

We receive dozens of reports from ACLU affiliates all across the nation documenting the rapidly growing menace of this new anti-liberties force.

There is no question in my mind that these activities represent a persistent, planned pattern to erode individual rights and impose the Christian Right's anti-liberty "morality" on every American.

We must also insist on *exposing the links* between the *violent* religious right and the so-called *respectable* religious right.

Now is the time...to alert the public to their dangerous, anti-liberty agenda and to fight them everywhere.

The letter ends with the emotional appeal: "This is your opportunity to stop the new wave of extremism before it does even more damage to liberty...So please join us today. You will be making a crucially important investment in preserving our nation's most deeply cherished liberties for yourself and for all Americans."

"And yes," came the tongue-in-cheek clincher, "*you'll receive your own personal membership card*! Believe me, we need as many 'card-carrying members' of the ACLU as possible."

The Strangest Kind of War

In case you haven't heard the latest news bulletin, there's a war going on out there. A cultural war. A religious war. For some—on both sides—an almost holy jihad. And the rhetoric can be deafening. (You may even have heard a few rounds exploding in this book.) Each side is trying desperately to advance its front lines into enemy territory. To gain ground. To take captives. To win a war.

Sometimes, regrettably, wars are necessary. Sometimes, too much is at stake—like liberty, or life itself—to sit back and do nothing. There are noble causes worth defending. (But when does a war *not* involve someone's idea of a "noble cause?") In this case, the "noble cause" of the ACLU and the liberal-Left is liberty, while the "noble cause" of the conservative-Right is...*also liberty*!

You mean, both sides in the cultural war are fighting for the same thing? Well, almost. They are both fighting for the right to maintain (and even promote) their own world view, and they are both fighting to prevent "the other side" from imposing its contrary values on them. In this regard, at least, all that's really different between the two sides are their distinct values, which, so it seems, are mutually-exclusive. Yet, if it is sometimes easier to identify the differences (and, without question, they are significant), it may also be possible to identify certain shared concerns.

In the school prayer controversy, for example, both sides appeal to the First Amendment guarantees in support of their cause. Both sides are fighting for the right to freely exercise religion, or non-religion, as they understand that right. And both sides would agree that the Establishment Clause prohibits the ordaining of a national church. Nobody, but *nobody* wants to tear down *that* "wall of separation."

If you are the least bit in doubt about that (and want to view a great spectator event), just tell the Baptists that the Presbyterians are going to become the official church of the nation! Or, spread the word that Roman Catholicism is to be officially preferred over Protestantism; or that Buddhism is going to be named as America's official faith! The idea of a State Church headquartered in Washington D.C. is just as repugnant to Christians as it is to Jews, Muslims, Buddhists, and atheists.

Another seemingly irreconcilable issue—abortion—is contested on the basis of two competing commitments. However, neither of those commitments is a complete stranger to the other side's thinking. The ACLU's commitment to "choice," for instance, is an appeal to liberty not unlike what many in the conservative-Right also desire when it comes to the issue of school vouchers. It's not that conservatives don't understand the "choice" argument. When it involves their children's education, they, too, want the right to choose. It's just that, when abortion is the particular choice under consideration, they see more at stake.

On the pro-life side, the commitment of the conservative-Right is to *life*, a commitment not wholly unlike the concern of many in the pro-choice camp when it comes to capital punishment. So, it's not that pro-choice supporters can't be touched by an argument based upon the value of human life. In fact, the potential loss of innocent life is what motivates death penalty opponents to stand vigil outside the gas chamber on the eve of an execution.

When considering the commitment of the civil libertarian to life on death row, pro-life's concern for the wrongful taking of innocent life through abortion can't exactly be seen as coming out of left field. And, if the truth be known, most people who are "pro-choice" have no more love for abortion than they have for capital punishment. The issue of "choice" aside, the overwhelming majority of Americans of all stripes find abortion personally unacceptable.

When the issue is free speech, there's no question but that everybody on both sides wants it! Just because the conservative-Right opposes obscenity and pornography, doesn't mean they want to shut down free speech. In fact, conservatives have joined with the ACLU in opposing politically-correct censorship (on campus and off) and restrictions on hate speech, even when (as vilified "homophobes," for example) they themselves might be the intended target. Certainly with regard to *political* free speech, the conservative-Right shares with the ACLU a deep commitment to its inviolability.

On these and other issues, what the ACLU and the conservative-Right have in common could turn out to be as significant as that over which they divide. Perhaps somewhere amid the rubble of bombed-out dogmas and ideologies are some fragments large enough to be used in building a bridge between the two sides.

A Shared Personality?

In an earlier chapter, I observed that the two extremes, both left and right, tend to meet each other on the back side of any continuum. Even without going so far as to talk about radical or militant extremes, it is interesting to observe the personalities of activists on both sides, and to see just how similar they are. To make the observations as graphic as possible, simply compare everyone's stereotype of a "left-wing liberal" with everyone's stereotype of a "religious fundamentalist."

With each there is a sense of elitism and "chosenness," which is generally shared with others of like persuasion in a kind of enclave mentality. Like Roger Baldwin, who kept a tight rein on the circle of leadership within the fledgling ACLU, both the "religious fundamentalist" and the "left-wing liberal" tend to prefer a cadre of true believers to sharing the power base. Whether by virtue of feeling intellectually superior or perhaps divinely chosen, these two personalities are pretty sure that they are *just that bit above* everyone else.

Pride, therefore, is a common trait. Perhaps this explains the thread of self-righteous posturing on either side, as if they, and they alone, are the sole repositories of *liberty*, on the one hand, or *truth*, on the other. The "religious fundamentalist" (invariably typecast as being a Pharisaical moralist) has nothing on the "left-wing liberal" when it comes to expressing moral indignation. (In his recruitment letter, Glasser spoke disparagingly of Pat Robertson for choosing the name "American Center for Law and Justice" (ACLJ) "deliberately to mock...*our moral stance* [emphasis added].") Though neither personality likes to admit it, moral superiority comes as naturally to the "left-wing liberal" as it does to the "religious fundamentalist."

Perhaps that feeling of moral superiority explains why both the "left-wing liberal" and the "religious fundamentalist" tend also to reject authority, whether (for the liberal) it be civil authority or perhaps moral authority; or (for the fundamentalist) human authority as opposed to divine authority. In whatever way it might be more precisely delineated, there is a touch of anarchy in both personalities.

The "left-wing liberal" and the "religious fundamentalist" also share a sense of being counter-cultural. As the fundamentalist might say (quoting Scripture), "*In* the world, but not *of* the world." Ideologically swimming against the tide, they often feel alienated from society and suspicious of its values. (For the "liberal," traditional bourgeois values seem threatening; for the fundamentalist, the battle is against ungodly, secularist values.) In each instance, then, they seem always to be looking from the outside in. Never quite accepted. Never quite *wanting* to be accepted, as if acceptance would confirm an unprincipled conformity on their part.

A spin-off from that trait is an "interesting" aversion to hierarchy and an insistence on egalitarian rights. *Interesting*—particularly for the "religious fundamentalist"—because his great *respect* for hierarchy when it involves divine authority is matched only by his great *disdain* for hierarchy when it involves human institutions. The more fundamentalist the believer, the more likely he will honor divine (biblical) authority, but reject both clerical hierarchy within a particular denomination and governmental hierarchy represented by "big government." While the "left-wing liberal" might not fully appreciate such a spiritually-based dichotomy, he would certainly understand hostility towards hierarchy in general. And in that, they have much in common.

Perhaps what the "religious fundamentalist" and the "left-wing liberal" share most in common is their way of thinking about issues. As Stephen Carter suggests in part, the beliefs of both are driven less by purely rational thought (even if they happen to be intellectuals) than by ideology and bias. This may explain why each finds it difficult to make subtle (and sometimes not-so-subtle) value distinctions. If the caricatured "religious fundamentalist" sees issues only in stark black and white, the "left-wing liberal" follows closely at his side, apparently unable to distinguish between, for instance, political speech and pornography.

The point of all this is that—simply by virtue of personality—the ACLU and the conservative-Right may have much more in common than either would have guessed, or would ever wish to acknowledge. (We have met the enemy, and he is us!) Oddly enough, the intensity of civil wars of all types tends to show that, the more alike the adversaries, the greater the conflict. Like magnets, whether both positive or both negative, they repel each other. Yet, even that truth is not without hope. It just might also be true (and well worth exploring) that, the more alike the adversaries, the greater the potential for resolution. When you think about it, middle ground ought to be easier to find when there is less distance between two enemies. If on some issues the distance separating us would require a quantum leap, it should not stop us from walking the few steps it would take to meet each other where we easily can. Do not even quantum leaps require a running start?

Shades Along the Spectrum

In the foregoing analysis of the two warring personalities, it was almost necessary to compare exaggerated caricatures of two greatly-over-generalized personalities. How else does one cut through the myriad of nuances that threaten to stand in the way of any attempt to make concise arguments? As a practical matter, one simply cannot constantly be making the kind of careful distinctions that really ought to be made. So we use shorthand instead. And labels. And broad-sweeping generalizations. And over-inclusive categories.

That's why we speak generically of the "liberal-Left" or the "conservative-Right." Or "secularists" and "fundamentalists." Or "left-wingers" and "right-wingers." But who *are* these people? Do they all, in each category, come out of the same cookie cutter? Are they really so homogeneous? Is there no continuum, no spectrum of philosophies, values, commitments, and motives?

Time and time again we have seen that civil libertarians are not necessarily one and the same with political liberals. (It is even possible for a civil libertarian to be a political conservative, and vice versa.) Civil libertarians and political liberals disagree on any number of issues, including: so-called political correctness; hate speech; sexual harassment; double jeopardy; capital punishment; and pornography. When it comes to pornography, just watch the fur fly when the ACLU's Nadine Strossen debates Michigan law professor Catharine MacKinnon, an outspoken feminist who campaigns against pornography. (For those in the know, "debates" isn't actually the right word. MacKinnon won't even share the podium with Strossen or any other female critic!¹)

However, if civil libertarians and political liberals don't always see eye to eye, they do far more often than they *don't*. And, because political liberals are unquestionably left of center, it is *usually* fair to speak of the "liberal-Left" (and to include civil libertarians), just as we have done in this book.

But it is not *always* fair. In fact, it is the very lumping together of civil libertarians and political liberals—not linguistically, but organizationally—that threatens the historical mission of the ACLU. The recent ascendance of political liberalism is precisely that which most deeply divides the ACLU. Listen, for instance, to Harvard's Alan Dershowitz: "The ACLU is caught in a tug-of-war between civil liberties and the politics of the left, and the politics of the left is winning. It's a terrible tragedy."²

Today in the ACLU, there is a battle-within-a-war between hard-core civil libertarians (First Amendment absolutists) and civil rights advocates who have stretched the meaning of "civil rights" to a breaking point. (It is no longer race, but *racism*; not sex, but *sexism*.) Their concept of "victims" includes virtually any special interest group, from feminists to homosexuals, that fits under an ever-expanding umbrella of politically-correct victimism.

Therefore, when those in the "conservative-Right" challenge various policies of the ACLU, the target is not always easily identifiable. Is it hard-core civil libertarians or political activists-slash-radicals who are pushing the contested agenda? Indeed, is it the national board or one of the local affiliates which is behind the shocking headline? An interesting combination of those two critical distinctions has even led to the Ohio chapter filing an amicus brief opposing the national ACLU in a Supreme Court hate crime case!³

If we could just get the right area code for each issue we are confronting, we might end up talking with people whom we have more in common with than we think. In fact, that has been one of the purposes of this book: to be a wake-up call from an outsider to those within the ACLU who never intended for the ACLU to be anything other than a defender of fundamental constitutional liberties; and to give aid and comfort in the fight against the ACLU becoming an advocate for unworthy causes. In opposition to those unworthy causes, we have every reason to stand together in solidarity.

Remarkably, that solidarity extends even to the very arguments that the conservative-Right would make to civil libertarians about the importance of transcendent spiritual verities. When we listen through the keyhole to the ACLU's domestic dispute regarding sexual harassment, we hear executive committee member Mary Ellen Gale saying to her traditionalist colleagues, "You can't have a nice clean set of abstract rules when you have an imperfect world. Your noble principles may not do good. In fact, they may do harm."[4] As reporter Dennis Cauchon observes, "That's the type of talk that makes purists shiver."[5]

If, indeed, civil libertarian purists shiver at such nouveau libertarianism, then there is hope for dialogue with those on the conservative-Right who also shiver at such talk. Their common enemy is not each other, but a slippery slope of unprincipled pragmatism leading wherever its proponents want it to go. When Playwright Lillian Hellman refused to name names before the House Un-American Activities Committee in 1951, she spoke for all who value principle above pragmatism: "I cannot and will not cut my conscience to fit this year's fashion."[6]

Civil libertarian purists might find it equally interesting to listen through the keyhole to the family arguments going on in church after church these days. *They are the same arguments!* Principle versus pragmatism; fundamentals versus innovation; anchors versus slippery slopes. As "Yogi" Berra would say, "It's déjà vu all over again!"

The cynical observer might say that the battle on both sides is pretty much "old guard" versus "young turks." (To the chagrin of many of us, the latest article in the paper is all about the baby boomers filling out AARP applications!) Maybe it is time for the "old guard" on both sides to sit down together among themselves, and see if there isn't some way of carrying the dialogue further to their respective younger colleagues.

What that dialogue might reveal is that, like civil libertarians and the liberal-Left, the conservative-Right is also a mixed bag of folks who definitely do *not* come from the same cookie cutter! For starters, they are not all "Bible-thumping religious fundamentalists" (or even Bible-believing evangelicals); nor Republicans; nor members of the Christian Coalition; nor members of the NRA; nor, especially, members of the Michigan Militia.

Surely, not even Rush Limbaugh's "ditto heads" are marching in completely uniform lockstep.

For proof, just listen to the conservative-Right when they are fighting among themselves. When it comes to gun control, school vouchers, or even school prayer, there is not total unanimity. The spectrum covered by the conservative-Right is no less broad than the spectrum covered by the liberal-Left. Who among us wants to be labelled so indiscriminately that we are identified with beliefs we don't hold, and perhaps even vehemently oppose?

Never is the disagreement among the conservative-Right more ago-nizing than when it comes to choosing which methods to pursue in protesting legalized abortion. If it needs to be said one more time, the killing of abortion doctors and the bombing of abortion clinics is a method of protest supported by only a minuscule number of pro-life activists. Tarring all pro-life protesters with the same brush (especially by invoking the RICO anti-racketeering statute in derogation of free speech) merely serves as an excuse for the extremists to be even more extreme.

Whether on the left or right, we have much to lose by lumping together the adversary. If there is a war—and of course there is—the oppos-ing troops are not all in the same regiment. Or are wearing exactly the same uniforms. Or have the same reasons for fighting. Or are unwilling to honor a white flag of truce long enough to go to the negotiating table.

It is important to remember that the worst civil war this nation has ever known is now over. Wars always last too long, but they never last for-ever. Surely, then, the road to peace is out there somewhere, if we'll only stop fighting long enough to look for it.

CHAPTER 18

De-escalation and Disarmament

PEACE IS NOT AN ABSENCE OF WAR, IT IS A VIRTUE, A STATE OF MIND,
A DISPOSITION FOR BENEVOLENCE, CONFIDENCE, JUSTICE."
BENEDICT SPINOZA

I f there is any hope at all for a de-escalation in the cultural war, both the ACLU and its allies on the Left and those of us marching in from the Right must agree upon a strategy of disengagement. It will take an enormous infusion of goodwill to initiate the process. Someone or some group needs to take the first step. If anyone is listening, perhaps each side can offer a token of good faith—something that isn't crucial to the cause. A symbol. A gesture. A signal that beckons the way forward.

In the meantime, those of us on the conservative/religious Right must examine ourselves as well as our principles. Are we coming to the negotiating table with clean hands? Do we decry the secular policies of the ACLU, yet have within ourselves a secular self that overshadows what we proclaim? Do we rail against the ACLU's blinkered view of church-state separation, while drawing distinct lines in our own lives between our sacred commitments and our secular practices? How can we hope to convince the ACLU that its morally-debased social policies are an affront to civil liberties if our own moral practices are an affront to our professed faith?

Liberal or conservative, Right or Left, the time has come to recognize that we are engaged, not just in a cultural war, but in a cosmic spiritual battle in which the enemy is both without and within. In this great battle of heart and mind, both God and the devil are keenly interested spectators.

De-escalation and Disarmament

In a war of the magnitude we are facing—a war between fundamental cultural assumptions and competing world views—it is not to be assumed that peace is just around the corner. Only a fool would minimize the seriousness and dimensions of the conflict. Yet there are steps which thoughtful people on both sides could take, with little risk to their respective positions, that would at least narrow the field of conflict.

What's nice to know is that it has happened before, on an even grander scale. Against all odds and expectations, the Cold War ended and the Berlin Wall finally fell. But the end did not come overnight. It began years earlier with a behind-the-scenes initiative here, and a symbolic summit talk there; a round of goodwill visits one year, a cultural exchange program the next. Perhaps as much as anything, both sides realized that they had a common enemy greater than their mutual differences—a flagging world economy unable to support the hugely expensive arms race. And, of course, there was the ever-present risk of mutual destruction.

Is our cultural war really so different? Do we not have a common enemy which supersedes our differences: a disintegrating society which we can no longer afford to maintain, either financially or psychically? Are we not foolish to be fighting each other while the ship of state sinks beneath our feet? Surely, now is the time for "goodwill visits" and "cultural exchanges"—to get to know each other better. Surely, the time has come for a behind-the-scenes initiative here, and a quiet summit talk there.

In order to lay the foundation for a growing sense of mutual trust, we could begin simply, perhaps with something like disarmament talks. What weapons can we lay down? What missiles can we aim in a different direction? What tokens of good faith can we exchange?

Just to get the ball rolling, maybe we could begin by exchanging acts of good faith in areas that are not really crucial to either side. Why not give up something that doesn't cost the cause of civil libertarianism or conservatism all that much, but which could be highly symbolic? Why not send each other (and a watching nation) some clear signal of a new rapprochement?

On the conservative-Right, for example, why not give up the annual push for nativity creches and Hanukkah menorahs in city halls and public parks? Are there not plenty of locations on private property where those religious symbols could be displayed with equal effectiveness to the passing public? Can it be said that those particular symbols are crucial to the maintenance or advancement of religious belief in America? In fact, are not those symbols of the sacred actually trivialized (as the ACLU suggests[1]) by having to surround them with Santa Claus and his reindeer in order to satisfy the Court's requirement that they be part of a *secular* display? Maybe there are other ways to celebrate the religious holidays. Maybe even *better* ways.

As for the ACLU, why not lay down your arms used in the defense of kiddy porn? (If you must, continue to defend other forms of pornography until you are satisfied that there is no sinister conspiracy afoot to prohibit any form of free speech that would be crucial to the maintenance of liberty.) Kiddy porn has never been a defensible position in any event, and having to employ tortured logic in an attempt to justify it only serves to make you look bad. It's one of those "weak arguments" that permits the opposition to believe that your other free speech arguments are equally contrived. So, why give them that opening?

As for your "slippery slope" argument, give it some time. If it starts looking like you were right, there will be plenty of time to retrench before irreversible damage has been done to the First Amendment. In the meantime, as the bumper sticker says, "Give peace a chance."

And what a peace dividend that would be! Besides making the ACLU look better, there will be some children no longer at risk who will rise up and call you blessed!

How to Woo a Homophobe

If headway could be made by these initial symbolic overtures, there is no reason why other doors could not also be opened. Take gay rights, for example. Is it not clear by now that anti-gay rights initiatives from Colorado to Oregon to Georgia are a reaction to pro-gay-rights legislation? That may seem sophomoric, but consider the realities of the struggle.

As late as 1961, every state made sodomy a misdemeanor, and occasional prosecutions were lodged accordingly. Since then, however, sodomy has been decriminalized in over half the states; and in the remaining states where sodomy laws are still on the books, the statutes are rarely, if ever, enforced. Contrary to rumor, there are simply no bedroom police out there invading anyone's sexual privacy.

In the landmark *Bowers v. Hardwick* case (which held state sodomy laws constitutional), the arrest of Michael Hardwick was merely coincidental to the investigation of another offense, and the prosecuting attorney had even declined to prosecute.[2] It was only because gay activists seized upon the fortuitous arrest in order to take a test case to the courts that the case ever saw the light of day.

So why the push to get sodomy statutes off the books, if not to gain *official acceptance* of conduct which most people find offensive? That, of course, is the one thing which those who are conscientiously opposed to homosexual behavior cannot concede. They cannot be asked to repeal sodomy laws if such a repeal will be taken to mean that society thereby *condones* and *gives moral approval* to sodomy. On the other hand, if it is *tolerance* that the gay community seeks, then that tolerance has already been shown by not enforcing the law.

It is only when gay activists and civil libertarians do not respect society's legislated (yet still restrained) moral conscience that the anti-gay backlash begins to take the form of state-wide initiatives and referenda. Had it not been for gay activists pushing the envelope for special-interest rights, there never would have been Amendment 2 in Colorado nor Proposition 9 in Oregon.

The moral of the story is this: sometimes more is less and less is more. In the case of gay rights, the more the ACLU presses for official acceptance of homosexual behavior through laws which are unrelated to *actual legal jeopardy*, the less the conservative-Right will be willing to exercise tolerance. Likewise, the less pressure the ACLU puts on society to give its *official* blessing to the homosexual lifestyle, the more latitude and even personal acceptance homosexuals are going to have in practice. If, as we are told, morality can't be legislated, neither can love.

The irony of the present conflict is that criminal laws against sodomy might have gone the way of criminal laws against adultery had it not been for the implications attached to repeal by the gay lobby. (There was no similar adulterers-rights lobby demanding that society give adulterers special legal status and implied moral approval.) We may now be far beyond the point of no return, but a trade-off is still remotely possible. If the gay community would be willing to keep its homosexual activity *truly private from a legal standpoint*, then there would be no compelling reason for retaining criminal sodomy laws, any more than laws criminalizing adultery.

If, short of such a trade-off, the ACLU and its gay rights activists wish to engender goodwill from the conservative-Right, it would be a good beginning simply to honor religious conscience (read, free exercise of religion) in matters of housing, hiring, and education. It is unrealistic to demand tolerance while at the same time exercising intolerance. Though it may sound too religious for some, the give and take of political reality, no less than good neighborliness, is a matter of doing unto others what you would have them do to you.

Compromise in the Classroom

That same principle could be applied to the classroom. No one can speak for the entire conservative or religious-Right, but headway might also be made in the creation-evolution controversy, perhaps along the lines suggested in an earlier chapter. Creationists might well be willing to forego efforts to teach what has been called "creation science," if they could be assured that public schools would teach the general theory of evolution as just that—a *theory*—complete with its own set of yet-to-be proven assumptions.

Is the ACLU willing to permit free academic inquiry in the public classroom? If high school biology textbooks were allowed to ask the hard questions that creationists have asked of Darwinian or other evolution theory, then the cause of Creation belief will have been served without running afoul of current Court restrictions. Such a compromise may not be all that parents from the religious-Right would like, but it would go a long way toward easing the conflict. If naturalistic science alone is to be the only game in town, then let's at least agree to teach science the way it ought to be taught—with complete intellectual honesty.

Toward that end, what better opportunity could the ACLU have to demonstrate good faith than by dropping its opposition to the disclaimer being read by science teachers in Tangipahoa Parish in New Orleans before teaching evolution to their students? The disclaimer reads, in part, that the lesson is intended "to inform students of the scientific concept and [is] not intended to influence or dissuade the Biblical version of creation or any other concept....Students are urged to exercise critical thinking and gather all information possible...."[3] Whatever else one may think about it, the disclaimer fits squarely within the ACLU's official policies related to free speech, classroom autonomy for teachers, and students' rights.

And while we are in the classroom, let's take advantage of any moment of silence either side in the school prayer controversy can muster. Is it school prayer that is crucial to the religious-Right? Or is school prayer mostly symbolic of deeper concerns about the inculcation of basic moral values in America's young people? Is it being able to acknowledge God in prayer that prompts calls for a constitutional amendment, or is it the concern of parents that their children's education is being robbed entirely of a spiritual dimension? Surely, in each instance, it is the latter.

The call for reinstatement of school prayer is a cry for help from parents and teachers who see their children and students facing an increasingly uncivil society without having the strength of character to stand against its evils. They are not asking for church worship services, or opportunities to proselytize others' children to their own faith, or requirements forcing the children of atheist parents to recant the disbelief they have been taught at home. There is no hidden agenda on the part of the Christian Coalition or anyone else to turn public schools into taxpayer-supported parochial schools.

The conservative-Right is not asking that teachers read the Bible to their students at school, but that texts such as William Bennett's *Book of Virtues* be available in the classroom—even if such books happen to include passages from the Bible. It's not the Ten Commandments that parents insist be tacked on the classroom wall, but an effort to instill within the heart of each student moral parameters that constitute the basic "thou shalts" and "thou shalt nots" without which no society can long function.

Can civil libertarians really say that those kinds of parental concerns are anti-liberty? Do not civil libertarians themselves want those same core values of morality, decency, and civility taught to their own children? How far apart can we be? What a tragedy that the children have become the innocent victims in a cultural war they cannot yet understand!

Can we not agree to teach core values in primary and secondary schools, and then help high school students see that religious faith for most people is a significant part of their understanding of the universe? Indeed, it is practically impossible to teach about the history and values of Western Civilization—or African or Latin American culture—without reference to the faith that has played such a significant role in politics, art, music, and science—even civil liberties.

As long as there remains open hostility to such teaching (and activist promotion of radical political ideology such as the gay-inclusive "Rainbow Curriculum"), no progress is likely to be made. But, if parents in the conservative and religious-Right could see a consensus for value-based education in the public schools (and be assured that "political correctness," as it is currently promoted, has been chucked out forever), then even school prayer might be re-prioritized. Unless and until that happens, unfortunately, school prayer will remain the token issue while the real issue for parents on both sides—*value-based education*—gets shoved aside.

Abortion—The Last Great Struggle

This brings us to the battle over abortion. Without question, the way forward here is far less clear. To this point, pro-choice advocates say they *will* not budge, and pro-life advocates respond that they simply *cannot* budge. Unlike other issues, this one (if abortion opponents are right) is a matter of life and death.

To civil libertarians who defend abortion as a constitutional right, one can only plead that you recheck your Constitution, your libertarian instincts, and your heart. Something must be terribly wrong with one or more of the three to justify your strong pro-choice commitment.

As Samuel Walker's invaluable history of the ACLU reminds us, not even the ACLU's founders would ever have dreamed that the Constitution contained a generalized right of privacy permitting women to terminate pregnancies in the womb or restricting the government from proscribing such an act.

In fact, as late as 1963 it could still be said that "many ACLU members were hesitant about embracing the abortion rights issue, *as the legal foundations were uncertain* [emphasis added]."[4] The necessary creation of abortion rights from "uncertain legal foundations" became such a fast development at one point that the ACLU itself got left behind. "In one curious footnote," Walker points out, "the ACLU awoke in 1985 to discover that its abortion policy had never been revised since 1968 and did not go as far as *Roe v. Wade* in upholding the right to third trimester abortions." The board then took corrective action.[5]

If the ACLU is proud of the fact that it helped give birth to the right of privacy, then why the great pretense that such a generalized right of privacy is *unquestionably* constitutional?

As for your libertarian instincts, do they not fairly scream for the protection of the defenseless against those who have it within their power to bring about death in the womb? Isn't the cause of the unborn to be identified far more closely with your hallowed causes of equal protection, due process, racial justice, and minority rights—even *privacy*—than anything possibly related to the mother? (If "choice" is a matter of privacy, where is the right of choice for the unborn, who, in virtually every other arena apart from abortion are recognized as legally protectable persons?)

Samuel Walker speaks proudly of the ACLU's concern for the underdog: "The powerless and despised have been the ACLU's most frequent clients, for the simple reason that they have been the most frequent victims of intolerance and repression."[6] Considering that each year in America alone 1.5 million powerless babies suffer the ultimate form of repression, surely, civil libertarians have taken the wrong side on this one!

If the ACLU would rather not listen to the preaching of the religious-Right, that's understandable. But it should at least give a closer ear to some of its own, including former board member Nat Hentoff, who is outspoken in his opposition to abortion. It is not just a concern of the religious-Right. For at least some civil libertarians, the rights of the unborn are as fundamental a question of liberty as free speech.

And then there are concerns of the heart. For many pro-choice advocates, the crucial issue is whether or not, in fact, the unborn fetus is a human life. One can only appeal to the obvious. If the mother *wants* it to be a baby, it is a baby. If the grandparents are told with excitement that, "We're pregnant!"—it is a baby. If the happy mother-to-be miscarries, she has "lost her baby," and everyone grieves for her. If a "preemie" makes an earlier-than-normal entrance into this world, doctors and nurses make heroic efforts to make sure that "baby Doe" survives (sometimes while a more fully-developed "fetus" is being aborted in another wing of the same hospital).

Nor is there any currency in talking about a "glob of cells," or the beginning of brain activity, or viability. According to *Roe v. Wade* (with which ACLU policy is squarely aligned), a state *may*, but *need not*, intervene to protect a third-trimester baby.[7] Absent state intervention, there is no *constitutional* barrier that would prevent a mother from aborting a fully-developed nine-month-old the day before he or she otherwise would be naturally born.

To say that a baby is a baby when we want it to be, but not a baby when we don't want it to be is sheer madness. If we listen to our hearts as well as our minds, we will understand why pro-life advocates really don't have an option.

Or do they?

In point of fact, pro-life activists are faced every day with a number of options related to the abortion struggle. No, not *whether* to defend the unborn, but *how?* The options run the gamut from writing letters to the editor; faxing their representatives in Congress; volunteering clothes, money, and time to help in crisis pregnancy centers; joining in Life Chain demonstrations; picketing abortion clinics; and "rescuing" babies scheduled for abortion by talking their mothers into changing their minds. (As indicated earlier, neither bombing abortion clinics nor killing doctors who perform abortions is a viable option for any but a tiny fraction of pro-life activists.)

This is not the place to flesh out a full-scale discussion of anti-abortion strategy. But, if pro-choice civil libertarians are being asked to rethink their basic approach to abortion, it is only fair that pro-life advocates do the same. It is just possible that unwise decisions about anti-abortion strategy have led many pro-choice folks to take more unyielding positions than they themselves would prefer in the defense of an issue that, for them, isn't all that comfortable to defend.

We are talking here, first of all, about organizations like Operation Rescue, whose commitment to the cause has earned them unquestioned credentials. Front line advocates, they put many of the rest of us to shame with their energy and unflagging dedication to preventing abortion. (If we *really believe* that 1.5 million babies a year are being destroyed in the womb, how can we content ourselves with little more than token, ivory tower opposition?) And, indeed, they *have saved* hundreds of babies directly, and perhaps thousands more indirectly, through their controversial abortion clinic confrontations.

It's a close call. Would the more moderate pro-life movement be as successful as it has been to date if it weren't for the more aggressive anti-abortion activists on the street? (They believe, certainly, that they play an important role in being the noisy, but necessary, radicals who keep the media's attention focused on the issue.) Or, to the contrary, would we be much further along in convincing Americans to do the right thing if they felt less offended and threatened by such militant protesters?

Sometimes it is good just to "crunch the numbers." Suppose through the efforts of a "rescue" operation that we managed to save, say, 10,000 babies a year. As long as abortion is legal and acceptable, that still leaves 1.4 million-plus babies being aborted in the same period. But what if we could make abortion morally unacceptable, even without changing the law? (Something like, "Suppose they threw a war and nobody came.") Wouldn't that be a far better result? Isn't that what the protest is all about—to stop abortions? And is it possible that, at this point, radical protest is counter-productive in the effort to achieve that broader result?

How, then, can we justify saving the relatively *few* when we might risk jeopardizing the *many* by any off-putting strategy we might pursue? Can we really be more concerned about winning the legal battle over abortion laws than in winning the hearts and minds of America? It is not only a matter of commitment, but of strategy.

Herein lies the potential for a win-win victory for both sides: If the laws of every state permitted abortion, but no one took advantage of them, each side would win. Freedom of choice coupled with moral responsibility is always the noblest ideal.

Where Peace Talks Break Down

Is the ACLU willing to work together towards that end? So far, of course, the ACLU has not spoken out against the immorality of abortion. Nor is it likely to. (ACLU Policy 263 says, "The Union itself offers no comment on the wisdom or the moral implications of abortion....") And that is the *real* roadblock to progress—not just the ACLU's defense of "choice" in the abstract, for indeed the exercise of all morality is a choice.

Which brings us to the crux of the matter. As seen so clearly in the abortion issue, peace talks are likely to break down when form is elevated above substance; when liberty is divorced from values. The conservative-Right is no less concerned about liberty than the American Civil Liberties Union, but it is also concerned about the morality which must of necessity accompany that liberty if liberty itself is to survive. Unfortunately, the ACLU has not demonstrated a shared understanding as to the importance of such fact-value cohesion.

There was once a civil libertarian who did understand that crucial link...his name was Thomas Jefferson. Of all the quotes attributable to Jefferson, this one may be the most memorable: "That government governs best which governs least." What could be more libertarian? (What could be *less* politically liberal?) But that famous quotation is not complete. The complete quotation is: "That government governs best which governs least, *because its people discipline themselves* [emphasis added]."

Jefferson understood that civil liberties cannot be maintained or exercised in a vacuum. The less government there is, the more self-discipline is required on the part of each citizen. That is where basic morality becomes so important. In the absence of public and private morality, a decrease in government leads not to greater freedom, but to deterioration of the entire social fabric, resulting in *less* freedom.

Never in recent history has that lesson been so important. For it is not only civil libertarians who need to be reminded, but the new revolutionaries in the conservative-Right whose agenda is the reduction of government in the shared belief that "that government governs best that governs least." If in opposing "big government" the conservative-Right finds itself once again having surprising common ground with traditional civil libertarians, there is also a shared duty to promote the kind of moral responsibility that will lead to self-discipline.

It is easy for the conservative-Right to criticize the politically-hijacked ACLU for putting America in a double bind: on one hand, calling for less government; on the other hand, actively promoting policies which undermine both public and private morality. And that is a battle worth fighting. Indeed, it is the most crucial political battle of all.

However, because *speaking* morality and *doing* morality are not always the same, the conservative-Right itself may also be at risk despite its much-touted moral stance. It's the apostle Paul's warning that ought to sober the mind: "You, therefore, have no excuse, you who pass judgment on someone else, for at whatever point you judge the other, you are condemning yourself, because you who pass judgment do the same things."[8]

Is it possible, after roundly condemning the ACLU and the liberal-Left for loosening the moral underpinnings of our society, that those of us in the conservative-Right bring to the bargaining table our own brand of secular thinking which is equally inimical to sound moral practice? The kind of moral self-discipline to which Jefferson referred is not satisfied merely by political rhetoric related to abortion, gay rights, pornography, and school prayer. Moral self-discipline gets much closer to home. It has little to do with whether we are Republican or Democrat, conservative or liberal; and everything to do with whether, as individuals, we are any different from the morally-debased culture in which we find ourselves.

The War Within

Pollster George Barna tells us that, with regard to ethical and lifestyle choices, Christian evangelicals do not live much differently from other Americans.[9] Whereas there may be significant differences in ideology and public policies between the liberal-Left and the conservative/religious-Right, the common ground we most share is what social analyst Daniel Yankelowich described as a radical "duty to self" strain of ethics.[10] If perhaps our political and religious rhetoric aims at a higher road, nevertheless in our private actions we too often travel by the lower road of crass self-fulfillment. Whether we are liberal or conservative, whether "secular" or "religious," our lives are driven mostly by ego, money, and passion.

When culture's unrestrained "self-fulfillment" becomes our own guiding light, then those of us who condemn the secularism of the Left can find ourselves caught up in the same trap. Professor John Woodbridge of Trinity Evangelical Divinity School bluntly chides our false sense of spiritual smugness: "We may sincerely profess orthodox doctrine yet think that our primary interests revolve around ourselves rather than the neighbors we are called to love or the God we are commanded to honor."

What this means in terms of culture wars is that The Great Culture War is not between liberalism and conservatism; or between ideological secularists and doctrinal believers; or between the Christian Coalition and the ACLU. On both sides of the conflict, The Great Culture War is the moment-to-moment struggle between the secular self and the spiritual self within each of us.

In support of this proposition, Professor Woodbridge minces no words. "We may bemoan a moral decline in the country," he says, but "our actual concern, if the truth be known, is not to see a vital Christianity flourish, but rather to secure a more orderly and less violent society in which to live out comfortable and self-satisfied lives."[11]

If Woodbridge is right about this being the level from which we normally operate, then our public and political pronouncements relative to constitutional and moral issues count for little. We come to the negotiating table with unclean hands and an agenda little different from those with whom we claim to be at war.

Perhaps on one level the war has already been fought and won. So thinks Jewish scholar Irving Kristol, who listened to the same speech by Pat Buchanan at the 1992 Republican convention, but had a different reaction from Ira Glasser. Lamented Kristol: "In his convention speech, Pat Buchanan referred to the 'culture wars.' I regret to inform him that those wars are over, and the Left has won....The Left today completely dominates the educational establishment, the entertainment industry, the universities, the media....There is no point in trying to inject 'family values' into these institutions. They will debase and corrupt the very ideal while pretending to celebrate it."[12]

Although Kristol did not himself make this application, it is clear that even those of us on the conservative/religious-Right have succumbed in our personal lives to a tidal wave of secularism. We see it in our materialism, our popular forms of entertainment, our language, our dress, and even our religious habits. We may decry pornography, but we willingly watch shades of it on major-channel television every day. We may rail against gay rights, but we have not always disciplined ourselves to heterosexual purity. We may shout and scream about abortion, but we possess the same have-it-your-way mentality that leads to pro-choice thinking. And we may demand the right for students to pray in public schools, but too often we fail to bend the knee to God in the quiet privacy our own homes.

Separation of church and state may have been grotesquely distorted by the ACLU and the liberal-Left. But on what grounds may we legitimately protest when in our own lives we have unjustly separated faith from practice; the sacred from the secular; our moral pronouncements from our moral life?

It is not constitutional argument, nor the waving of Bibles, flags, and motherhood, that will win the cultural war or even pave the way for greater understanding between the two warring sides. For those of us on the con-servative/religious-Right, our lives and actions are the "epistles known and read by all men"—especially by those on the liberal-Left. Not until we each win The Great Culture War within ourselves can we expect anyone else to listen. Why should the enemy defect if, in our normal course of conduct, we're not really all that different?

Not Just a Cultural, but a Spiritual War

In the introduction, we asked whether the American Civil Liberties Union was playing the honorable role of devil's advocate in the defense of constitutional liberties; or whether, by its current, morally-debased policies, it has truly become an advocate for the devil? Neither that question nor the title to this book was meant to demonize the ACLU, as if to win the battle merely through guilt by the worst possible association.

What lies behind the many references to the devil and those who do his bidding is an attempt to show that the struggle in which we are engaged as a society is not simply and solely a *cultural* war, but in truth a *cosmic* war. A war that is being fought on a wider field than simply the courts or legislative halls. This is a war being waged, not just in classrooms, art galleries, gay bars, and abortion clinics, but deep within each of us. This is an intergenerational global war reaching far beyond our own shores to every culture and people that have ever existed.

Unlike any other merely human conflict, this is a *spiritual* war, being fought on a *spiritual dimension*. Raging world wars cannot begin to describe it. Nor cold wars bristling with nuclear warheads. Nor even the most bitter ideological struggles. This is a Herculean struggle between the cosmic forces of Darkness and the hosts of Light. It is an apocalyptic conflict taking place in far-flung worlds beyond worlds, galaxies beyond galaxies, universes beyond universes.

At stake is nothing less than the ultimate victory of right over wrong, the triumph of good over evil. Not that the outcome is in doubt, but the battle is no less fierce.

To the strictly secular mind, of course, none of this makes the slightest sense. The world of the ideological secularist is a closed world—purely naturalistic, purely rationalistic. For that secularist—the purist—there is no such thing as a spiritual dimension. God, the devil, demons, and angels are but fanciful myth—the ultimate proof of religion's irrationality.

But the secularism of the liberal-Left and the ACLU is not, by and large, an outright denial of the spiritual dimension. Indeed, counted among each group would be people of faith—*churched* people, *synagogued* people, *religious* people—people who acknowledge God, people who fight for what they believe to be right and oppose that which they believe to be wrong. If nothing more, civil liberty itself is a religious expression embodying faith in the sublime importance of truth and justice.

It is, then, to those eternal verities that this appeal has been made. In the cosmic battle between good and evil, with which side is today's civil libertarianism most closely allied? Can the policies of the ACLU withstand the scrutiny of the spiritual dimension? Indeed, can the rest of us measure up?

It is important that we get this brief right. In the short term, our nation hangs in the balance. What shall we say to the next generation if we get it wrong? Yet, the long-term repercussions are even more sobering. For in the divine Temple of Justice, there is no further appeal; and, despite a Judge renowned for his mercy, leniency cannot be assured for those who would dare to become advocates for the devil's ignoble cause.

Notes

Introduction

1. ACLU Briefing Paper, "Guardian of Liberty: American Civil Liberties Union," no. 1.
2. New Catholic Encyclopedia (New York: McGraw–Hill, 1967), 829–830; New Encyclopedia Britannica, 15th ed., 47.
3. Richard Vigilante and Susan Vigilante, "Taking Liberties—The ACLU Strays From Its Mission," Policy Review, vol. 28, (Fall 1984), 38.
4. Ibid., 38.
5. Alexis de Tocqueville, Democracy in America, trans. George Lawrence (Garden City, NY: Anchor Books, 1969), 291–292. The Lawrence translation is based on the 12th edition, which was published in 1848.

Chapter 1

1. Richard Lacayo, "Rushing to Bash Outsiders," Time, 1 May 1995, 52.
2. Laurence McQuillan, "Clinton Vows Capture of Oklahoma Bombers," Reuters World Service, 19 April 1995.
3. As reported by Bryant Gumbel, The Today Show, NBC, 28 April 1995.
4. John Omicinski, "Before Passing Terrorism Law, Let's Take a Deep Breath," Gannett News Service, 27 April 1995.
5. Bruce Frankel, "New sides to old debate on surveillance," USA Today, 26 April 1995, A1.
6. Lacayo, 52.
7. "Would a Crackdown Be Worth It?," Time, 1 May 1995, 53.
8. ACLU Policy 270, Policy Guide of the American Civil Liberties Union, revised through October, 1992.
9. Ibid.
10. Richard Benedetto, "Americans would give up liberties for safety," USA Today (International Edition), 26 April 1995, A1.
11. Ibid.
12. Ibid.
13. James Q. Wilson, "The Case for Greater Vigilance," Time, 1 May 1995, 57.

14. Judi Hasson, "The fine line between protection, persecution," USA Today (International Edition), 5 May 1995, 2A.
15. Ibid.
16. Ibid.
17. Samuel Walker, In Defense of American Liberties (New York: Oxford Univ. Press, 1990), 193.
18. Walker, 141.
19. Omicinski.
20. Ibid.
21. Hugh Davies, "Wrong men arrested in Oklahoma bomb hunt," The Daily Telegraph, 4 May 1995, 10.
22. New York Senate, Joint Committee, Revolutionary Radicalism, 1982.
23. U.S. House Special Committee to Investigate Communist Activities in the United States, 71st Cong., 2d and 3d sess., Hearings, 409–412.
24. Anne Applebaum, "A blast that put America in touch with its past," The Daily Telegraph, 25 April 1995, 18.
25. Leslie Phillips and Judi Hasson, "Parties' vow on FBI power worries some," USA Today (International Edition), 26 April 1995, 2A.
26. Simon Sebag Montefiore, "Warlords come to America," The Sunday Times (London), 30 April 1995, News Review, 7.
27. Hasson, 2A.
28. Paul Greenberg, "Views of 'Iron Lady' still carry a keen edge," The Commercial Appeal (Memphis), 4 May 1995, 13A

Chapter 2

1. ACLU Briefing Paper, "Guardian of Liberty: American Civil Liberties Union."
2. Samuel Walker, In Defense of American Liberties (New York: Oxford Univ. Press, 1990), 132–133.
3. Ibid., 127.
4. In 1924, the Union filed a libel suit when it was accused by the Chicago Tribune of selling out to the Communists and taking "Moscow gold." The inappropriateness of the ACLU's suit seems to have escaped the attention of Samuel Walker when he briefly noted the unseemly litigation in his book. Ironically, in the immediately preceding paragraph, Walker says of the ACLU's former labor movement allies who had joined in the attacks on its ideology: "Powerless groups repeatedly sought the ACLU's assistance when their own rights were violated but then turned anti–civil libertarian in the face of groups or ideas they did not like." One might indeed question such a hypocritical turnabout on the part of a labor union. But surely it was more hypocritical for a civil liberties union to turn anti–civil libertarian when criti-cism was dumped in its own backyard.

Another libel suit was filed in 1936 when Harold Lord Varney castigated the ACLU and its founder Roger Baldwin in the American Mercury. Varney's article, entitled "The Civil Liberties Union—Liberalism à la Moscow," quoted from Baldwin's book, Liberty Under the Soviets, and excoriated the Union for its Communist leanings. "Under Mr. Baldwin's artful leadership, [the ACLU] is a mobilization of unsuspecting Liberal idealism to the materialistic services of the Kremlin," Varney wrote boldly. The ACLU did not like this particular free speech and promptly sued.

5. ACLU Policy 516, Policy Guide for the American Civil Liberties Union, revised through October, 1992.
6. Gellhorn, Memo to Board, 30 November 1949, ACLUP, 1949, Box 32.
7. Walker, 206.
8. Ibid., 359.
9. ACLU Policy 271, Policy Guide of the American Civil Liberties Union, revised October, 1992.
10. Alex Beam, Globe staff, "Double Jeopardy," Boston Globe, 21 April 1993, op. ed., 19.
11. Ibid.
12. Richard Vigilante and Susan Vigilante, "Taking Liberties—The ACLU Strays From Its Mission," Policy Review, vol. 28, (Fall 1984), 32–33.
13. In some respects, the ACLU's trendy denunciation of Communism was as pragmatic as Roger Baldwin's tolerance for civil liberties violations in aid of the working class struggle. In a 1934 Soviet Russia Today article, Baldwin freely admitted his pragmatism, even to the point of accepting dictatorship as a necessary evil. "If I aid the reactionaries to get free speech now and then," said Baldwin, "if I go outside the class struggle to fight against censorship, it is only because those liberties help create a more hospitable environment for working class liberties....When that power of the working class is once achieved, as it has been only in the Soviet Union, I am for maintaining it by any means whatever. Dictatorship is the obvious means in a world of enemies, at home and abroad."

Baldwin's disillusionment following the Hitler–Stalin pact quickly cooled his love–affair with Soviet–style Communism and considerably toned down his rhetoric. But, following in Baldwin's footsteps, the ACLU has continued to pursue a course of pragmatic and leftward–leaning politics in support of the cause. If civil libertarian inconsistencies abound, the one great consistency—modern liberalism—remains.

Chapter 3

1. Samuel Walker, In Defense of American Liberties (New York: Oxford Univ. Press, 1990), 31.
2. Ibid.
3. Ibid., 46.
4. Ibid.
5. Ibid., 69.
6. Ibid.
7. Ibid.
8. Ibid.
9. Roger Baldwin, Memorandum on ACLU Program, 27 December 1948, ACLUP, 1948, vol. 4. Isbell, interview.
10. Walker, 204.
11. Ibid., 21.
12. Ibid., 267.
13. Ibid., 206.
14. Herbert McCloskey and Alida Brill, Dimensions of Tolerance (Russell Sage Foundation).
15. Jeremy Rabkin, "Class Conflict over Civil Liberties," The Public Interest, vol. 77, (Fall 1984), 120.
16. William J. Bennett, The Devaluing of America (New York: Summit Books, 1992), 26.
17. Walker, 269.
18. Ibid., 210.
19. Robert H. Bork, The Tempting of America (New York: The Free Press, 1990), 242.
20. Ibid., 250.
21. Bennett, 27.
22. As quoted in P. Hollander, The Survival of the Adversary Culture (1988), 151–52.
23. Ibid.
24. Irving Howe, The Decline of the New (New York: Harcourt, Brace & World, 1970), 5.
25. Charles J. Sykes, A Nation of Victims (New York: St. Martin's, 1992), 66.
26. Richard Grenier, "The Elite and 'Intellectual Hubris,'" International Herald Tribune, 30 May 1994.
27. Ibid.
28. Walker, 268.
29. Barbara Amiel, "Unto us is born...petty tyranny," The (London) Sunday Times, 20 March 1994, 4.4 Opinion.
30. Ibid.

31. Bennett, 28.
32. Daniel Bell, The Cultural Contradictions of Capitalism (New York: Basic Books, 1976), 41.
33. Norman Podhoretz, Breaking Ranks (New York: Harper & Row, 1979), 81.
34. Sykes, 37.
35. James Coleman, "Self–Suppression of Academic Freedom" (Address to the National Association of Scholars, New York, 19 June 1990).
36. Sykes, 73.
37. Kenneth Keniston, "The Sources of Student Dissent," The Journal of Social Issues 23 (1967), 108–137.
38. Sykes, 91
39. Nat Hentoff, "Them and Us: Are Peace Protest Self–Therapy?" Evergreen Review 2, no. 48.
40. Gerd Behrens, "Africa's Uphill Battle," Time, 15 August 1994, 56.
41. Stephen L. Carter, The Culture of Disbelief (New York: BasicBooks, 1993), 246.
42. 2 Cor. 11:14.

Chapter 4

1. Roger Baldwin, "What Is the Truth About Constitutional Rights?," ACLUP, vol. 904, 14 December 1936.
2. Ibid.
3. Samuel Walker, In Defense of American Liberties (New York: Oxford Univ. Press, 1990), 111.
4. Ibid., 4.
5. Baldwin [on Brandeis], The New Leader, 18 October 1941; Baldwin memo, Impressions of Judge Brandeis, 24 April 1942, RNBP, Box 8.
6. Walker, 65, 109.
7. Ibid., 73, 75.
8. Ibid., 135.
9. Ibid., 27.
10. Ibid., 249.
11. Mapp v. Ohio, 367 U.S. 643 (1961).
12. Walker, 68, 107.
13. Ibid., 178, 252.
14. Ibid., 280.
15. Ibid., 66, 67, 73.
16. Ibid., 106.
17. Felix Frankfurter, "Can the Supreme Court Guarantee Toleration?," The New Republic, 17 June 1925, 85–87.
18. "White House Releases Letters of Support for Judge Ginsburg," U.S. Newswire, 14 June 1993.

19. Religious Freedom Restoration Act of 1993, Pub.L. 103–141, 107 Stat. 1488, 42 U.S.C. sec. 2000bb.

20. Employment Division, Department of Human Resources of Oregon v. Smith, 494 U.S. 872 (1990).

21. Walker, 112.

22. Ibid., 306.

23. Ibid., 221.

24. Charles Morgan, Jr., interview with Samuel Walker, 269.

25. Walker, 35.

26. Ramona Ripston, "ACLU/SC Takes Lead in Colorado Boycott," Open Forum, vol. 68, no. 4, Winter 1993, 1.

27. Akron v. Akron Center for Reproductive Health, 462 U.S. 416 (1983).

28. Richard Vigilante and Susan Vigilante, "Taking Liberties—The ACLU Strays from Its Mission," Policy Review, vol. 28 (Fall 1984).

29. Ibid., 29.

Chapter 5

1. Senator Kennedy. 133 Congressional Record S9188–S9189 (daily ed. 1 July 1987).

2. Business reply letter from ACLU Foundation (31 August 1987), reprinted in Myers, "Advice and Consent on Trial: The Case of Robert H. Bork," 66 Den. U.L. Rev. 201, 215 n.68 (1989).

3. Samuel Walker, In Defense of American Liberties (New York: Oxford Univ. Press, 1990), 366–368.

4. Ibid.

5. ACLU, Board of Directors, Minutes, 29–30 August 1987.

6. The New York Times, 8 October 1987, A1.

7. Walker, 368.

8. Biden Report, 9 Cardozo L. Rev., 246.

9. Robert H. Bork, The Tempting of America (New York: The Free Press, 1990), 289.

10. Dothard v. Rawlinson.

11. Bork, 326–331.

12. Robert W. Jensen, "Churchly Honor and Judge Bork," DIALOG, vol. 27, Winter 1988, 3.

13. Ibid.

14. Jn. 8:44. New International Version. "You belong to your father, the devil, and you want to carry out your father's desire. He was a murderer from the beginning, not holding to the truth, for there is no truth in him. When he lies, he speaks his native language, for he is a liar and the father of lies." (New International Version)

15. Ibid.

16. The Washington Post, 14 September 1987, A9.
17. Gen. 3:1–5.
18. Walker, 318.
19. Paul Brest, "The Misconceived Quest for Original Understanding," Boston University Law Review 60 (1980): 204, 220–221.
20. Bork, 251–252.
21. Walker, 314.
22. Ibid.
23. Abrams v. United States, 250 U.S. 616, 624 (1919).
24. Walker, 78.
25. Ibid., 6.
26. Palko v. Connecticut, 302 U.S. 319,325,326 (1937).
27. Moore v. East Cleveland, 431 U.S. 494, 503 (1977).
28. Bork, 119.
29. Bowers v. Hardwick, 478 U.S. at 199 (Blackmun, J., dissenting).
30. Gerard V. Bradley, "The Constitution and the Erotic Self," First Things, October 1991, no. 16, 30.
31. Ibid.
32. Robert Williams, Just As I Am (New York: Crown Publishers, 1992), xviii.
33. Ibid., xv.
34. Elisabeth Schussler Fiorenza, Bread Not Stone: The Challenge of Feminist Biblical Interpretation (Boston: Beacon Press, 1984), xiii.
35. Williams, 42.
36. Ibid., 43.
37. Margaret A. Farley, "Feminist Consciousness and the Interpretation of Scripture," in Letty M. Russell, ed., Feminist Interpretation of the Bible (Philadelphia: Westminster Press, 1985), 43.
38. Stephen L. Carter, The Culture of Disbelief (New York: BasicBooks, 1993), 73.
39. James R. Edwards, "Eros Deified," Christianity Today, 27 May 1991, 14–15.
40. David A.J. Richards, Sexual Autonomy and the Constitutional Right to Privacy: A Case Study in Human Rights and the Unwritten Constitution, 30 Hastings L.J. 957 (1979) at 1005.

Chapter 6

1. Lawrence A. Stanley, "The Child Porn Storm; How One Curious Legal Case Caused a Capitol Hill Stampede," The Washington Post, 30 January 1994, Outlook, C3.
2. William V. Roth, "Protecting the Child Victims of Porn," The Washington Post, 2 March 1994, A17.
3. Mark Genrich, "Defining Pornography; Arizona Appellate Court Buys Into Looser Interpretation," The Phoenix Gazette, 23 November 1994, B5.
4. Julie Cohen, "A Legal About–Face Into a Minefield; Clinton Approach to

Child Porn Pleases No One," Legal Times, 22 November 1993, 2.

5. Genrich, B5.

6. Ibid.

7. Cohen, 2.

8. Ibid.

9. ACLU Policy 4, Policy Guide of the American Civil Liberties Union, revised through October, 1992.

10. Ibid.

11. Ibid.

12. ACLU Policy 16, Policy Guide of the American Civil Liberties Union, revised through October, 1992.

13. Ibid.

14. Samuel Walker, In Defense of American Liberties (New York: Oxford Univ. Press, 1990), 82.

15. Ibid.

16. Ibid.

17. Ibid.

18. Roth v. United States, 354 U.S. 476 (1957).

19. Jacobellis v. Ohio, 378 U.S. 184 (1964).

20. Marjorie Heins, Sex, Sin, and Blasphemy (New York: The New Press, 1993), 34.

21. ACLU Policy 4.

22. "Larry King Live," Cable News Network, 31 January 1992.

23. ACLU Policy 4.

24. Genrich, B5.

25. Heins, 125.

26. Ibid.

27. Walker, 217.

28. Ibid., 318.

29. Walter Berns, "Pornography vs. Democracy; The Case for Censorship," The Public Interest (Winter 1971), 3–24. Walter Berns, The First Amendment and the Future of American Democracy (New York: BasicBooks, 1976).

30. Cohen v. California, 403 U.S. 15 (1971).

31. Texas v. Johnson, 491 U.S. 397 (1989).

Chapter 7

1. Susan Carpenter McMillan, "Ultra–Liberals Fight Morality in the Schools," Los Angeles Times, 15 November 1994, B7.

2. Margarette Driscoll and Geordie Greig, "The Art of Saying No," The (London) Sunday Times, 1 May 1994, 14.

3. Phillip E. Johnson, Reason in the Balance: The Case Against Naturalism in Science, Law and Education (Westmont, IL: Intervarsity, 1995), 163.

4. ACLU Policy 211, Policy Guide of the American Civil Liberties Union, revised through October, 1992.

5. Ibid.

6. "The ACLU Commitment to Defend The Rights Of Gay Men And Lesbians And Fight AIDS Discrimination," flyer, ACLU of Southern California.

7. Ibid.

8. Ibid.

9. ACLU, Board of Directors, Minutes, 7 January 1957. Vern L. Bullough, "Lesbianism, Homosexuality, and the American Civil Liberties Union, Journal of Homosexuality 13 (Fall 1986), 23–33.

10. Ibid. Also, Samuel Walker, In Defense of American Liberties (New York: Oxford Univ. Press, 1990), 312.

11. ACLU Policy 110, Policy Guide for the American Civil Liberties Union, revised through October, 1992.

12. ACLU Policy 246, Policy Guide of the American Civil Liberties Union, revised through October, 1992.

13. Ibid.

14. Walker, 32.

15. See Rosalyn Fraad Baxandall, Words on Fire: The Life and Writing of Elizabeth Gurley Flynn (New Brunswick, NJ: Rutgers UP), 41

16. Walker, 31.

17. Ibid., 34.

18. Ibid., 83.

19. Russell Hittinger, "When the Court Should Not Be Obeyed," First Things, October, 1993, no. 36, 12–18

20. Ibid., 16.

Chapter 8

1. US Const, Amend IV (1791).

2. Ibid.

3. Ramona Ripston, "Poll, Blacks' confidence in police plummets," USA Today, 22 March 1995, 3A.

4. Rochin v. California, 342 U.S. 165 (1952).

5. Mapp v. Ohio, 367 U.S. 643 (1961).

6. Gideon v. Wainwright, 372 U.S. 335 (1963).

7. Escobedo v. Illinois, 378 U.S. 478 (1964).

8. Miranda v. Arizona, 384 U.S. 436 (1966).

9. Weeks v. United States, 232 U.S. 383 (1914).

10. Samuel Walker, In Defense of American Liberties (New York: Oxford Univ. Press, 1990), 250.

11. Walker, 246–252.
12. Ibid., 251.
13. Ira Glasser, "Can't Beat Crime? Just Blame ACLU," Wall Street Journal, 25 January 1994, A13.
14. ACLU Policy 270, Policy Guide of the American Civil Liberties Union, revised through October, 1992.
15. Paul Glastris, "The ACLU and the right to die in a train wreck," Washington Monthly, March 1988.
16. William A. Donohue, The Politics of the American Civil Liberties Union (New Brunswisk: Transaction Publishers, 1990), 264.
17. "The Chief's Justice and Crime," editorial, New York Times, 11 February 1981, A26.
18. Ibid.
19. Linda Greenhouse, "Burger's Talk: Quick Dispute," New York Times, 10 February 1981, B9.
20. ACLU Policy 239, Policy Guide for the American Civil Liberties Union, revised through October, 1992.
21. Ibid.
22. Ibid.
23. ACLU Policy 242, Policy Guide for the American Civil Liberties Union, revised through October, 1992.
24. Barton Bean, "Pressure for Freedom: The American Civil Liberties Union" (Ph.D. diss., Cornell University, 1955), 271.
25. Gen. 2:17.
26. Gen. 3:4.
27. ACLU Policy 47, Policy Guide for the American Civil Liberties Union, revised through October, 1992.
28. Ibid.
29. Ibid.
30. Joe Urschel, "When 'just living for today' ends in murder," USA Today, International Edition, 13 April 1995, 5A.
31. John Keegan, "Who says a Hitler could never happen again?" Daily Telegraph (London), 23 March 1995, 18.
32. Mk. 2:27.
33. Grant Gilmore, "The Age of Anxiety," The Storrs Lectures, Yale University Law School, 31 October 1974.

Chapter 9

1. Samuel Walker, In Defense of American Liberties (New York: Oxford Univ. Press, 1990), 17.
2. Roger Baldwin, "The Individual and the State: The Problem As Presented

by the Sentencing of Roger N. Baldwin," (November, 1918), privately printed and circulated by Baldwin's friends; reprinted in The Survey, 9 November 1918, 253; The Nation, 9 November 1918, 54.

3. Walker, 41.

4. Roger Baldwin to his mother, 10 October 1918, 3 November 1918, AUAMP, Box 3, Lamson, Roger Baldwin, 84–91.

5. "American Civil Liberties Union and Communist Activity," Law and Labor, February 1931, 24.

6. Walker, 119.

7. "Robert W. Dunn, 81, a Co–Founder of American Civil Liberties Union," New York Times, 23 January 1977, 28.

8. Baldwin, as quoted in, Peggy Lamson, Roger Baldwin: Founder of the American Civil Liberties Union (Boston: Houghton Mifflin, 1976), 141.

9. Ibid., 192.

10. Walker, 193.

11. Baldwin, as quoted in, Lamson, Baldwin, 86.

12. Ibid., 203.

13. Walker, 53.

14. ACLU Policy 7, Policy Guide of the American Civil Liberties Union, revised through October, 1992.

15. ACLU Policy 8, Policy Guide for the American Civil Liberties Union, revised through October, 1992.

16. ACLU Policy 11, Policy Guide for the American Civil Liberties Union, revised through October, 1992.

17. ACLU Policy 42, Policy Guide for the American Civil Liberties Union, revised through October, 1992.

18. G.K. Chesterton, "Defense of Patriotism," Defendant, 1901.

19. Jeremy Rabkin, "Class Conflict over Civil Liberties," The Public Interest, vol. 77, (Fall 1984), 122.

20. Richard Vigilante and Susan Vigilante, "Taking Liberties: The ACLU Strays From Its Mission," Policy Review, vol. 28, (Fall 1984).

21. ACLU Board of Directors, minutes, 30 January 1966.

22. ACLU Board of Directors, minutes, 2 June 1970. ACLU Policy 116, Policy Guide for the American Civil Liberties Union, revised through October, 1992.

23. Walker, 285.

Chapter 10

1. Roberts et. al. v. Madigan and Adams County School Dist. No. 50, 921 F.2d 1047 (1990).

2. Tinker v. Des Moines Indep. Community School Dist., 393 U.S. 503 (1969).

3. ACLU Briefing Paper, "Church and State," no. 3.

4. ACLU Policy 62 (a), Policy Guide for the American Civil Liberties Union, revised through October, 1992.

5. Ibid.

6. ACLU Policy 60, Policy Guide for the American Civil Liberties Union, revised through October, 1992.

7. Ibid., 113.

8. Roberts, 33.

9. *Zorach et. al. v. Clauson* et. al., 343 U.S. 306 (1952).

10. Roberts, 38.

11. "Help employers fight religious harassment," USA Today, 14 June 1994, 8A; "Don't curb religious liberty," Louis P. Sheldon, USA Today, 14 June 1994, 8A.

12. Ibid.

13. ACLU Briefing Paper.

14. Witters v. Washington Department of Services for the Blind, 474 U.S. 481 (1986).

15. Zobrest v. Catalina Foothills School Dist., 509 U.S. 1 (1993).

16. Rosenberger et. al. v. Rector and Visitors of the University of Virginia, 115 Sup.Ct. 2510; 1995 U.S. Lexis 4461 (1995).

17. ACLU Policy 71 (b)(5), Policy Guide for the American Civil Liberties Union, revised through October, 1992).

18. Fordham University v. Brown, 856 F. Supp. 684 (D.D.C. 1994).

19. Kim Murphy, "Students Sue Saddelback Schools," The Los Angeles Times, 7 May 1985, part 2, 14.

20. Perumal et. al. v. Saddelback Valley Unified School Dist., 198 Cal. App. 3rd 64 (1988).

21. *Perumal et. al. v. Saddelback Valley Unified School Dist.*, 488 U.S. 933 (1988).

22. See Everson v. Board of Education, 330 U.S. 1 (1947) [government "cannot exclude individual Catholics, Lutherans, Mohammedans, Baptists, Jews, Methodists, Non–believers, Presbyterians, or the members of any other faith, because of their faith, or lack of it, from receiving the benefits of public welfare legislation."]; McDaniel v. Paty, 435 U.S. 618 (1978) [violation of Free Exercise Clause to exclude ministers or others with religious vocations or identities from eligibility to hold public office or participate in political sphere]; McDaniel at p. 641 (Brennan, J., concurring) ["Religionists no less than members of any other group enjoy the full measure of protection afforded speech, association, and political activity generally. The Establishment Clause...may not be used as a sword to justify repression of religion or its adherents from any aspect of public life"]; Widmar v. Vincent, 454 U.S. 263 (1981) [violation of Free Speech Clause to exclude religious student group from equal access to university facilities on same basis as other student groups]; Board of Education v. Mergens, 496 U.S. 226 (1990) [violation of federal Equal Access Act to exclude religious Bible study club

from equal access to public high school facilities on same terms as other student groups].

See also analysis of these and other cases by Professor Michael Stokes Paulsen, University of Minnesota Law School, in testimony before the Subcommittee on the Constitution of the Committee on the Judiciary, U.S. House of Representatives, 8 June 1995.

23. Lamb's Chapel v. Center Moriches Union Free School Dist., 113 Sup.Ct. 2141 (1993).

24. Bob Edwards, "Schools Are Not Required To Be 'Religion–Free' Zones," National Public Radio, Morning Edition, 13 July 1995.

Chapter 11

1. Stephen L. Carter, The Culture of Disbelief (New York: Basic Books, 1993), 117.

2. Church of Holy Trinity v. U.S., 143 U.S. 457 (1892).

3. Note, "Rethinking the Incorporation of the Establishment Clause: A Federalist View," Harvard Law Review, vol. 105, no. 5, March 1992, 1700, 1704.

4. Everson v. Board of Education, 330 U.S. 1 (1947).

5. Berkey v. Third Avenue R. Co., 244 N.Y. 84, 94; 155 N.E. 58, 61 (1926).

6. Quote by Thomas Jefferson in response to an address given by a committee of the Danbury Baptist Association (1 January 1802), reprinted in 8 Writings of Thomas Jefferson 113 (H. Washington, ed., 1861).

7. Thomas Jefferson, Second Inaugural Address, 1805.

8. Akhil Reed Amar, "The Bill of Rights as a Constitution," 100 Yale Law Journal 1131.

9. In addition to the Harvard Law Review note cited above, see also William K. Lietzau, "Rediscovering the Establishment Clause: Federalism and the Rollback of Incorporation," 39 DePaul Law Review 1191.

10. Harvard Law Review note, 1704.

11. Amar, 1158.

12. Wallace v. Jaffree, 472 U.S. 38 (1985).

13. Lietzau, 1214.

14. Jaffree v. Board of School Commissioners, 554 Fed. Supp. 1104 (S.D. Ala, 1983).

15. Laurence H. Tribe, American Constitutional Law (2nd Ed., 1988), sec. 14–3, 1161.

16. Harvard Law Review, 1701. James Iredell was responding to these fears when in the North Carolina convention he stated: "They [Congress] certainly have no authority to interfere in the establishment of religion whatsoever...." 4 Elliot's Debates, at 194.

17. The Constitutions of All the United States According to the Latest

Amendments (Lexington, KY: Thomas T. Skillman, 1817), 60, 62.

18. John J. McGrath, ed., Church and State in American Law: Cases and Materials (Milwaukee: Bruce Publishing, 1962), 375.

19. Harvard Law Review, 1701.

20. Abington School Dist. v. Schempp, 374 U.S. 203, 309–310 (1963), (Stewart, J., dissenting).

21. Ibid., 310.

22. Lietzau, 1207.

23. U.S. Term Limits, Inc., Et Al. v. Thornton Et Al., 1995 U.S. LEXIS 3487; 63 U.S.L.W. 4413 (1995).

24. Lietzau, 1223.

Chapter 12

1. Samuel Walker, In Defense of American Liberties (New York: Oxford Univ. Press, 1990), 224.

2. Engel v. Vitale, 370 U.S. 421 (1962).

3. Barbara Amiel, "Heaven save us from these high priests of confusion," The Daily Telegraph, 30 January 1994, sec. 4, 5.

4. McCollum v. Board of Education, 333 U.S. 203 (1948).

5. The point at which the Court went astray on the issue of coercion is this statement: "The Establishment Clause, unlike the Free Exercise Clause, does not depend upon any showing of direct governmental compulsion and is violated by the enactment of laws which establish an official religion whether those laws operate directly to coerce non–observing individuals or not." (Engel, 430.) The relevance of that statement would attach only if the Establishment Clause had been intended to apply to the individual states, which, as shown, it was not. Failing that, the Court's only remaining interest would be state coercion in the matter of religious liberty. Absent any showing of coercion, the states have the right to promote and encourage religious expression as deemed proper.

6. ACLU Policy 81, Policy Guide for the American Civil Liberties Union, revised through October, 1992.

7. Editorial, "Religious indigestion," The Daily Telegraph, 26 January 1994, 18.

8. ACLU Policy 80, Policy Guide for the American Civil Liberties Union, revised through October, 1992.

9. ACLU Briefing Paper, "Church and State," no. 3.

10. Lee v. Weisman, 112 S.Ct. 2649 (1992).

11. Tony Mauro, "Many students don't want to graduate without a prayer," USA Today (International Edition), 6 June 1994, A3.

12. Ibid.

13. Ibid.

14. Joint School District 241 v. Harris, 1995 U.S. Lexis 4292 (1995).
15. Sheila Wissner, "Principal seeks end to graduation prayer confusion," The Tennessean, 23 January 1994, B1.
16. Tracy Wilson, "Junior High Student Challenges Simi Valley Dress Code," The Los Angeles Times, 4 October 1994, A3.
17. Walker, 342.
18. Tony Mauro, "School prayer amendment on slow track," USA Today (International Edition), 16 May 1995, 4A.
19. Ibid.

Chapter 13

1. Lucille Milner, Education of an American Liberal: An Autobiography (New York: Horizon, 1954), 161.
2. Roger Baldwin to R. Fosdick, Rockefeller Foundation, 21 October 1925; Arthur Garfield Hays to Walter Nelles, 9 September 1925, ACLUP, 1925, vol. 274.
3. Arthur Weinbert, ed., Attorney for the Damned (New York: Simon & Schuster, 1957), 187–188.
4. Samuel Walker, In Defense of American Liberties (New York: Oxford Univ. Press, 1990), 74–75.
5. Ray Ginger, Six Days or Forever? (Chicago: Quadrangle Paperbacks, 1969).
6. Walker, 76.
7. Ibid., 72.
8. Epperson v. Arkansas, 393 U.S. 97 (1968).
9. Walker, 342, citing Glasser interview.
10. McLean v. Arkansas Board of Education, 663 F.2d 47 (8th Cir. 1981), aff'g No. LRC 81–322 (W.D. Ark. 20 August 1981).
11. Edwards v. Aguillard, 482 U.S. 578 (1987).
12. ACLU, Board of Directors, minutes, January, 1987.
13. Stephen Jay Gould, Wonderful Life (New York: W.W. Norton, 1989), 45–52.
14. Quoted in Terry Spencer, "Parents Protest Reprimand of Teacher over Creationism," Los Angeles Times, 2 April 1991, B8.
15. Ibid.
16. David Crews, "Animal Sexuality," Scientific American, (January 1994), 108–114.
17. Kathleen Stein, "Censoring Science," Omni (February 1987), 42.
18. Harold Bloom, The American Religion: The Emergence of the Post–Christian Nation (New York: Simon & Schuster, 1992), 56.
19. Quoted in untitled article, Proprietary to UPI, Feb. 13, 1989, Regional News section [NEXIS].
20. Stephen L. Carter, The Culture of Disbelief (New York: BasicBooks, 1993), 159.

21. Carter, 161.
22. Carter, 160. His footnote: The figures are calculated from a table in George Gallup, Jr., and Sarah Jones, 100 Questions and Answers: Religion in America (Princeton, NJ: Princeton Religious Research Center, 1989), p. 26. A 1991 survey found more impressive numbers. See Jim Dawson, "Evolution Fight Has New Form, But Emotions Have Endured," Star Tribune [Minneapolis], 22 June 1992, 1A (47 percent agree that "God created man in his present form at one time within the past 10,000 years"; 40 percent agree that "humans developed over millions of years, but God guided the process"; only 9 percent say "man evolved without God").
23. Ibid., 160.
24. Ibid., 169.

Chapter 14

1. Arthur Weinbert, ed., Attorney for the Damned (New York: Simon & Schuster, 1957), 187–188.
2. Richard Vigilante and Susan Vigilante, "Taking Liberties—The ACLU Strays From Its Mission," Policy Review, vol. 28, (Fall 1984), 31.
3. Ibid.
4. Thomas Paine, The Age of Reason, Part First.
5. Michael Hudson, "Science is Science and Faith is Faith," Los Angeles Times, 8 November 1989, op–ed page.
6. McLean v. Arkansas Board of Education, 529 F. Supp. 1255, 1266, (E.D. Ark. 1982), aff'd, 723 F.2d 45 (8th Cir. 1983).
7. Stephen L. Carter, The Culture of Disbelief, (New York: BasicBooks, 1993), 111, 162, 165.
8. Paine.
9. Ibid.
10. Anselm Atkins, "Human Rights Are Cultural Artifacts," The Humanist, (March/April 1990), 15f.
11. Ibid.
12. Ibid.
13. Surveys prepared by the author and administered over a period of years to students in his Law and Morality and Criminal Law classes at Pepperdine University, Malibu, CA. Students indicated religious backgrounds of all types and represented a broad cross–section geographically and politically.
14. Robert Wright, "Our Cheating Hearts," Time, 15 August 1994, 36–44. (Article adapted from his forthcoming book, The Moral Animal: Evolutionary Psychology and Everyday Life, Pantheon.)
15. William J. Bennett, De–Valuing of America (New York: Summit Books, 1992), 60.
16. Gen. 4:2–9.

Chapter 15

1. Martin Luther King, Jr., "Letter from Birmingham City Jail," in James M. Washington, ed., A Testament of Hope: The Essential Writings of Martin Luther Kings, Jr. (San Francisco: Harper and Row, 1986), 27.

2. Stephen L. Carter, The Culture of Disbelief (New York: Basic Books, 1993), 227.

3. Tony Snow, "Oh, those faint–hearted Republicans," USA Today, 22 February 1994, 7A.

4. Carter, 228.

5. Ibid., 229.

6. Roach, "War of Words on Abortion," Origins 20 (1990), 88,89, quoted in Michael Perry, Love and Power, 136.

7. Carter, 228.

8. ACLU Policy 41, Policy Guide for the American Civil Liberties Union, revised through October, 1992.

9. ACLU Policy 54, Policy Guide for the American Civil Liberties Union, revised through October, 1992.

10. ACLU Policy 123, Policy Guide for the American Civil Liberties Union, revised through October, 1992.

11. Samuel Walker, In Defense of American Liberties (New York: Oxford Univ. Press, 1990), 341.

12. ACLU Policy 263, Policy Guide for the American Civil Liberties Union, revised through October, 1992.

13. Ibid.

14. Robert H. Bork, The Tempting of America (New York: The Free Press, 1990), 243.

15. Ibid.

16. Bork, 245.

17. Ibid., 246.

18. ACLU Policy 60, Policy Guide for the American Civil Liberties Union, revised through October, 1992.

19. Jn. 8:32.

20. Clifford Longley, "Guidelines for the survival of civilization," The Daily Telegraph, 10 March 1995, 25.

21. Janet Daley, "Death of the 7th Commandment?," The Sunday Times (London), 26 March 1995, 10.

22. Brigitte Berger and Peter Berger, The War Over the Family: Capturing the Middle Ground (New York: Anchor Books, 1984), 112.

23. Richard John Neuhaus, "All Too Human," National Review, 2 December 1991.

24. Ibid.

Chapter 16

1. Samuel Walker, In Defense of American Liberties (New York: Oxford Univ. Press, 1990), 21.
2. Ibid.
3. William J. Bennett, The Devaluing of America (New York: Summit Books, 1992), 213.
4. Walker, 222.
5. James M. Barrie, The Twelve–Pound Look and Other Plays, (1921), 28.
6. Walker, 67.
7. Charles J. Sykes, A Nation of Victims (New York: St. Martin's, 1992), 68.
8. John Murray Cuddihy, quoted in "Losing Our Moral Umbrella," Newsweek, 7 December 1992, 60.
9. Jacob Neusner, quoted in "Losing Our Moral Umbrella," Newsweek, 7 December 1992, 60.
10. Stephen L. Carter, The Culture of Disbelief (New York: BasicBooks, 1993), 88.
11. Jonathan Miller, as quoted in The Harper Book of Quotations, Robert I. Fitzhenry, ed. (New York: Harper Perennial, 1993), 389.
12. Peggy Lamson, Roger Baldwin: Founder of the American Civil Liberties Union (Boston: Houghton Mifflin, 1976), 132.
13. Walker, 206.
14. Engel v. Vitale, 368 U.S. 924; 82 Sup.Ct. 367; 7 L.Ed. 2d 189 (1961).
15. Walker, 220.
16. Interview by William A. Donohue, The Politics of the American Civil Liberties Union (New Brunswick, NJ: Transaction Publishers, 1990), 256.
17. Ibid.
18. Walker, 305, 330.
19. Ibid., 330.
20. Isa. 61:1,2; Lk. 4:16–30.
21. Mt. 5:39–41.
22. Jn. 3:16.
23. Jn. 18:36,37.
24. Mt. 22:21, King James Version.

Chapter 17

1. Clint Bolick, "Hard–Core First Amendment Activist Speaks," Wall Street Journal, 30 January 1995, A18.
2. Dennis Cauchon, "Civil Dispute Within the ACLU," USA Today, 31 March 1993, 1A.
3. Ibid.
4. Ibid.

5. Ibid.
6. Victor Navasky, Naming Names (New York: Viking, 1980). Lillian Hellman, Scoundrel Time (New York: Bantam, 1977), 89–91.

Chapter 18

1. ACLU Briefing Paper, "Church and State," no. 3.
2. Bowers v. Hardwick, 478 U.S. 186 (1968).
3. Mona Charen, "ACLU takes confusing stand against 'sincere prayer,' 'critical thinking,'" Gazette Telegraph (Colorado Springs), 28 May 1995.
4. Samuel Walker, In Defense of American Liberties (New York: Oxford Univ. Press, 1990), 302.
5. Walker, 348. ACLU Executive Committee, minutes, June, 1985. ACLU, Board of Directors, minutes, January, 1988.
6. Walker, 5.
7. Roe v. Wade, 410 U.S. 113 (1973), at pp. 163–165. "For the stage subsequent to viability, the State, in promoting its interest in the potentiality of human life, may, if it chooses, regulate, and even proscribe, abortion, except where necessary, in appropriate medical judgment, for the preservation of the life or health of the mother."
8. Rom. 2:1.
9. John D. Woodbridge, "Culture War Casualties," Christianity Today, 6 March 1995, 20.
10. Ibid.
11. Ibid.
12. Ibid.

Index